FAMILY, POWER, AND POLITICS IN EGYPT

Sayed Marei, 1959

ROBERT SPRINGBORG

FAMILY, POWER, AND POLITICS IN EGYPT

SAYED BEY MAREI—HIS CLAN, CLIENTS, AND COHORTS

UNIVERSITY OF PENNSYLVANIA PRESS PHILADELPHIA 1982

Photographs courtesy of *al Ahram,* Cairo
Map of Minya al Qamh and environs on p. xxiv is reproduced courtesy
of the Library of Congress.

Library of Congress Cataloging in Publication Data

Springborg, Robert.
  Family, power, and politics in Egypt.

  Includes bibliographical references and index.
    1. Egypt—Politics and government—1952–
2. Marei, Sayed.   3. Statesmen—Egypt—Biography.
4. Elite (Social sciences)—Egypt.   5. Marei,
Sayed—Family.   5. Family—Political aspects—
Egypt.   I. Title.
DT107.827.S7   306'.2'0962   81–43527
ISBN 0–8122–7835–6   AACR2

Printed in the United States of America

For George and Mildred,
Patricia and Ziyad

CONTENTS

LIST OF
ILLUSTRATIONS

LIST OF TABLES

PREFACE

Numerous works on the contemporary Middle East state that the family is a crucial unit of interaction in virtually all areas of collective human activity. Having asserted this, few then go on to utilize the family as a basic conceptual tool for understanding political systems.[1] This work is intended primarily to fill that gap with regard to Egyptian politics and, by extension, Middle Eastern and Third World politics more generally. But that cannot be accomplished by extracting out of the dynamics of politics and then analyzing in a vacuum only one of the many social units in which Egyptians gather in pursuit of political goals. Instead, the family must be cast in the ongoing drama of Egyptian politics, so that its relative importance and relation to other contending units can be evaluated. In short, this is a political anthropology of contemporary Egypt, dealing mainly with national-level politics and according the family a central, but not exclusive, importance.[2] As such, it should be of interest both to social scientists specializing in the Middle East or other areas of the Third World and to laymen who want to know more about modern Egypt.

To analyze better the political roles of the family and other relevant social collectivities, a single prominent politician has been selected as the central focus of this work. He is Sayed Ahmad Marei, known informally in Sadat's Egypt, where Ottoman honorific titles have reemerged in daily discourse, as Sayed Bey Marei, and among his friends simply as Sayed Bey. From a prominent rural family that habitually sent at least one of its members to parliament, Sayed Marei began his political career in 1944–45, inheriting his family's seat in the Chamber of Deputies. Following a five-year term in parliament and a brief but successful career as a businessman-financier, Sayed Marei became in 1952 the new revolutionary government's director of agrarian reform. During the Nasser era he went on to become the undisputed overlord of the agricultural sector and eventually the Arab World's most prominent agronomist. Simultaneously he carved out a niche for himself in Nasser's political elite, becoming a leading figure in the single party, in parliament, and in numerous cabinets. His transition to Sadat's Egypt was even smoother than his earlier one from ancien régime to Nasserite politics, due in large part to his intimate friendship with the new president. Probably Sadat's closest confidant, Marei in the 1970s served in numerous capacities, including cabinet minister, leader of the party, parliamentary speaker, diplomat *extraordinaire,* special advisor to the president, and secretary-general of the much publicized 1974 World Food Conference.

Sayed has not been the only successful Marei of his generation. His elder brother served in one of Nasser's early cabinets and then went on to a long career in business, academia, and government. His younger brother became a leading administrator of the nationalized economy, while his half brother, who barely escaped execution for plotting to overthrow Nasser, emerged in Sadat's Egypt as a prominent banker. Sayed's children have similarly promising careers, with the youngest son having become President Sadat's son-in-law in 1975.

An ideal subject for study because of his and his family's political prominence and durability, Sayed Marei is also more of a known and knowable quantity than most other Egyptian politicians. He has written several books as well as scores of articles and pamphlets. His speeches and contributions to parliamentary debates have been part of the public record since 1945. Moreover, in 1976 he began writing his memoirs, part of which were serialized in *al Ahram* before finally being published in three volumes in late 1978.[3] Most important, approached through intermediaries, Sayed Marei proved willing to grant interviews to the author and to urge members of his family to do likewise. Augmented by interviews with a large number of Egyptians who have had casual or sustained contact with Sayed or other members of the Marei family, these are among the most extensive sources a foreign observer could hope to have for any single member of the political elite.

The material so gathered is presented in this book in two parts. In Part One the dramatis personae, in the form of politically relevant units of behavior, are introduced and analyzed. The family, being the most significant of those units, is the subject of the first four chapters. Chapter 5 introduces those nonfamilial units of behavior that have proved to be of importance to Sayed Marei in his political career. Part Two is a political biography of Sayed Marei, tracing his career from his student days in the 1920s to his semiretirement from political life in October 1978. The central theme around which the biographical material is organized is provided by one question: What strategies and tactics, given various and constantly changing political circumstances, did Sayed Marei adopt to exercise and enhance his personal power? It is for the purpose of answering this question that the behavioral units discussed in Part One are introduced.

While standard footnote form has been followed with reference to the Egyptian public record and secondary sources, the autobiography, ghost-written by a team of six from material dictated by Sayed Marei, has been cited sparingly in order to avoid cluttering the text. Unless otherwise indicated, attribution of motives to Sayed Marei is based on his autobiography or on information provided in interviews with him or his closest confidants. Information obtained from other Egyptians is generally not specifically attributed, in part because it is frequently derived from interviews with several different individuals, and in part to avoid complications or embarrassment for the interviewees. Virtually all the information presented on intrafamily affairs was obtained directly from family members, none of whom is specifically identified for the same reasons as mentioned above. The family tree, presented in Appendixes A and B, was constructed from information provided by the Mareis. Their own family tree, no longer kept up-to-date, lies in some forgotten dusty closet in one of the family's decaying rural villas.

ACKNOWLEDGMENTS

This book is the product of a continuing interest in Egyptian elite political culture first stimulated in the early 1970s while I was researching and writing a Ph.D. thesis on that topic. Because its preparation has been operationally and intellectually inseparable from that earlier work, its indebtedness to individuals and institutions dates back more than a decade. Stanford University's Center for Research in International Studies provided the financial support which made it possible to spend 1971–72 in Cairo. I was able to return there in 1977, thanks to a grant from Macquarie University in Sydney, Australia. On both occasions the American Research Center in Egypt provided warm hospitality and useful assistance, practical and intellectual. While in Cairo in 1977, the staff of the Australian Embassy and especially the ambassador, Robin Ashwin, facilitated my work in a variety of ways. Several weeks at the Public Records Office in London in 1978 were also made possible by support from Macquarie University. The University of Pennsylvania has likewise been generous in support of the project, enabling me to visit Cairo briefly in 1980 and to work on the manuscript in the summer of 1980, and providing the facilities and finances necessary to process the manuscript. The Hoover Institution, at which I was a Visiting Scholar in 1980, provided an excellent environment, in which the bulk of Part

Two was written. To all these institutions I express my deepest gratitude, for without the assistance of any one of them the book would either have been impossible to complete or very much inferior.

Those individuals without whose help the work could simply not have been done and whom I would therefore most like to thank are the Mareis themselves, and particularly Sayed. He and numerous members of his nuclear and extended families gave graciously of their time, being extremely indulgent of my intrusions into their personal affairs. It is all the more commendable that they were willing to do this without detailed knowledge of the purpose or the outcome of the study. I hope that they will accept my apologies for the inconveniences caused them by my research and for whatever awkwardness may result from its publication. In that the only compensation any of them will receive is that of seeing their family history pieced together and made publicly available, I can but express my sincerest desire that this will be sufficient reward for their cooperation. I further apologize to the Mareis for any errors of fact or interpretation they may find herein. If any do exist, they reflect an honest mistake rather than malicious or other intent.

Many other Egyptians contributed graciously and generously to the project by granting interviews, engaging in thought-provoking discussions of Egyptian society and politics, providing warm hospitality, and in general making my research experiences highly enjoyable from all standpoints. These individuals, regrettably, must with one exception remain anonymous, lest my recognition of their cooperation cause them embarrassment or worse. That exception is my very dear friend Ahmad Fawzi, who, despite his personal reservations about the advisability of pursuing this topic and his desire not to become involved in the research, did everything he could to ensure its success. I want to thank him for his individual efforts on my behalf and as a representative of a much larger group of his countrymen.

My greatest debt of intellectual gratitude is owed to Clement Henry, who has been a mentor and friend from the outset of my work on the Egyptian elite. Without the benefit of his keen insights into Egyptian politics, his voluminous knowledge of its inside workings, and his constant encouragement and careful reading of the manuscript, the resulting book would have been much inferior. It would also have suffered immeasurably had not my wife, Patricia, made herculean efforts to aid in the research, engaged in discussion on theoretical and substantive issues, and improved the manuscript almost beyond recognition with her careful editing.

Others have contributed variously and significantly to the project. Gabriel Almond and George Lenczowski stimulated my thinking on political elites, provided assistance in numerous ways for the research and writing, and read and commented on the manuscript. Gough Whitlam, former prime minister of Australia, kindly provided my initial introduction to Sayed Marei. Peter Duignan ensured that my stay at the Hoover Institution would be as productive as possible. Don Reid, John Damis, and John Waterbury made useful comments on part or all of the manuscript, as did some ten anonymous readers selected by the Political Science Department of the University of Pennsylvania, the University of Pennsylvania Press, and Syracuse University Press. My colleagues at the University of Pennsylvania, and most particularly Henry Teune, likewise offered advice on improving the manuscript. Kay Dilks typed it expertly and expeditiously. Malcolm Call, Peggy Hoover, and others at the University of Pennsylvania Press facilitated publication in a cooperative and professional manner. To all these individuals and institutions I express my heartfelt thanks, while simultaneously excusing them from responsibility for the work's shortcomings, for which I alone must take the blame.

NOTE ON
TRANSLITERATION

The system of transliteration adopted in this book is intended to balance the interests of both readers and nonreaders of Arabic. Diacritics have not been used, and the 'ayin and hamza have been omitted, except in titles of publications, and in the commonly known Arabic word *ra'is* (president). Widely known names are transliterated as they are found in the Western press, and authors' names are retained as printed. The names of the Mareis appear as they are transliterated by the family members themselves.

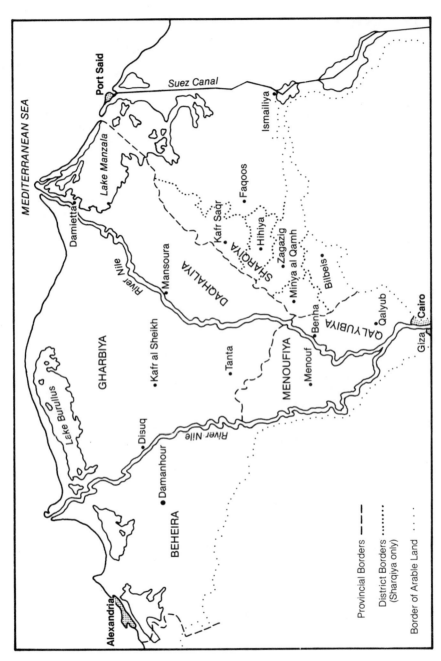

MEDITERRANEAN SEA

Port Said

Suez Canal

Ismailiya

Lake Manzala

Faqoos

Damietta

Kafr Saqr

Hihiya

River Nile

Mansoura

Zagazig

Minya al Qamh

DAQAHLIYA

SHARQIYA

Bilbeis

GHARBIYA

Benha

Kafr al Sheikh

Qalyub

QALYUBIYA

Cairo

Lake Burullus

Tanta

MENOUFIYA

Giza

Menouf

Disuq

Damanhour

River Nile

BEHEIRA

Alexandria

Provincial Borders

District Borders
(Sharqiya only)

Border of Arable Land

Lower Egypt in the 1930s

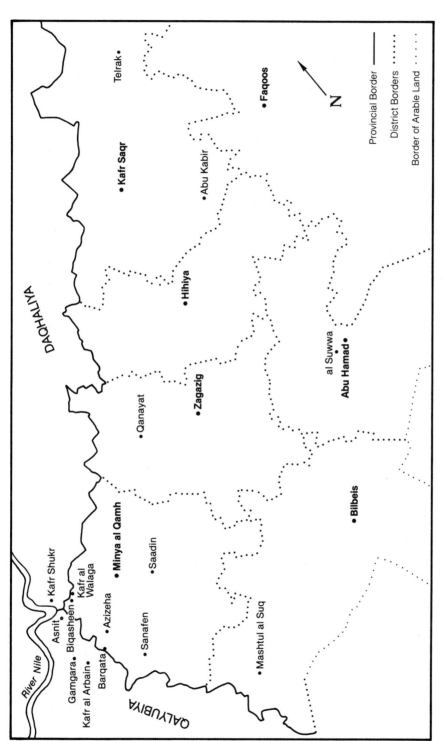

Western Sharqiya

DAQHALIYA

QALYUBIYA

River Nile

Telrak

Faqoos

Kafr Saqr

Abu Kabir

Hihiya

al Suwwa
Abu Hamad

Zagazig

Qanayat

Bilbeis

Minya al Qamh

Saadin

Kafr Shukr
Asnit
Biqasheen
Kafr al Walaga
Gamgara
Kafr al Arbain
Azizeha
Barqata
Sanafen
Mashtul al Suq

N

Provincial Border ———
District Borders ·········
Border of Arable Land · · ·

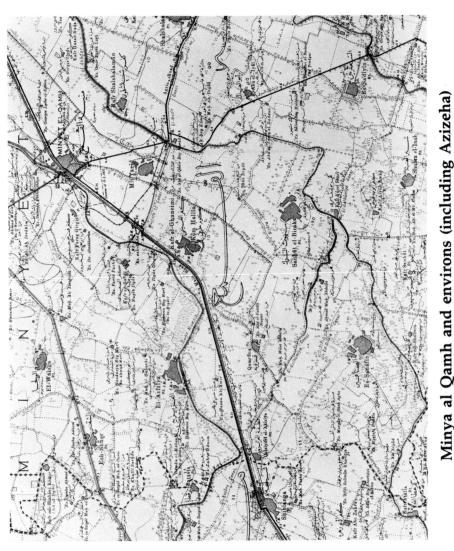

Minya al Qamh and environs (including Azizeha)
(Government of Egypt, Survey Department, 1915)

INTRODUCTION

There is little doubt that Sayed Marei is an interesting, indeed fascinating, Egyptian politician. There may, however, be some question as to how representative he is of the Egyptian elite and, by implication, whether generalizations based upon his career are valid at the macro level. Because he hails from the landowning notability, for example, it might be argued that he was an atypical member of the Nasser and Sadat regimes—but this is not at all the case. The provincial notability has throughout this century provided a majority of the members of the political elite. The transition from ancien régime to Nasserite politics did provide new social forces access to the elite, but as a recent detailed study of the rural notability suggests,[1] that class nevertheless continued to play the dominant political role throughout the Nasser period. Members of the elite from such backgrounds have, if anything, enhanced their political standing in Sadat's Egypt. Thus, while it is fair to say that Sayed Marei and his family are not representative of all social types constituting the elite, they clearly do represent a crucial element within it.

There is, moreover, little evidence to suggest that there are clear and predictable differences in political outlook and behavior between those in the elite springing from the notability, on the one hand, and those from other social origins, on the other. While the family, for example, may be a less significant unit of politically relevant action to nonnotables of urban and especially lower- and middle-class origins, impressionistic evidence suggests that even for these individuals the family, and the connections it provides, is a significant political resource. It might also be hypothesized that the newly acquired elite status of these individuals will enable them through new marriage alliances to capitalize their families as repositories of intergenerational class, status, and power resources. In short, even though the elite may become more heterogeneous, it is premature to predict the decline and eventual demise of the family as a politically relevant unit of social behavior.

It should also be pointed out that the polarities implied by distinctions between officers and civilians, technocrats and provincial notables, businessmen and politicians, urbanites and rural residents, and so on, are not as sharp as the terms suggest. Sayed Marei entered ancien régime politics as a provincial notable, but he made his career under Nasser as a technocrat. During the Sadat era, he has legitimized his presence in the elite through claims to political, not technical, expertise. Similar flexibility has characterized innumerable military officers as they have floated in and out of the various administrative, economic, and political institutions of public life. Less incorporated and institutionalized than larger, more developed political and economic systems, Egypt imposes fewer categorical restraints on its citizens, especially those active in politics. Political strategies and tactics, therefore, cannot be deduced only from vocational roles or ascribed positions in a class hierarchy. Their genesis instead must also be sought in the comparatively complex informal associational life characteristic of the Egyptian social and political systems.

It is curious that some previous endeavors to determine which collectivities are of greatest relevance to the political process have been labeled as Orientalist,[2] by which a great deal is implied, but most importantly that the work, instead of conceptualizing the political process in a priori and universal class terms, has done so in terms that are culturally and historically specific.[3] The unique, in other words, is to these critics suspect, for it implies Western misconceptions of the Orient and the desire to draw distinctions between cultures and people as they exist to the mind of an outsider. This quixotic campaign against presumed Orientalism, understandable in light of the historically oppressive relationship of dominance and subordination that characterizes interaction between the Middle East and the West, is, however, at least in the case of some of its standard-bearers, fundamentally misguided.

In the first instance it is erroneous, to say nothing of the misreading of Marx involved, to assume that the economic is in all cases determinant. Humans group together in pursuit of mutual goals out of numerous and not just economic considerations. This is particularly so in the Middle East, given its history of localized, primordial loyalties and its as yet far from complete process of industrialization. Proper research procedure therefore demands that the determination of politically meaningful units of collective action be an empirical, not a definitional, undertaking. The concept-formation stage is thus an integral part of the empirical research process, for those concepts which must relate to subjectively as well as objectively meaningful collective units cannot be derived by any other method. In this sense most scholarship and especially most good scholarship on the Middle East is essentially pretheoretical, concerned as it is or should be with the difficult task of concept formation. Those doing battle with Orientalism, by failing to recognize this, are paradoxically more a victim of cultural imperialism than some of their presumed enemies. Having extracted from scholarship relating to Western experience concepts essential for its understanding, they demand cultural equality through the misapplication of those nonindigenous concepts.

Those who have cast themselves as anti-Orientalists and who are to a greater or lesser degree committed to class analysis are guilty of a further oversight in failing to appreciate the very significance of the autonomy of the state from its hypothetical economic substructure. In the Middle East, and in Egypt in particular, Marx's characterization of the capitalist state as "a committee for managing the common affairs of the whole bourgeoisie"[4] is inappropriate, and he would be the first to agree. Control over the state apparatus is, in this area of the world—which according to Marx falls under the Asiatic mode of production—a general prerequisite for the acquisition of wealth. But the obverse is not true. Unlike the capitalist mode of production, a monopoly of wealth does not presuppose control of the state apparatus by an economically dominant class, as Marx quite well explained. Political power paves the way for economic success, not vice versa.[5] Government is insufficiently institutionalized to protect economic interests in an impersonal, regularized, and predictable fashion. Such protection can be obtained only through continuous and successful political activity, as the following study of Sayed Marei and his family will suggest. In the case of Egypt, the state, and within it the political elite, is autonomous from class structure in the sense of not being determined by it, while yet being dominant over it.

Even if conflict between social classes were the principal dynamic of politics, it would still remain to be determined how class
interest is formulated and acted upon within those arenas in which
significant policies are made. If, for example, the state is to be labeled
as petit bourgeois, the process by which that class dominates the state
apparatus is a fit and necessary subject for study. Classes do not act
as organized wholes—they are hypothetical constructs based on the
observable pursuit of interest by individuals, families, and possibly
other small social units. To focus, as we do in this work, on the
behavior of an individual and the groups in and with which he has
pursued his goals does not involve, therefore, an implicit denial of the
relevance of class. The political significance of social groups varies
from culture to culture and over time in the same setting, and to
ignore those variations is to imply that class interest operates in a
universally identical fashion, which is nonsense. Neither Orientalism, if by that term is understood the study of social units and
processes indigenous to the Middle East, nor class analysis, should
therefore be seen as irreconcilable or mutually exclusive approaches.
Each should, in fact, benefit from the other's insights.

PART I

THE FAMILY AND OTHER UNITS OF POLITICAL ACTION

1 | THE MAREI FAMILY: FROM BEDOUIN TO TECHNOCRATS

The biblical land of Goshen, lying directly astride the land route from the fertile Nile Valley to the arid Arabian Peninsula, has since time immemorial provided temporary refuge or permanent domicile for countless Arabian tribes seeking escape from the rigors of their harsh environment. Known today as the Egyptian Delta Province of Sharqiya (literally, eastern), the demography of the area still reflects its history as a land bridge and point of entry into Egypt for Arabs of the Peninsula.[1] On the eastern fringe of the province, where the lush green of the Nile Delta gives way to desert, reside the Tahawi, who of the many descendants of Arab tribesmen in the area retain most fully the Arab bedouin life-style. Several thousand strong, the Tahawi remain primarily pastoralists and animal breeders, preferring to build their homes on the sandy hilltop known as Gezirat al Saud (the island of Saud) rather than in the green valley below.[2]

Farther to the west, descendants of most other Arab tribesmen have long since abandoned the rigors of a semibedouin, semidesert existence in favor of agriculture and a settled life-style, but they remain identifiable family units within the native Egyptian population of Sharqiya.[3] They are, moreover, not disadvantaged latecomers to the province and the agrarian life-style, but the most significant element in the provincial elite. Granted large tracts of land by various rulers of Egypt in exchange for military and other services, large Arab families, the most numerous and well known of which is the Abaza, have dominated Sharqiya politics since at least the reign of Muhamed Ali (1805–48).[4] Aggressive, ambitious, cohesive, and wealthy, at least by the standards of the local peasant population, these Arab families have been a force to be reckoned with for almost two centuries, and every Cairo-based government during this period has had to come to terms with them, most frequently by attempting to balance one off against another.

More or less in the middle of this Arab-descended elite, by virtue of size, wealth, and political prominence within Sharqiya, is the Marei family, or, more accurately, the Marei lineage of the Nasr tribe. Descended from one Sheikh al Arab, Nasr Ibrahim Nasr, who migrated along with his tribe from the Nagd in the Arabian Peninsula to Minya al Qamh in western Sharqiya in the beginning of the eighteenth century, the Marei trace their ancestry as a distinct and separate lineage within the Nasr tribe to Marei Ibrahim Nasr, who was born at the time of the Napoleonic invasion of Egypt (1798) and who by virtue of his acumen as a wood merchant amassed considerable wealth, thereby becoming one of the two most prominent sons of Ibrahim Nasr, leader of the Nasr tribe. Converting his assets to land in the environs of Azizeha, a village in the Minya al Qamh district, Marei Ibrahim Nasr on his death, about the time of the Orabi Rebellion in 1881–82, owned some 350 feddans* of prime agricultural land, making him the largest landowner in Azizeha.[5]

Land acquisition by Marei Ibrahim Nasr reflected one of the many trends which were bringing about fundamental economic, social, and political changes in Egypt in the latter half of the nineteenth century. As Ottoman power receded in the face of European colonial penetration, a class of predominantly non-Turkish landowners began to emerge, a class which in Sharqiya included not only native Egyptians but, at least as important, Arabs recently, or not so recently, arrived from the Peninsula. Augmenting their newly acquired wealth in land with political power, members of this emerging class began the process of political osmosis by which they were quickly to rise to the top of the Egyptian political system by first taking over the village headship position known as *umdah*. [6] Representing this trend, Marei Ibrahim Nasr, after a term in office by one of his brothers and a short but, according to the contemporary male elders of the family, disastrous period of tenure by his sister, became *umdah* of Azizeha.

*One feddan equals 1.038 acres.

The key social adhesive binding together individuals within the newly emerging class of landowners was that of intermarriage. Prior to the economic transformations of the mid-nineteenth century, Arab families of Sharqiya evinced a very pronounced tendency toward endogamy. The Nasr virtually always found marriage partners within their own family, as did the Tahawi, the Abaza, and so on. By the mid to latter part of the nineteenth century, however, as land became increasingly sought after, the economic advantages of exogamous marriages became apparent to larger landowners, and they began to link their fates by intermarrying their sons and daughters. The immediate benefit to be gained thereby was the reinforcement of family power bases, while the long-term effect was to weld these families into a cohesive social class capable of successfully accumulating land, then the primary and virtually only source of capital in the country. In Sharqiya, as the scramble for land intensified after 1870, only the very largest of Arab families could afford to go it alone; so, for example, the Abazas continued to find spouses within their own tribe or on occasion to make the trip to Istanbul, where much-sought-after Turkish-Circassian brides were to be found. The Tahawis likewise remained recalcitrant in their desert fastness and continued to practice endogamy almost exclusively. The Nasr, however, were neither as large as the Abaza nor as isolated as the Tahawi and had, in fact, suffered reverses during the reign of Muhamed Ali, when one lineage within the tribe, having somehow engendered the wrath of the ruler or one of his courtiers, fled to Palestine, never to return, taking with it the name of Ezza (shortened from Azizeha). Some of the Nasr thus began to mix their bloodlines and link their economic and political fates with other prominent families, a strategy which the Mareis pursued to greatest effect, rapidly becoming the most prominent and wealthy of the various sublineages of the Nasr tribe.

The marriage strategy of the Mareis involved a judicious mixture of endogamy, by which the lineage's cohesion was maintained, and of exogamous marriages, the majority of which were contracted with two neighboring families, the Abdillas and the Nosseirs. Both families inhabited villages a short donkey ride away from Azizeha. And whereas the Abdilla were the *umdah* family in Sanafen, the Nosseirs, being larger, wealthier, and politically more powerful, had two villages—Gamgara and Kafr al Arbain—at their disposal, and the positions of *umdah* therein. The Abdillas, also of Arab stock, had been a prominent family in western Sharqiya since at least the beginning of the nineteenth century, Muhamed Abdilla serving in the Maglis al

Mashwara (Advisory Council) of Muhamed Ali, and his son Muhamed represented Sanafen in the Maglis Shura al Nuwwab (Consultative Council of Deputies) of 1866–79 and again in the Maglis al Nuwwab (Council of Deputies) of 1881. Another branch of the family, based in Biqasheen, a village lying close to Azizeha, was also represented in the Maglis Shura al Nuwwab of 1870–73.

But the Nosseirs were of considerably greater account than either the Mareis or the Abdillas. This family claims to be descended from Abu Nosseir, one of the Arab conquerors of Spain, and his descendant, another Abu Nosseir, who was a leading general in the army of the famous Salah al Din al Ayyubi (Saladin). Ismail Abu Nosseir, true to the family's putative militant heritage, was Muhamed Ali's son Ibrahim's top commander in the campaign against the Wahhabis in the Arabian Peninsula from 1811 to 1820. He was rewarded for his services with a grant of land, which became the nucleus of the family estates in Sharqiya.[7] From that time until well into this century, the Nosseir were one of the major forces to be reckoned with in Sharqiya Province. Virtually every delegation from Sharqiya to national parliaments, beginning with the Maglis al Mashwara of Muhamed Ali from 1824 to 1837, through the Maglis Shura al Quwanein of 1883 to 1890, and up to the various Gamiat al Ummumiya of 1891 to 1914, included Nosseirs, who by virtue of having supported the British too openly at the time of rising Egyptian nationalism during and after World War I, had to wait until the election of 1930—which was carefully stage-managed by Ismail Sidqy and the king—before regaining access to parliament.[8] The Nosseirs won parliamentary seats on two other occasions prior to 1952 and, after Nasser's rise to power, provided a cabinet minister with some influence. But despite these successes and their ability to hang on to the positions of *umdah* in Kafr al Arbain and Gamgara, declining family fortunes, due mainly to an extremely extravagant life-style, gradually undermined the family's political and economic position during the course of the twentieth century.

While the Nosseirs' fortunes were on the wane, the Mareis' were on the rise, the trajectory of the latter's passing the former's more or less at the time of the purchase by Ahmad Marei in 1923 of the Nosseir family home and surrounding land.[9] By that time, though, the families were so interlinked that the Nosseirs could take pride in, as well as count on the support of, the Mareis. While the linkage of the Marei, Abdilla, and Nosseir families through intermarriage predated the generation of Marei Ibrahim Nasr, it was during his lifetime that the connections became firmly established. This former wood merchant, landowner, and onetime student at al Azhar took as his second wife Sedaata Nosseir, his sister marrying an Abdilla. By his first wife, Marei Ibrahim Nasr had two sons and a daughter: Hassanein-2, Huseyn-3, and Steta-4; while by the second he had two sons and three daughters: Amna-5, Fawzi-6, Halima-8, Fatma-9, and Ahmad-10, in order of birth.*

The marriages of this generation in particular reflect with great accuracy attempts by members of this newly emerging landowning class to consolidate their hold over the countryside and, subsequently, over national politics. Five of the eight offspring of Marei Ibrahim Nasr married Nosseirs. Ahmad, the youngest son, although already married to Zeynab Nosseir, took as a second wife in 1919 his brother Fawzi's beautiful young widow, Nabawiya Nosseir, who was also the cousin of his first wife. The second son, Huseyn, had the most successful match, marrying Nemet Shamsi of the wealthy Sharqiya landowning Shamsi family, which was to provide Ali Shamsi Pasha, Nemet's brother, one of the leading political and financial figures in parliamentary Egypt. Steta, the eldest daughter of Marei Ibrahim Nasr, married the son of a middle-ranking Sharqiya landowning family, one Hassan Qandeel, while the youngest daughter, Fatma, married Ahmad Abdilla, whose mother was a Nosseir. In short, between 1848, the year in which Hassanein, the eldest son, was born, and 1919, the date at which the last marriage of this generation took place, the Mareis succeeded not only in inextricably intertwining their fates with the most prominent family in their immediate neighborhood, the Nosseirs, but also in consolidating the tie to the Abdillas, as well as establishing linkages to the Qandeels, a family of somewhat lesser status than the Abdillas.[10] It was the marriage into the Shamsi family, however, a family geographically more distant in its village of Qanayat, and socially, politically, and economically more prestigious, which most clearly demonstrated the Mareis' passage to prominence in the new elite of Sharqiya.[11]

While marriages to the Qandeel and Shamsi were of course exogamous, those to the Nosseir were endogamous by virtue of matrilineality, and that to the Abdilla was endogamous because of intermarriage in one or more ascending generations. The fact that none of the offspring of Marei Ibrahim Nasr married into any other sublin-

*The Mareis, following Egyptian custom, constantly reuse the same first names, so considerable confusion can arise when examining the family tree. To avoid this, each Marei mentioned in the text, if there is any ambiguity about his or her identity, is assigned a number, the key being provided in the family tree that appears as Appendix A and Appendix B.

eage of the Nasr tribe marked either the beginning, or more probably the continuation of, a process of encysting the Marei lineage within the Nasr tribe, while at the same time further opening it up to new outside lineages, chief of which was the Nosseir. The most probable explanation for the Mareis turning their back on their own tribesmen in favor of neighbors either not connected, or only recently linked, by affinity is that of economic and therefore political and social mobility. The Nasr, as a lineage of much less account than the Shamsi or Nosseir, or even the Abdilla or Qandeel, were a dead end as far as the ambitious Mareis were concerned. Poor country cousins, as indeed most ended up, they were to prove useful as peasants working the Marei estates and as loyal political supporters, but hardly desirable as marriage partners. Thus, while the Mareis today proudly trace their lineage back some eight generations to the noble Sheikh al Arab, Nasr Ibrahim Nasr, and even, occasionally, one step beyond to a bedouin of the Nagd, one Sharif Nasr, they make little reference to the contemporary Nasrs of Sharqiya outside the context of their economic and political dependency.

A process of expansion and consolidation, suggested indirectly by the marriage patterns of the Marei family, is demonstrated in starker terms by their rapid acquisition of land, especially within the economically active life spans of Marei Ibrahim Nasr's children. For convenience' sake we may date this period from about 1870, when Hassanein, the eldest son, had reached his majority, to the late 1930s, when most of the siblings had either died or simply grown too old to take an interest in further financial or political endeavors. Shortly before his death, around 1880, Marei Ibrahim Nasr divided his estate between his four sons, giving the two eldest, Hassanein and Huseyn, 100 feddans each, Fawzi 80 feddans, and his youngest son, Ahmad, 60 feddans. The total exclusion of the four daughters from the patrimony gave rise to considerable family conflict, and after Marei Ibrahim Nasr's death the sons made limited adjustments in favor of their sisters. As it turned out, there was little need for argument, for the landholdings of the Marei lineage expanded rapidly after that time. Hassanein succeeded in parlaying his 100 feddans into some 750 feddans by the time of his death in 1925, while Ahmad did just as well, beginning with some 60 feddans and leaving on his death in 1944 more than ten times that much. The estates left by Huseyn and Fawzi were somewhere between 200 and 600 feddans each. The four brothers together, therefore, accumulated land probably well in excess of 1,750 feddans in total, a very considerable figure by the standards of Sharqiya Province prior to 1952, and one exceeded only by the royal estates in the province and by the holdings of a few very prominent families, such as the Abazas, Tahawis, and Shamsis.

By the early twentieth century, therefore, the Mareis had become prominent local squires in Sharqiya Province. But from that time on they were to be caught up in a continuous process of rapid modernization which within a generation undermined not only the aristocracy but the squirarchy as well, separating members of this class from their rural base. The most obvious and consequential socioeconomic aspects of this modernization were urbanization, education, and change in economic and vocational structures, all of which had profound effects on rural elite families, leading at first to their rise to prominence and later to their decline. In the political arena the Egyptianization of politics, particularly after 1882, and their ever-increasing concentration in the national capital, provided opportunities for rural notables. At the same time, these developments led eventually to the demise of the notability as the dominant class, although not by any means to their total exclusion from Nasserite or post-Nasserite politics.

EDUCATION AND URBANIZATION OF THE MAREIS

Cairo, lying at a distance of slightly more than one hundred kilometers from Azizeha, was well known to Marei Ibrahim Nasr. Prior to the mid-nineteenth century, in his capacity as a wholesaler and retailer of timber in Sharqiya Province, he regularly visited Rod al Farrag, then as now a large entrepôt on the Nile lying just north of the main part of the city. He was, moreover, familiar with the city in other than a commercial context, having been a onetime student at al Azhar, the city's venerable institution of Moslem learning. Impressed by his educational experience, and especially by the modernists led by Muhamed Abduh, who were vying for power and influence at al Azhar with the entrenched, traditionally minded sheikhs, Marei Ibrahim Nasr ensured that the benefits of Western civilization, chief of which was secular education, would be available to his sons. But Marei Ibrahim Nasr himself was essentially a provincial figure. His primary place of residence remained his village of Azizeha, where he and his family occupied a splendid manor house set one hundred meters back from the Bahr al Muweiss, a large irrigation canal flowing through Azizeha and referred to literally as "a sea" by the overly impressed landlocked native inhabitants.

Serving as vehicles for their father's ambitions and reflecting their marginal social status in an Egypt still dominated by the Turkish-Circassian ruling elite, the male offspring of Marei Ibrahim Nasr sought upward mobility by obtaining modern, secular education. It must, however, have been adjudged unwise to commit all of the family too heavily in the more or less unknown direction of modernization and to abandon the traditional rural base entirely. So Hassanein-2, the eldest son, chief inheritor of the patriarchy and main defender of the family's interest, was taught to read and write at home. Not wishing to separate Hassanein for an extended period from the family's rural stronghold, Marei Ibrahim Nasr groomed his eldest son to follow in his footsteps by instructing him in estate management. He likewise taught his eldest progeny the fine art of practical politics, handing down to him the position of *umdah* of Azizeha while Hassanein was still a relatively young man.

With intergenerational continuity in the family's status thereby secured, the younger sons were encouraged to sail on broader and as yet untested waters. Huseyn-3, the second son by Marei Ibrahim Nasr's first wife, was duly sent off to Paris and enrolled in the Polytechnique in preparation for a career in engineering. But he returned to Azizeha before completing the degree and took up residence with his elder brother in his newly constructed mansion, immediately adjacent to, and grander than, the ancestral family home.

It was then left to Fawzi-6, the first son by his father's second wife, to make his and the family's mark in the modern sector. Said to be the most intelligent of the four sons and the apple of his father's eye, Fawzi was also dispatched to Paris, where he eventually obtained a law degree. While in France he made the acquaintance of Abd al Aziz Fahmy and Lutfi al Sayyid, who were likewise studying law and later to become prominent figures in the Egyptian nationalist movement.[12] Armed with a prestigious degree and valuable political contacts, Fawzi returned home to begin his legal and political careers and to start a family with his new wife, Nabawiya Nosseir-7, daughter of Mansour Pasha Nosseir, the patriarch of the branch of the Nosseirs centered in the village of Kafr al Arbain. Fawzi and Nabawiya had three offspring before tuberculosis caused his untimely death while he was yet in his mid-thirties. Ahmad-10, the last child of Marei Ibrahim Nasr, born less than ten years before his father's death, was not encouraged to pursue even a secondary education. However, he invested his considerable intellectual talents in teaching himself English, French, and basic agronomy, augmenting his scholastic knowledge of the latter by extensive experimentation in animal breeding and citrus cultivation on his estates.

The Marei family failed to emerge as a prominent force in national politics in the parliamentary era because as landowners with large but not immense estates they, like their class cohorts, needed to bolster their prestige and augment their connections through secular professional educations. This transition to the status of urban professionals was not really achieved until the generation of Marei Ibrahim Nasr's grandchildren. Huseyn's disinterest in the engineering profession, Fawzi's early death, and Ahmad's youth at the time of his father's death served to delay by one generation the entrance of the Mareis into the modern professions and hence into prominence in national politics. As it turned out, this delay proved to be a blessing in disguise, for had the Mareis achieved national political stature prior to 1952, they would have been forced into political obscurity after that date by the new military government, which did not wish to share the limelight with formerly prestigious political figures.[13]

Urbanization for the Mareis was a gradual process rather than an abrupt step. For each of the sons of Marei Ibrahim Nasr it was accomplished in the same fashion. Establishing temporary residence in Cairo when their children grew to the age of intermediate school (about age ten), they gradually reversed the ratio of time spent in Sharqiya to that spent in Cairo, so that, by their deaths between 1925 and 1944, they had all become Cairenes, owning and occupying villas in the smart new quarters. Hassanein, the eldest, purchased a house in the fashionable new quarter of Qasr al Aini in 1911, which he shared, like the mansion in Azizeha, with his full brother Huseyn and his family. Fawzi died before taking up residence in Cairo, while his younger full brother Ahmad spent the latter half of his life gradually urbanizing. Purchasing a home in the Cairo suburb of Abbasiya just after World War I, Ahmad and his family migrated back and forth between Cairo and Sharqiya, spending considerably more time in the latter than the other Mareis because of Ahmad's greater attachment to the land and the rural life-style. In 1923 he reinforced his ties to the province by purchasing his maternal grandparents' estate in Kafr al Arbain, the splendid mansion and surrounding gardens of the Nosseir family, who had fallen on increasingly hard times. In 1919 Ahmad had married his brother Fawzi's widow and ensconced her and her children in yet another dwelling close to Minya al Qamh in Sharqiya, before eventually purchasing for them a villa on Ahmad Hishmet Street, one of the most fashionable addresses in the European quarter of Cairo, Zamalek. Thus by the early 1930s all the Mareis had become Cairenes, owning valuable real estate in the city and taking part in its social, economic, and political life. Their rural estates in Sharqiya, which they still occupied for at least some period during the summer months, consumed less of their time and interest as the years passed, a trend made evident by the gradual decay of their Italianate rural villas. This physical decay was paralleled by the erosion of their political predominance in the Azizeha-Kafr al Arbain-Sanafen area of Sharqiya, which was not, however, made obvious until Nasser seized power in 1952 and revealed to one and all the relatively fragile political base of the newly urbanized rural gentry. Having maintained neither their rural villas nor their extended networks of peasant clients, the gentry were to find that urbanization had, by 1952, undermined their rural power base to the point that it was no longer a crucial resource in Egyptian national politics. The Mareis, or more specifically, the sublineage of Ahmad and his children, did maintain closer ties to the countryside than many of their class cohorts, however, and as a result had a political power base of some significance even after 1952.

The generation of Hassanein-2, Huseyn-3, Fawzi-6, and Ahmad-10 (hereafter referred to as the second generation) was sociologically, geographically, economically, and politically transitional for the Marei family. Beginning life in Azizeha in the household of their father, Marei Ibrahim Nasr, members of this generation witnessed from their earliest days the customary deference of peasants dismounting from their donkeys when they passed by the walls of the Marei mansion lest, by riding on, they show disrespect for the owners. As notables occupying the top rung in the local status order, the Mareis were as yet unknown beyond the confines of the Minya al Qamh district of the province of Sharqiya. They were, moreover, at the time of their births ethnically marginal, because the country's elite was Turkish-Circassian, and Egyptians, including those of Arab descent, were just beginning their ascent into the elite. By the time the second generation of Mareis reached middle age, however, the Turkish-Circassian ruling elite had been almost completely submerged in a demographic sea of native Egyptians. The Mareis themselves had by then become respected notables at the provincial level, although not as yet attaining national prominence, an achievement to be gained in the succeeding generation.

This second generation became urbanized, a unilinear process which altered irrevocably not only their life-styles but the life-styles of all their descendants. The second generation also began the vocational shift from landowners to modern professionals, although again it was the succeeding generation that completed this process. When asked to specify their vocations in order to submit their names for political candidacy, second-generation Mareis identified themselves as landowners, an occupation which was of only secondary interest to almost all their sons, who were to obtain professional credentials. Politically, the second generation began life at a time when the Mareis could aspire to an office no higher than that of village *umdah,* but ended it having occupied seats in parliament for several terms, an achievement which implied considerable standing within Sharqiya and carried with it the promise of power and influence on the national level.

In sum, having begun life in the rural surroundings and traditional style which Mareis and Nasrs had known since their ancestor had emigrated to Sharqiya in the early eighteenth century, members of this second generation ended it as at least partially Europeanized gentlemen living among British, French, Germans, and other Westerners in a rapidly modernizing metropolis. Because these transitional processes, including that of expansion and consolidation through marriage, are crucial to understanding the development of the Marei family and, by implication, Egyptian politics more generally, they will now be reviewed in the context of the male sublineages. The sublineages established by Marei Ibrahim Nasr's daughters, being of lesser importance to the family as a whole, are discussed in Appendix C.

HASSANEIN AND HIS SUBLINEAGE

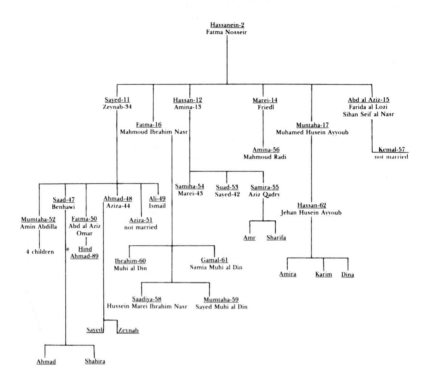

In 1886 at the age of thirty-three, Hassanein, the eldest son of Marei Ibrahim Nasr, married Fatma Nosseir, who by virtue of her fecundity was later to earn the nickname of Um al Rizq (Mother of Riches). Fatma, some sixteen years of age at the time of her marriage, was the elder sister of Zeynab Nosseir, who was later to marry Hassanein's younger brother Ahmad. Fatma and Zeynab's four brothers were to become the main standard-bearers of the Nosseir family.[14] Thus Hassanein Marei, having inherited from his father the position of *umdah* of Azizeha, married into the more powerful branch of the Nosseir, thereby reinforcing his and his family's dominant position in Azizeha, but simultaneously precluding the option of attempting to win a seat in any of the prewar parliaments. The limited size of those parliaments, and the large electoral districts which resulted, meant that the Mareis of Azizeha were thrust together with the Nosseirs of Kafr al Arbain, and given that the latter were in the nineteenth century of considerably more account than the Mareis, there was no question which family would ride the other's coattails. It was only in the next generation, after the Nosseirs had succeeded in dissipating the larger part of their fortunes and had to sell off the bulk of their lands, that the upwardly mobile Mareis were able to turn the tables.

Between 1887 and 1903 Hassanein's wife Fatma gave birth to four sons and two daughters who lived to maturity. The family continued to live in the luxurious villa adjacent to the Bahr al Muweiss in Azizeha until 1911, when it was decided that instead of dispatching the younger sons to board in Cairo while obtaining their intermediate and secondary educations, as their elder brothers had done, it would be preferable for the whole family to live together in Qasr al Aini, the new and bustling district of Cairo. By that time the eldest son, Sayed-11,* following in his Uncle Huseyn's and Uncle Fawzi's footsteps, had already departed for advanced study in France. Returning to Egypt at the time of World War I, Sayed, his degree in medicine newly acquired, first established a practice in the provincial town of Mansoura and then moved on to Alexandria. Despite Sayed's geographical separation from the Marei family in Cairo and Sharqiya, and his acquisition of an M.D. and a modern profession, he married his father's sister Fatma's daughter, Zeynab-34, who had lived most of her life until then in the Abdilla village of Sanafen.

But Sayed, having moved into the new professional world of rapidly Westernizing Egyptian elites in Cairo and Alexandria, and despite being the eldest male of the third-generation Mareis, was to take little interest in Marei family economic and political affairs, although socially he and his relatives remained on close terms. He was uninterested in assuming the mantle of political leadership which he might have inherited from his father Hassanein, nor did he endeavor to expand his landholdings. On his death in 1944 he left a parcel of some 120 feddans which he had inherited from his father and which his father had before him inherited from Marei Ibrahim Nasr.

It was Hassanein's second son, Hassan-12, to be referred to significantly in adult life as Hassan Hassanein, who was to lead this branch of the family. Born in 1892, Hassan completed a degree in

---

*Not to be confused with Sayed Ahmad Marei-42, the principal focus of Part Two of this study.

agronomy in England before returning to Azizeha to manage the family's estates. Like his elder brother, he too married a cousin, his father's brother Huseyn's eldest daughter Amina-13, thereby linking through endogamy in the third generation the sublineages of the two full brothers Hassanein and Huseyn. At the age of thirty-one, Hassan made his claim to political leadership of the entire Marei family, demanding that he be nominated as the Wafdist candidate for the district of Azizeha in the 1923 parliamentary elections, the first held in nominally independent Egypt. The effect of generational skewing was such, however, that his father's youngest half brother, Ahmad-10, was at this time only in his early forties, and he too coveted the roles of family leader and M.P.* The rivalry between Hassan and Ahmad split the Marei family along the lines of maternal descent, the sons, daughter, and grandchildren of Marei Ibrahim Nasr through his first wife lining up behind Hassan, and the rest of the family, which was descended from the second wife, Sedaata Nosseir, supporting Ahmad. In the end it was the younger Hassan, backed by his father Hassanein and his uncle Huseyn, who carried the day and won the endorsement of the Wafd for the Azizeha constituency.

Hassan spent a good deal of his adult life jousting with his uncle for political prominence because, despite being of the third-generation Mareis, he was, as the second eldest son of Marei Ibrahim Nasr's eldest son, closer in age to the younger members of the second generation. His life-style reflected this, for he, like members of the older generation, spent several months a year in Azizeha until 1935, when he purchased a villa in Heliopolis and became increasingly reluctant to journey out to Sharqiya. Lacking a profession, despite his degree in agronomy, Hassan's vocation was listed as "Min al Ayan" (notable) on election registers. He died in 1961, his greatest disappointment in life having been his wife's failure to have a son— although she did have three daughters who were to play a crucial role in healing the split in the family's solidarity, a subject to be discussed below.

Hassanein's third son, Marei-14, was born in 1897 and sent to England for a university education at the end of World War I. Feeling victimized by English prejudice against Egyptians in the wake of the 1919 nationalist uprising, he left England that year for Germany, where he completed his degree. Eventually marrying a German woman, Marei made his career in the Egyptian foreign service and

---

*Reflecting English usage, Egyptians use the term member of parliament for legislators.

lived most of his life in Europe. Having but one daughter, he died in 1948, leaving an estate of only some 50 feddan.

Hassanein's youngest son, Abd al Aziz-15, was born in Cairo in 1903, the first of the family not to enter the world in Azizeha. Like his three brothers, he too was educated in Europe, taking a B.Sc. in commerce from the University of Lyons and a Ph.D. in economics from the University of Lausanne. Returning to Egypt in the early 1930s, he was appointed to the faculty of economics at Ain Shams University, where he remained throughout his life. In 1939 he married Farida al Lozi, daughter of the wealthy al Lozi family of Damietta, which ran a silk-weaving business in Alexandria.[15] Of their four sons, only one lived to maturity. On the death of his wife in 1952, Abd al Aziz married Sihan Seif al Nasr, daughter of Hamdi Seif al Nasr, a prominent Wafdist and frequent cabinet minister in the 1930s and 1940s.[16]

Fatma-16, Hassanein's eldest daughter, was married to Mahmoud Ibrahim Nasr, her grandfather's brother's son and the only connection between the Marei lineage and the Nasrs in this generation. Fatma's husband was in fact the most powerful of the Nasr not in the Marei lineage, and on occasion he served as *umdah* of Azizeha, thereby further reinforcing the hold of Hassanein Marei's lineage on the rural political base. The endogamous marriage of Fatma was balanced by the exogamous marriage of her sister Muntaha-17, who was matched with Muhamed Pasha Hussein Ayyoub, later to become the second chamberlain of King Fuad and then governor of Alexandria. The Ayyoub family from al Suwwa, a village close to Zagazig, capital of Sharqiya, was one of the leading families in the province. Muhamed Ayyoub's older brother Ali Ayyoub served as a Wafdist M.P. in the 1925, 1926, 1930, and 1936 parliaments and as a Saadist in 1945 and was the leader of the Sharqiya parliamentary delegation and a minister of state in 1939 and minister of social affairs ten years later. This affinal tie to the Ayyoubs was, like the link to the Shamsis, a connection which Muntaha's brother Hassan drew on in his struggle to ensure that his Uncle Ahmad would not short-circuit his tie to the Wafdist elite and hence to electoral success.

Of Hassanein's six children, only the elder daughter, Fatma, remained permanently in Sharqiya, where her Nasr husband looked after the family's estates and political fortunes. The sibling with the next strongest tie to the land was Hassan. By virtue of his degree in agronomy, which made him the ideal son to manage the family estates, and because of his political ambition, which necessitated his being on the scene in Sharqiya at least part of the time to weave alliances among surrounding notable families as well as to keep the peasant clientele loyal, he delayed the last step in his process of urbanization until the mid-1930s. In the meantime, the other children had become residents of Cairo, Alexandria, or Europe, returning to Sharqiya infrequently and taking little if any interest in the management of the family estates, from which most derived only a secondary source of income, the primary source being their professions. In short, Hassanein's children, of whom but one is still living, more or less completed the process of transition begun by their parents from rural gentry to urban, Westernized professionals.

HUSEYN AND HIS SUBLINEAGE

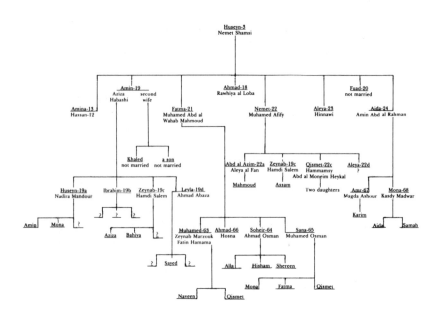

Huseyn, recalled from Paris by his father Marei Ibrahim Nasr before finishing his engineering degree, was consoled by his marriage to Nemet Shamsi, daughter of Sheikh Ali Shamsi. Merging his household with that of his brother Hassanein, Huseyn lived the life of a gentleman landowner, first in Azizeha, where he served briefly as

umdah, and then, after 1911, in Cairo. The only son of Marei Ibrahim
Nasr to be married out of the Marei/Nasr, Nosseir, Abdilla tripartite
marriage alliance, Huseyn founded what was to become the highest-
status sublineage of the Mareis. His eldest son, Amin-19, who did
not bother with a university degree, assumed responsibility for the
economic and political fortunes in Sharqiya of Huseyn's children and
their families. Utilizing his connection to the Wafd hierarchy through
his mother's brother Ali Shamsi Pasha, Amin Marei secured the
Wafd's nomination for the Senate in 1938, defeating Senator Abd al
Aziz Radwan, a successful industrialist, cotton broker, and landowner from Zagazig. Equally successful in finances, politics, and
matrimony, Amin married Aziza Habashi of the extremely wealthy
landowning family of Habashi from Damanhour, which produced
Saba Habashi, a leader of the newly emerging financial/industrial
sector and an occasional minister of commerce and industry.

Amin's younger brother, Ahmad-18, took an M.D. specializing
in radiology at Edinburgh University, returning to establish a clinic
in Cairo after an extended period of training in Vienna. In 1943 he
married Rawhiya al Loba, daughter of Muhamed al Loba Pasha, one
of the several large landowners from Upper Egypt who were the main
force behind the Liberal Constitutionalists, a party with a reputation
for being generally pro-British, economically conservative, and
representing the interests of the country's largest landowners.

While the two elder brothers reflected the status and affluence
of this branch of the Marei family by virtue of political and professional success and by marriages into two of the country's leading
families, the younger brother Fuad-20 also mirrored his family's high
status by managing to lead a life of complete frivolity. Failing out of
both Oxford and Cambridge universities, he returned to Cairo to live
with his sister Aida-24 and her husband for the next twenty-five
years, spending with gay abandon the considerable revenues which
were his share of the earnings from the family estates. Enjoying a
bachelor playboy's existence, he died prematurely of liver disease in
1957 without having worked a day in his life.

The lives of Huseyn's five daughters similarly reveal the upper-
class status which he attained. Amina-13, the eldest, was married off
to Hassan-12, son of Hassanein. Three other daughters married doctors, one of the favorite professions for the sons of rural notable
families like the Mareis. The youngest daughter, Aida-24, married
her brother Fuad's close friend Amin Abd al Rahman, whose family
village was Kafr al Walaga, a short drive from Azizeha. A nephew of
the *umdah* of that village, Amin Abd al Rahman took a commerce

degree in England before embarking on a successful career in business and government administration.

In sum, Huseyn's offspring, like his elder brother Hassanein's, moved successfully into the new urban professional elite, with one of the sons taking charge of the family's political and economic affairs in the countryside. Huseyn's children, however, being the sons and daughters of a Shamsi mother, had a claim to higher social status than their cousins, as is reflected by the preponderance of physicians in the sublineage.

FAWZI AND AHMAD AND THEIR SUBLINEAGE

Ahmad-10, the youngest son of Marei Ibrahim Nasr, was the battler in the family. Whereas his elder half brother Hassanein was the chief inheritor of the family patrimony, his other half brother, Huseyn, was favored by an education in Europe and marriage into the notable Shamsi family, and his full brother Fawzi was likewise armed for a professional career with a French law degree, Ahmad, not benefiting from paternal guidance, his father having died before he was ten, was left more or less to his fate on the family estates in Sharqiya. Intelligent and ambitious, he turned his talents to agriculture and succeeded admirably, using his profits to acquire more land. Although he moved his large family to Cairo in 1919 so that his sons could enroll in intermediate and secondary schools in Abbasiya, he continued to manage his estates actively and to add to them. Having become by the 1930s the largest landowner in the family as a result of his own efforts, Ahmad felt entitled to become the family's standard-bearer in the provincial political arena. Ahmad's young nephew Hassan, son of Hassanein, felt differently, however, and almost to the end of their lives these two men were to fight a running battle over the parliamentary seat centered on Azizeha.

In the 1923 election, despite Hassan's victory in securing the Wafdist endorsement for Azizeha, Ahmad Marei did manage to pull family strings so that his honor and political aspirations were salvaged. Although his sister Fatma-9's daughter was married to Hassan's older brother, Sayed-11, Ahmad succeeded in winning Fatma's and, more important, her husband's support for his candidacy from the neighboring electoral district centered on the village of Sanafen. This village and the surrounding countryside were the preserve of the

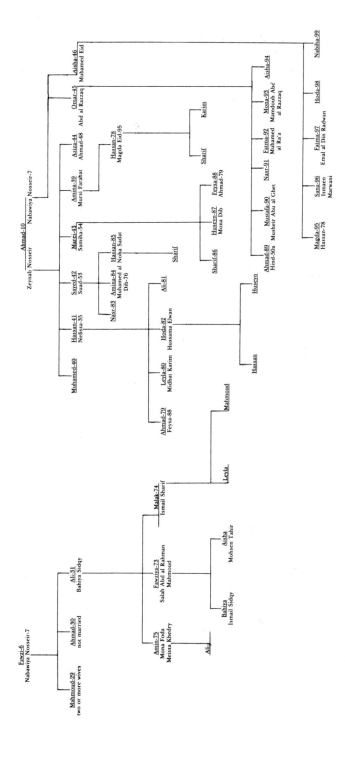

Abdilla family. Fatma's husband, Ahmad Abdilla, the son of the sister of Marei Ibrahim Nasr, was the leader of that family. So with the backing of his Abdilla in-laws, Ahmad Marei succeeded in defeating the incumbent prime minister and representative of the foundering Turkish-Circassian elite, Yehia Ibrahim Pasha, causing a British political officer in Cairo to comment that the prime minister had been defeated "by a Zaghloulist of no standing."[17] Saad Zaghloul himself referred to Ahmad Marei's surprise victory in a postelection speech in Cairo.

Over the long haul, however, Hassan was to prove too powerful for his Uncle Ahmad, for not only did he have the support of his father Hassanein and his uncle Huseyn, but, more important, he had Huseyn's brother-in-law, Ali Shamsi Pasha, one of the leading figures in the Wafd, pushing his political career along. So Ahmad, precluded from receiving Wafdist endorsement by his nephew's alliance with Ali Shamsi Pasha, had to wait until 1937–38, when Ahmad Maher Pasha and Nuqrashy Pasha split from the Wafd and founded the Saadist Party, which duly endorsed Ahmad Marei's candidacy in the Azizeha district for the 1938 election, which the Saadists won handily. Ahmad thus replaced his nephew in parliament. But if revenge was sweet, it was also short. Hassan, once again with Wafdist support, won back the Azizeha seat in 1942. In short, throughout his life, despite achieving considerable financial and political success, Ahmad had to live with the fact that his two elder half brothers and their children were, by virtue of age and marriage connections, of higher status than himself. In the eyes of Hassanein's and Huseyn's children and grandchildren, Ahmad and his children were, and despite their national prominence still are, the country cousins of the family.

Had his full brother Fawzi lived, Ahmad would have been able to draw on his support in the family feud, but Fawzi's premature death prior to World War I left Ahmad with only sisters as full siblings. As the surviving male kinsman closest to Fawzi, he assumed responsibility for raising Fawzi's three sons and eventually married Fawzi's widow, Nabawiya Nosseir, by whom Ahmad had a son Omar-45 and daughter Aisha-46, bringing to eight the total number of his children. In the early 1920s tragedy struck Ahmad and his family when the eldest son, sixteen-year-old Muhamed-40, drowned while swimming in the Bahr al Muweiss in front of the ancestral family home in Azizeha. This tragedy, in combination with the family feud, led Ahmad to abandon Azizeha as the scene of his summer residence and to move to Kafr al Arbain, the estate of his maternal grandparents, which he had acquired after the Nosseir family had been forced by financial difficulties to sell.

The next eldest son of Ahmad, Hassan-41, born in 1906 and reflecting his father's practical-mindedness and interest in agricultural equipment, took a degree in mechanical engineering at Birmingham University, remaining overseas for such an extended period that the task of assuming the family's political burden in Sharqiya had to fall to the next son, Sayed-42. Hassan, who is now the patriarch of the entire Marei family, eventually did enter the cabinet in the early years of the Nasser era, but that brief sortie into top-level politics was the result of his technical expertise and, more important, his brother Sayed's personal connections within the Revolutionary Command Council and is not an indication of political prowess or even particular interest on Hassan's part. Hassan's marriage to his father's full sister Fatma-9's daughter Nefissa-35 reinforced the connection between these sublineages but did nothing to bridge the gap between the two wings of the family based on descent from the two wives of Marei Ibrahim Nasr and exacerbated by the conflict between Hassan-12 and Ahmad-10.

It was Ahmad's third son, Sayed-42, whose political career is the subject of Part Two, who was simultaneously to heal the wound to the family's solidarity and catapult the family name into national political prominence. Beginning life in Azizeha, Sayed was transferred from the village *kuttab* (Quranic school) to a primary school in Abbasiya when the family moved there in 1919. But Sayed, unlike most of his cousins and his elder brother, was to retain strong links to Sharqiya, largely as a consequence of his father's commitment to rural life. Spending five months a year in Azizeha, and then after his brother Muhamed's death, in Kafr al Arbain, Sayed was taught the rudiments of agriculture by his father, especially horse-breeding and a love for horses. On completing his secondary certificate, he entered the faculty of agriculture at Cairo University, where he obtained his B.Sc. summa cum laude in 1937. Immediately upon graduation, he made two decisions that were to be crucial for his future political career. The first and most important was his decision to become engaged to marry Suad-53, daughter of Hassan-12, his father's nephew and political rival. This was a stroke of brilliance, for in one move it terminated the open hostility and rivalry between the Hassanein/ Huseyn and Fawzi/Ahmad sublineages and placed Sayed in the key position of inheriting not only his father's political mantle but also that of Hassan, who was without a male heir. Moreover, in that the three daughters of Hassan stood to inherit considerable estates from

their father, it meant that Sayed would have doubly large landholdings on which to practice his newly learned agricultural science, an
opportunity which probably would not have materialized had he
married outside the family.

Sayed's second decision was to center his newly formed household in Kafr al Arbain and to become a practicing farmer, rather than
to enter the bureaucracy, as most of his classmates chose to do. The
years Sayed was to spend in Kafr al Arbain prior to 1950, when he
moved to Cairo, enabled him to learn practical agriculture and to
become well acquainted with the local population, both gentry and
peasants. His knowledge of agriculture and the intricacies of Sharqiya family relations and politics were resources which served his
later career admirably.

Sayed's younger full brother, Marei-43, following in Sayed's
footsteps, likewise took a degree in agriculture from Cairo University and married in June 1942, some eighteen months after Sayed,
Samiha-54, another daughter of Hassan and the older sister of
Sayed's wife, Suad. The two brothers and two sisters set up a joint
household as their uncles Hassanein and Huseyn had done before
them. Marei worked with Sayed managing the family estates before
embarking on a career in business and government administration,
which was eventually to culminate in his appointment as director of
the Chemical Mouassassat (Organization), the governmental administrative body created to oversee the chemical industry during
Nasser's experiment with Arab Socialism.

Ahmad also had two daughters, Amina-39 and Aziza-44, by his
first wife, Zeynab Nosseir. The eldest, Amina, was married to Mursi
Farahat, a prominent Wafdist from Sharqiya, who was to serve as
minister of supply in the 1950 Wafdist cabinet. Aziza was married
to Hassanein's grandson, Ahmad-48, the eldest male of the fourth
generation in the patrilineage. Thus Sayed, Marei, and Aziza all married grandchildren of Hassanein, thereby closing the rift that had
opened up between their father Ahmad and his nephew Hassan.[18]

But while this series of well-executed marriages reunited the
branches of the family descended from the two wives of Marei
Ibrahim Nasr, a similar problem caused by different and conflicting
matrilineages was being recreated in the generation of Ahmad's children. When Nabawiya Nosseir, wife of Fawzi, married her husband's
brother, Ahmad, she brought with her to their newly established
household, purposely at a considerable distance from both Azizeha
and Kafr al Arbain, three sons. Young and attractive, Nabawiya,
much to the dismay of Ahmad's first wife, Zeynab Nosseir, was to

become the favorite of the two. Increasingly the preferred companion of Ahmad, Nabawiya was eventually moved from Sharqiya to Ahmad's newly acquired luxurious villa in Zamalek, the most prestigious suburb of Cairo, while Zeynab was left in her older residence in the declining quarter of Abbasiya. In 1924, Nabawiya provided Ahmad with a son, Omar-45, and somewhat later a daughter, Aisha-46. Omar and Aisha were raised with their half brothers, the three sons of their mother, Mahmoud-29, Ahmad-30, and Ali-31, and not with their paternal half brothers or sisters. Presumably Zeynab Nosseir's jealousy affected her children's attitudes, for to this day there is evidence of friction between the offspring of Zeynab and Nabawiya, and although this division has not given rise to open conflict and is not unbridgeable for political and economic purposes, it does form an obstacle to social interaction.[19]

The marriages of Nabawiya's offspring reflect her slightly marginal position in the Marei family and her ambition for social status, for they were arranged exclusively with prominent outsiders. Omar, Nabawiya's son by Ahmad, married the daughter of Mustafa Abd al Razzaq of the wealthy and powerful Abd al Razzaq family centered in Abu Girg in Minya Province.[20] Omar's sister Aisha married Muhamed Eid, a large landowner from Abu Sultan in the district of Ismailiya, where his uncle, Dr. Sulimani, a prominent jurist, had the distinction of defeating Hassan al Banna, founder and leader of the Moslem Brotherhood, in a parliamentary election. Successful as these two marriages were, they were overshadowed by the marriage of Nabawiya's son Ali (by her first husband Fawzi) to Bahiya Sidqy, daughter of Ismail Sidqy, one of the longest-serving prime ministers in parliamentary Egypt.[21]

But the propensity for high-status marriages did not erode the commitment to family solidarity, as endogamous and even exogamous marriages in the generation of Zeynab and Nabawiya's grandchildren suggest. Two endogamous marriages were contracted, one linking Zeynab's grandson Hassan-78 to Nabawiya's granddaughter Magda-95, and another linking Nabawiya's grandson Ahmad-89 to Hassanein's great-granddaughter Hind Omar. This latter marriage illustrates particularly well the complexity of the web tying together individuals within the family, and its reinforcement by overlapping affinal connections.

Hind Omar's father is Abd al Aziz Omar, a son of Dr. Abd al Rahman Omar, a former leading member of the Liberal Constitutionalist Party and nephew of Abd al Aziz Fahmy, one of the top figures in that party and in Egyptian politics generally in the interwar period.

Abd al Aziz Fahmy, it may be recalled, was a close friend of Naba-wiya's husband Fawzi as a result of their having been classmates in a French law school. Nabawiya and Fawzi's son Ali married Bahiya Sidqy, whose father had been a member of the Liberal Constitution-alists at the outset of his career and on good terms with Abd al Aziz Fahmy. A third close friend of theirs, Ali Abd al Razzaq, also of the Liberal Constitutionalists and famous as a result of his *Islam and the Principles of Government,* a treatise which challenged the authority of King Fuad and the religious establishment, was the uncle of the wife of Nabawiya's son Omar.

Yet another connection interlinking Nabawiya's sons and daughters, their second cousin Fatma-50 (mother of Hind Omar), and the elite of the Liberal Constitutionalist Party was established through the enormously wealthy Mahmoud family of Upper Egypt. Salah Abd al Rahman Mahmoud, nephew of Prime Minister Muhamed Mahmoud, leader of the Liberal Constitutionalists, mar-ried Nabawiya's son Ali's daughter Fawziya.[22] Salah Abd al Rahman Mahmoud's first cousin on his mother's side, a Mahfouz of the Assiuti Mahfouz family, which is extensively intermarried with the Mahmouds, was then married to Ahmad Nosseir-28, the banker-nephew of Ahmad Marei, who was brought up in the household of Ahmad and Zeynab Marei.

For this branch of the Fawzi and Ahmad sublineage, the wealthy families that composed the core of the Liberal Constitutionalist Party provided the social context within which suitable exogamous mar-riages were arranged. The density of these relationships, combined with the two crucial endogamous marriages, served to reinforce the sublineage and to maintain its linkage to the family as a whole. In turn, other members of the family could utilize the political connec-tions which these marriages made possible, as we shall see in the following chapters.

CONCLUSION: THE MAREI FAMILY TODAY

All the Mareis have now urbanized, and only a few maintain villas in Sharqiya. Even those who manage their own farms visit them not more often than once or twice a week for a few hours. There are no large regular family gatherings in the countryside, except on the occasion of parliamentary elections, when family members may journey up to Sharqiya to staff Sayed Marei's campaign organization. The Mareis have their permanent residences in villas and apartments scattered throughout Heliopolis, Zamalek, Garden City, and Qubbah, the most luxurious residential sections in Cairo. Without exception, all male members of these generations have gone to university, and many have taken advanced degrees abroad, as have some of the females. Vocationally, the Mareis, and those married to them, tend to be doctors, engineers, university teachers, businessmen, and/or bureaucrats, deriving their primary income from these vocations and not from their land.[23] Many, in fact, do not own rural real estate, and some have never been in Sharqiya. In short, the Mareis have become part of the highly Westernized urban and educated elite of the Third World and, like their class counterparts in Egypt and elsewhere, they behave accordingly. They tend to marry later, to marry spouses closer to their own age, and to have fewer children than their parents or ancestors.

The Mareis and other Egyptian families differ, however, from Western and most other Third World families in their propensity for endogamous marriage, which, in turn, has implications for family solidarity. Having undergone a fundamental transformation in lifestyle from the days when Marei Ibrahim Nasr journeyed to Rod al Farrag to purchase timber, the family remains nevertheless a constant in the lives of the Mareis of descending generations, continuing to be, largely as a consequence of endogamy, almost as important for the Mareis of today as it was for their ancestors.

2 | MAREI MARRIAGE PATTERNS: PRESERVATION OF CLASS, STATUS, AND POWER

THE ACT OF MARRIAGE

Since marriages are key indicators of the strategy by which a family attempts to preserve its power and privilege from one generation to the next, the process by which a marriage comes about is of more than just passing interest. It is, in fact, crucial, for modification of the marriage process due to systemic social change, often labeled Westernization or modernization, may wreak havoc with traditional family strategies predicated on marriage alliances. Specifically, if the right of a family to arrange the marriages of its offspring should be eroded in favor of the volition of the latter, then the pursuit of a systematic strategy for the renewal of wealth, status, and power in succeeding generations must contend with those chance factors associated with youth and youthful exuberance. The best-laid plans of careful parents can go up in smoke if their children assume the initiative in the marriage process. How then do marriages come about in the Marei family?

In the first instance, the dichotomization of marriages into those that are arranged and those that are the product of free choice by the marriage partners is a false one. Egyptian marriages should be seen on a continuum, ranging from those entirely arranged by the parents and family elders, in which the partners have no input in the decision-making and may in fact never have seen one another, to those very few marriages that are totally the product of the partners' instigation. The concept of a continuum is important, for while the Mareis themselves now say, and presumably believe, that their marriages are not arranged, most Europeans and Americans, operating with a different scale in mind, would consider them very much arranged. But to categorize all marriages as arranged would make it impossible to distinguish between marriages in preceding generations and those that are presently being made.

Until the post-World War II era the general practice was for parents, in consultation with other senior members of the extended family, to initiate the marriage process. The degree of participation in decision-making by those to be married varied between individuals, by type of marriage, and over time. One family story relates the plight of the handsome young Marei meeting on his marriage night for the first time his breathtakingly ugly bride, a story usually told to emphasize the distance that the family has traveled over the generations in the direction of modernity. But in fact that distance is not all that great if one finds the correct starting point. Prior to the 1940s and 1950s, marriages frequently took the form described in the story, but even then there was generally an input by the intended partners, in the form of a meeting arranged by the parents of the prospective spouses on neutral ground, usually in the house of a mutual friend. In this way the partners could see and possibly speak to one another. Marriages, and probably the majority of those that are exogamous, continue to be arranged in this fashion, although the meeting ground is now frequently one of Cairo's sporting clubs, and the number of occasions on which the families convene for their children to interact prior to entering into a marriage commitment has been increased. In other words, while in the majority of cases of exogamous marriages parents continue to initiate the process, the veto power of their children has increased through the generations.

There are now, and have been for half a century, other types of exogamous marriages. First, there are those that take place between Mareis and spouses known, at least originally, only to the persons being married, or in other words, marriages completely initiated by the partners. These marriages are of two subtypes: those contracted with foreigners, of which there are two in the lineage, and those in which a Marei male has taken more than one wife. While not all marriages to second wives are conducted beyond the jurisdiction of the family, many of them have been. Such marriages are considered to be a black mark on the family's record and are very much frowned upon by other members of the family. So, for example, Muhamed, grandson of Huseyn and father of two university-age children, took as a second wife Fatin Hamama, currently Egypt's leading movie star. His uncle Amin had also married two younger women while still married to his first wife, Aziza Habashi. In such cases the family ostracizes the new in-law and openly communicates its displeasure to the offending husband. In short, if the marriage partner is unknown to the family, and the family's blessing for the marriage is not sought or is not forthcoming, then the offending individual risks isolation from the family.

A more common type of exogamous marriage also began to occur some twenty years ago and now accounts for almost as many exogamous marriages as the type initiated by the parents. In this type the matrimonial connection is made not through the parents but through another somewhat older member of the family, usually a brother, a sister, or a first cousin. The procedure is that of a friend of the brother, sister, or cousin being introduced into one of the small groups of age cohorts in the family, usually with the idea in mind that he or she would make a good spouse for a specific member of that group. As this family-based group socializes over time on the university campus, at the sporting club, or in homes of the family, the couple who have been steered together by the family matchmakers may indicate a desire to marry. At this point the families of the prospective spouses, if previously not well known to one another, begin discreet inquiries to determine the family's suitability.

If this test is passed, approval for marriage is finally given by the family patriarch, who in the case of the Mareis is now Hassan-41. Although some two months younger than the oldest living male member of the family, Abd al Aziz-15, Hassan has for some years, by virtue of his strong personality and career success, served as the family's leader. If Hassan, acting as the family spokesman, is not pleased with the choice, then he may suggest that the wedding be delayed. In other words, family authority in the sphere of marriage is less than absolute, but it is nevertheless firm. If a marriage is conducted without the blessing of the family, it is understood that the benefits which flow on from family membership will be placed in jeopardy. This is no small threat, and in recent history no member of the Marei family following the pattern here outlined, and having been discouraged by Hassan from pursuing the matter, has continued to do so. Authority for initiating marriage contacts has thus passed in this case from the parents to other and younger members of the family, but the final right of approval remains with the parents and, ultimately, the family patriarch.

The act of marriage is primarily a family affair, then, except in those few cases when the spouses are foreign or are second wives. Whether initiation of the marriage process is begun by the parents or by other relatives, it is now the case that the prospective partners have a veto, although not the unilateral right to marry a spouse of their choice—at least not at a cost deemed acceptable by most, if not all, members of the family. Finally, marriage negotiations reveal most clearly the role of the family patriarch. Viewed as the custodian of the family's honor, his blessing implies family support for the proposed union and, in turn, reflects his power and authority within the family. For the Mareis, then, modernization has caused a modification of the marriage process while still permitting senior family members sufficient influence over matrimonial strategies to guarantee that what class, status, and power have been attained will not be jeopardized by ill-advised unions.

BETWEEN LINEAGE AND AFFINITY

The tendency among Middle Eastern and especially Arab Moslem families toward endogamy, or marriage within the kin group and, in its most extreme form, marriage between a man and his father's brother's daughter, has in the past been explained by anthropologists in terms of obedience to fixed rules. This legalistic conceptualization, as indicated, for example, by discussions of cousin-right marriage in the Middle East,[1] assumes that social practices constitute the execution of a plan deduced from and sanctioned by customary prescriptions. A similar legalistic rigidity characterizes much analysis of lineage, and particularly as regards the Middle East, patrilineality, sheer genealogy being viewed as the primary determinant of inter- and intrafamily behavior, including selection of spouse.[2] These conceptualizations reduce or remove altogether the act of individual choice by social actors, substituting in its place the notion of execution of a preordained model, much like the relationship between a musical score and its performance.[3] The desire to discover those laws which appear to govern marriage patterns and kin-group interaction, as well as other forms of social behavior in foreign societies, has led to the erroneous and almost unconscious assumption that those "laws," which are but generalizations from observed behavior, have in themselves causal significance.

The regularity with which Middle Easterners marry their relatives and form fairly sizable groups on the basis of kinship and affinity is best understood less as slavish adherence to a set of laws guiding social behavior than as a series of individual choices which reflect predispositions growing out of situational factors or, as defined by Pierre Bourdieu, "habitus." Habitus, the desire to reproduce in whole or in part extant structures and processes, consists of a "small number of implicit principles that have spawned an infinite number of practices and follow their own pattern, although they are not based on obedience to any formal rules."[4] With reference to marriage and kinship in the Middle East, this implies that endogamy and patrilineality are not goals in and of themselves, but are simply aspects of strategies conceived for the purpose of "biological, cultural, and social reproduction by which every group endeavors to pass on to the next generation the full measure of power and privilege it has itself inherited."[5] The drive to accumulate wealth, status, and power, and not slavish adherence to patrilineality and endogamy, thus constitutes the primary motivational force in explaining marriage patterns. And if the goal of perpetuating privilege through generations should require a change in marriage strategies and kinship identities, this too can readily be accomplished, as we have seen. It is this very flexibility, resulting from rational choice in pursuit of a conscious strategy, that characterizes endogamy and patrilineality in the Middle East. Rates for first paternal cousin marriage, while varying from subculture to subculture in the area, rarely exceed 12 percent, while that for all patrilineal parallel-cousin marriages is generally under 50 percent.[6] Endogamy, then, is less than half the story of Middle Eastern marriages, and the crucial question is how this mix of endogamy and exogamy is determined, and under what conditions the respective rates are modified.

With respect to patrilineality and lineage in general, it is likewise the case that what is said to be the dominant practice in the Middle East, namely, the formation of kinship groups on the basis of lineage, and especially patrilineage, is also only part of the story. While bedouin tribes may be true lineage systems, given that they explicitly trace kinship relations to common ancestors, most other kinship systems in the Middle East are based on renewal of kinship through affinity, causing Bourdieu to liken genealogical relationships to pathways which disappear if they are not used at least intermittently.[7]

Hildred Geertz, in her examination of the meanings of family ties in Morocco, comes to this conclusion:

> Within Moroccan culture, there is no kinship ideology taken in its literal sense, no culturally patterned genealogical or "organizational" chart by means of which Moroccans grant group membership in any simple way to the people around them, either directly or analogically. What counts to Moroccans are actual social ties, obligations, attachments, and loyalties, and the networks built up out of these.[8]

Christian Lebanese villagers, despite their interrelatedness through common descent, do not perceive kinship in this fashion. Instead, according to Peters,

> affinity is the instrument used to cut through a tangled undergrowth of relatedness, and it carves groups out of what would otherwise be an undifferentiated mass of kin. Without lineality of any sort, whether of a patrilineal, matrilineal, double descent or bilateral kind, affinity has the power to create groups, and it can do so with greater sensitivity.[9]

Peters goes on to observe that while the groups of kin so formed have no specific nominal designation, everyone in fact knows precisely their constitution. These groups are termed "affinal sets" by Peters:

> An affinal set is not a political group, not a complete power structure, but it makes an admirable starting point for anyone wishing to succeed politically. It is not an occupational group, but divers occupations interlock within it, and it also provides occupational opportunities. . . . It is not based on land ownership. It is not a jurally defined group, with exclusive control of specific relationships. But it is to be seen in sharp outline in marriages, funerals and partings, at municipal and national election times, in commercial activities and in the pattern of landholdings. It permeates the fabric of social life. It does not have a single aim, but aims at everything. As a general purpose group, it is elegantly constituted to meet a miscellany of needs.[10]

In the Middle East, then, it is less the completely deterministic aspect of lineage than the relatively free-will consequence of affinity that is important for the analysis of social cohesion and for an understanding of the perpetuation of class, status, and power.

Marei family history illustrates the flexibility of endogamy and lineage and their subordinate role in the Mareis' own thinking to the overriding concern of maintaining or enhancing personal standing. With respect to lineage, it probably was the case that the Nasr, ancestors of the Mareis, were entrenched in a rigid patrilineage. The Nasr were bedouin from the Arabian Peninsula, and older members of the Marei family can not only recite the genealogy at will, but can also readily describe their kinsmen in terms of their relationship to the founder of the family, Marei Ibrahim Nasr. Now, however, the lineage is more or less defunct as a coherent and all-embracing unit of social interaction. No younger members of the family can name all the descendants of Marei Ibrahim Nasr, nor do they regularly associate with all their age cohorts within the lineage. Instead, affinal sets within the lineage have sprung up; one consisting of many of the descendants of Huseyn; another of the descendants of Ahmad through his first wife, Zeynab, linked by kinship and affinity to the descendants of Hassanein; and a third composed of the descendants of Nabawiya through her husbands Fawzi and Ahmad. Within these larger affinal sets there are smaller groups, generally consisting of sets of brothers and/or sisters and their spouses, sharing domiciles, either permanently or in summer months, and having common economic interests. Although forming the primary basis for social, political, and economic interaction, affinal sets are not, however, self-contained units in the sense that they preclude interaction between their re-spective members; and for some purposes the entire family, and hence the lineage, constitutes the reference unit for its members' behavior.

An examination of the Mareis' mixture of endogamous and ex-ogamous marriages reveals a pattern indicating a combination of motivations: economic (class), social (status), and political (power)— all of which are highly interrelated and yet to some degree separable. If tradition were to determine adherence to the custom of patrilineal parallel cousin marriage, then the eldest members of the Marei lin-eage, namely Marei Ibrahim Nasr and his children, should show a greater propensity for it than their descendants. This is not in fact the case. Neither of Marei Ibrahim Nasr's wives was of his patrilineage, although it is probable that they were both of his descent group more broadly conceived, and of his matrilineage, if his father had indeed also married a Nosseir and/or an Abdilla. Of greater importance is the fact that Marei Ibrahim Nasr made no effort to renew his nuclear family's bonds to the extended family of Nasr, for the marriages he arranged for his children were exogamous or within the descent group based on the Abdillas and Nosseirs, which were matrilineages for his children. The explanation for this erstwhile traditionalist *umdah* of Azizeha rejecting his patrilineage when selecting marriage partners for his offspring can in all probability be found in the class, status, and power differentials between the patrilineage, on the one hand, and the matrilineage and exogamous patrilineages, on the other. Perceiving the Nosseirs, Abdillas, Shamsis, and possibly also the Qandeels to be more promising lineages than the Nasr, Marei Ibrahim Nasr did not feel bound by a cultural prescription of patrilineal endogamy, if indeed one existed, when deciding the fates of his children.

The marriage patterns of succeeding generations, reflecting the newly acquired wealth, status, and power of the Mareis, include a mixture of endogamous and exogamous marriages. These patterns in turn suggest what might be a functional division between offspring in the search for status and power. On the one hand, the eldest son of Marei Ibrahim Nasr, Hassanein, pursued a political career locally and handed down the reins of power in Azizeha to his second eldest son, Hassan-12, ensuring the support of the Marei and Nasr lineages for the continued predominance of his (the Hassanein) line by marrying his eldest son, Sayed, to his (Hassanein's) sister Fatma-9's daughter Zeynab-34; his second son, Hassan, to his brother Huseyn's daughter Amina-13; and his eldest daughter to a Nasr. Political prominence in Sharqiya was further ensured through the marriage of the younger daughter to Muhamed Pasha Hussein Ayyoub, brother of Ali Ayyoub, the longest-serving Sharqiya deputy in parliamentary Egypt.

On the other hand, Hassanein's brother Huseyn and his descendants were the primary possessors and defenders of the family's social status; consequently, of the twenty-eight marriages in this sublineage over four generations, only one was endogamous, that between Huseyn's daughter Amina-13 and Hassanein's son Hassan-12. By comparison, of the twenty-three marriages in Hassanein's sublineage, eleven have been endogamous, eight of which were in the descent group of Marei Ibrahim Nasr. The tendency toward endogamous marriage points to a strategy designed to preserve a political power base, while the tendency toward exogamy bespeaks a greater interest in status than in power.

The behavioral evidence also supports this conclusion. Of Huseyn's descendants, only his son Amin-19 was involved in politics, and Amin's onetime election to the Senate was more in the way of a confirmation of his status as the son of a Shamsi woman and husband of a Habashi than the reflection of political ambition. But Hassanein's descendants and their spouses have been keenly interested in politics, son Hassan-12 having served three times in parliament, son-in-law Mahmoud Ibrahim Nasr having served as *umdah* of Azizeha, and son-in-law Muhamed Pasha Hussein Ayyoub as second chamberlain to King Fuad and then as governor of Alexandria. Among Hassanein's grandchildren and their spouses are three Muhi al Dins of the Muhi al Din families which provided Zakariya and Khaled, two of the most prominent officer-politicians in the Nasser and Sadat eras. Hassanein's granddaughter Suad married Sayed, the political standard-bearer of the Mareis after 1952, while another of his granddaughters married into the Fahmy/Omar family, which had produced the famous nationalist Abd al Aziz Fahmy. In short, the political ambitions of Hassanein and his descendants resulted in a judicious mixture of endogamous marriages, through which the lineage remained united, and exogamous marriages, through which it made connections to other politically powerful families. The status ambitions of Huseyn and his descendants, by contrast, did not require that the family power base be nurtured through renewal, so exogamous marriages to wealthy individuals of high status, but from politically inactive families, greatly predominated.

The other main sublineage of the family, that of Ahmad and his descendants, reveals a similar duality. Ahmad's children through his first wife, Zeynab, were tied more closely to the land and encouraged to be the primary defenders of the family's political and economic interests. Thus his three sons were married to their cousins, including the marriages of Sayed-42 and Marei-43 to Saud-53 and Samiha-54, the classic alliance of nephews and their uncle through cousin marriage which Barth describes as the primary purpose of father's brother's daughter marriage.[11] Of all the marriages of Ahmad and Zeynab's descendants, of which there have been fourteen, eight have been endogamous, all within the descent group of Marei Ibrahim Nasr. Ironically, the sublineage with the highest rate of endogamy, a sublineage which is looked down upon by many other descendants of Marei Ibrahim Nasr as lacking status, has been politically and economically the most successful group within the family.

In contrast, the descendants of Nabawiya through her first husband, Fawzi, and second husband, Ahmad, were encouraged, especially by their ambitious mother, to seek social status. Thus her five children all had exogamous marriages, and her son Ali-31, who married Bahiya Sidqy but never attempted to convert that connection to Ismail Sidqy into political capital, had a family which for all intents and purposes has been matrilineal, preferring the higher-status Sidqy identification to that of the Mareis. Nabawiya's grandchildren, the offspring of Omar-45 and Aisha-46, her son and daughter by Ahmad, have had seven marriages, of which all but two have been exogamous. Omar and Aisha are themselves pillars of the religiously conservative branch of Egypt's high society.

In conclusion, marriage patterns within the Marei family suggest that the symbolic capital of status is acquired largely through exogamous marriages into "good" families, some of which may have politically active members, but whose appeal to the Mareis is primarily social status not political power. In contrast, those Mareis who by virtue of habitus, determined by affinal groups formed within and across specific sublineages, are politically ambitious rather than primarily status conscious are very careful to ensure the integrity of the family base through judiciously executed endogamous marriages. Moreover, an orientation toward either status or power determines the strategy to be adopted for the preservation and accumulation of wealth. Mareis who appear to be motivated primarily by the goal of status derive their income largely through the professions, especially that of medicine—which has long been legitimated as a high-status vocation—and to a lesser extent through land. Those Mareis attracted by political power show far greater diversity in their methods of acquiring capital, choosing to become businessmen, administrators, bankers, and generally following vocations that imply a higher degree of risk-taking than the professions. Wheeling and dealing in the general area of business and finance thus characterizes politically motivated Mareis, but a more cautious, incremental approach typifies those who prefer to enhance their social status.

ENDOGAMY IN THE MIDDLE EAST

Since endogamy in its most extreme form of patrilateral parallel cousin (Father Brother Daughter, hereafter FBD) marriage, is virtually nonexistent outside the Middle East, it is not surprising that anthropologists interested in this area of the world have devoted considerable attention to the phenomenon. Despite such attention, however, there remains ambiguity and controversy about its origins, function, and extent. While the reasons for its genesis in the Middle East are essentially unknown, anthropologists have offered several plausible functional explanations for its persistence: that it is a means of maintaining property within the family; that it is a strategy for enhancing political influence of the individual and his lineage; and that it is an essential ingredient in the segmented unilineal descent systems of Arabs.[12]

A further explanation grows out of role theory and argues that a member of the extended family who is intimately acquainted with the family of his or her spouse and already has structured role relations with its members will have fewer problems in adjusting to the new domestic situation that marriage creates.[13] Such explanations are of course not mutually incompatible, although those that emphasize endogamy and especially FBD marriage as a strategy for pursuing power, status, and wealth are most persuasive simply because the family in the Middle East, in the absence of other cohesive social, political, or economic units, has over time remained the crucial unit of interaction in almost all areas of human behavior. Any customary practice, therefore, which serves in one or more ways to reinforce the all-important family unit, is bound to be enduring and widespread. Endogamy, traceable to pre-Islamic times, has been practiced by adherents of virtually all Middle Eastern religions, major and minor, and presumably is therefore a vital ingredient in family solidarity and persistence.

Generalizations about the incidence of endogamy in various subpopulations of the Middle East raise difficulties, not only because there is an insufficient data base, but also because local variation appears to be very great and to fluctuate markedly within short periods. Patrilineal endogamy within certain Arab communities in Israel, for example, almost doubled between 1953–54 and 1969, rising from 31.5 percent to 57.7 percent among a sample of Moslem villagers.[14] Threatened economically, politically, and socially by the dominant Jewish community, the Israeli Arab response has been to turn inward to the family in time of need. In the Middle East more generally, however, it is probably safe to say that endogamy is on the decline, if nothing else the result of urbanization and the settling of bedouin tribes. Among many of the latter, cousin right in marriage is common, and the incidence of endogamy very high.[15] In the twentieth century, endogamy has been more common in rural than in urban areas, and within the latter possibly more frequent in the lower class than the middle class, although the data to support such conclusions is sketchy.[16] At least one observer of Syrian society has noted that endogamy among the urban upper class is more common than it is among the urban middle class, thereby suggesting that *ayan* (notable) families, with more wealth, status, and power to protect, use intermarriage for this purpose.[17] In Egypt, endogamy within village populations has traditionally been preferred, Jacque Berque reporting that in Fisha, a village in Menoufiya, marriage of cousins accounted for 26.2 percent of all marriages, while marriages within the *hamula* (extended family or clan) accounted for 84.4 percent of all marriages.[18] A study of an Egyptian family living on the outskirts of Cairo in Giza some thirty years ago reported that marriage was "almost exclusively within the family circle."[19] There are, unfortunately, no studies of which I am aware of marriage in contemporary urban middle- and upper-class Egyptian society.[20] A recent study of two suburbs of Beirut revealed that 11 percent of marriages among Moslems and 3 percent of those among Christians were FBD marriages,[21] while a study of a Lebanese Maronite mountain village in the 1960s revealed the unusually high figures (at least for Christians) of 19 percent for FBD marriages and 51 percent for marriages within the lineage.[22] Thus, while it is probably safe to conclude that urbanization militates against endogamy, there are insufficient data with which to determine its variable effect on different classes. Moreover, although lineage endogamy in the urban centers of the Middle East is probably declining, from the data available and from general impressions it is clear that it remains a very common practice, possibly accounting for as many as half, or even more, of marriages within some urban subpopulations in the region.

ENDOGAMY IN THE MAREI FAMILY

The term "endogamy," referring simply to marriage within a group, leaves open the precise delineation of the collectivity. With respect to studies of Middle Eastern kinship, it may refer either to the lineage descent group, which is the broadest category and includes all descendants, male and female, from a specified or frequently even unspecified ancester, or it may refer only to marriages within the patrilineage (i.e., a man and all his descendants through males). This ambiguity reflects the de facto state of affairs, for while Middle Eastern families are said to be patrilineal, it is clear that this is only an ideal-typical categorization from which in practice there is much deviation.[23] With respect to the Mareis, then, endogamy can in practice have two different meanings, and for this reason we will employ both operational definitions of the term. The definition used thus far has been inclusive, covering those marriages occurring within the overall lineage of the Marei/Nasr, as well as marriages to the Nosseir and Abdilla, which are included because the high degree of intermarriage between these three families—at least as far back as our data goes, which is some six generations from the present—has in effect created one large lineage. Marriages by descendants of Marei Ibrahim Nasr that are endogamous with reference not to the Marei/Nasr, Nosseir, or Abdilla, but to the affines with which the member of the Marei lineage is connected by marriage, will be tabulated separately. Finally, for the purpose of comparing the Marei descent group with the Marei patrilineage, the data on exogamous and endogamous marriages for the two will be presented separately.

Marei Ibrahim Nasr had eight children (second generation), thirty-six grandchildren (third generation), at least seventy-four great-grandchildren (fourth generation), and presently there are some fifty great-great-grandchildren (fifth generation). Table 1 presents marriages by type (whether endogamous or exogamous) of all those in the descent group of Marei Ibrahim Nasr.

Seven of the nine marriages of the children of Marei Ibrahim Nasr were endogamous, all seven being to either Nosseirs or Abdillas. In the third generation there were thirty-two marriages, of which ten were endogamous, or some 31.3 percent. Two of these were to Nasrs, one to an Abdilla, and one to a Nosseir, the remaining six marriages being contracted within the descent group of Marei Ibrahim Nasr. In the fourth generation, twelve of the fifty-three marriages were endogamous, or some 22.6 percent, while in the fifth generation there have been but five marriages to date, two of which have been endogamous. If the marriages of the fourth and fifth generations are combined, fourteen of fifty-eight have been endogamous, or 24.1 percent. In the fourth generation, three of the twelve endogamous

TABLE 1: MARRIAGES BY MEMBERS OF THE DESCENT GROUP OF MAREI IBRAHIM NASR BY TYPE

GENERATION	TYPE OF MARRIAGE		TOTAL MARRIAGES	ENDOGAMOUS MARRIAGES % OF TOTAL
	ENDOGAMOUS*	EXOGAMOUS		
Second	7	2	9	77.8
Third	10	22	32	31.3
Fourth	12	41	53	22.6 ⎤ 24.1
Fifth	2	3	5	40.0 ⎦
Total	31	68	99	31.3

*Defined as marriage by a member of the descent group of Marei Ibrahim Nasr to another descent group member; to an Abdilla or Nosseir; or to a member of another descent group of which the individual is a member.

marriages involved offspring in the descent group of Marei Ibrahim Nasr marrying into the descent group of their non-Marei parent; one of the twelve involved marriage to a Nasr; and another involved marriage to an Abdilla. Thus seven of the twelve were marriages within the descent group of Marei Ibrahim Nasr. In the fifth generation, one of the marriages involved a woman in the descent group of Marei Ibrahim Nasr marrying back into her maternal grandmother's lineage, that of the Sidqys.

To summarize, endogamous marriages of all types, be they within or outside the descent group of Marei Ibrahim Nasr, have tended to decline through succeeding generations, although if the two most recent generations are considered together, almost one quarter of marriages are still endogamous. The overall rate of endogamy for generations two to five is 31.3 percent.

The rate of endogamy is even higher if calculated on the basis of individuals rather than on marriages, as suggested by data presented in Table 2. In the second generation, six of the eight children of Marei Ibrahim Nasr had endogamous marriages, producing a rate of 75.0 percent, slightly lower than the rate of 77.8 percent for marriages in this generation (see Table 1), as a result of the youngest son having married endogamously twice. In the third generation, thirteen descendants of Marei Ibrahim Nasr had only endogamous marriages, while another had both an endogamous and an exogamous marriage. If this latter individual is counted in both the exogamous and endogamous categories, then fourteen of thirty-three grandchildren of Marei Ibrahim Nasr married endogamously, or 42.4 percent. In the fourth generation the overall rate of endogamy declined to 28.3 percent, fifteen of the seventy-four great grandchildren

TABLE 2: MEMBERS OF THE DESCENT GROUP
OF MAREI IBRAHIM NASR BY TYPE OF MARRIAGE

| | TYPE OF MARRIAGE | | INDIVIDUALS | % OF INDIVIDUALS WITH |
GENERATION	ENDOGAMOUS*	EXOGAMOUS	MARRIED	ENDOGAMOUS MARRIAGES
Second	6	2	8	75.0
Third	14	19	33	42.4
Fourth	15	38	53	28.3
Fifth	2	3	5	40.0
Total	37	62	99	37.4

*As defined in Table 1.

of Marei Ibrahim Nasr having endogamous marriages, thirty-eight having exogamous marriages, seventeen not as yet marrying, while for four members of this generation, all of them Qandeels through Marei Ibrahim Nasr's daughter Steta's sons, no information is available. In the fifth generation, two of the five so far married have married endogamously. To the present, then, Marei Ibrahim Nasr has had ninety-nine descendants who have married at least once, of whom thirty-seven, or 37.4 percent, have married endogamously, within either the descent group of Marei Ibrahim Nasr or the descent group of a parent or grandparent exogamous to the Mareis.

If the more restrictive definition of endogamy is adopted, namely of marriages within the descent group of Marei Ibrahim Nasr exclusively, and if the data is analyzed by individuals marrying rather than by marriages, then the rate of endogamy is lower, partly because of the necessity of excluding the second generation—for the sons and daughters of Marei Ibrahim Nasr could not of course marry among themselves. Nine of Marei Ibrahim Nasr's grandchildren married other of his grandchildren or great-grandchildren, while twenty-three married out of the descent group, for a rate of descent group endogamy of 28.1 percent (see Table 3). Six of the great-grandchildren (fourth generation) married descendants of Marei Ibrahim Nasr in their own generation, while three married one of his grandchildren and one married into the descending generation. Thus ten of the great-grandchildren had marriages within the descent group, forty-three marrying out of the lineage, to produce a descent-group endogamy rate of 18.9 percent. One of the great-great-grandchildren

TABLE 3: MEMBERS OF THE DESCENT GROUP
OF MAREI IBRAHIM NASR MARRYING WITHIN
OR OUTSIDE THE DESCENT GROUP

| | TYPE OF MARRIAGE | | TOTAL INDIVIDUALS | % OF INDIVIDUALS WITH |
GENERATION	ENDOGAMOUS*	EXOGAMOUS	MARRIED	ENDOGAMOUS MARRIAGES
Second	(not included because marriage within the descent group of M.I.N. impossible)			
Third	9	23	32	28.1
Fourth	10	43	53	18.9
Fifth	1	4	5	20.0
Total	20	70	90	22.2

*Defined as marriage within the descent group of Marei Ibrahim Nasr.

married her cousin in the ascending generation, while the other four members of the fifth generation have married into other lineages.

In sum, of the ninety descendants of Marei Ibrahim Nasr who married, and not including his own children, twenty have married cousins within the Marei lineage, twelve of them choosing spouses of the same generation. The overall rate of descent-group endogamy is 22.2 percent. If the fourth and fifth generations are considered jointly, their rate of descent-group endogamy is just less than 19 percent, compared to that of just over 28 percent for the second generation.

Marriage within the descent group of Marei Ibrahim Nasr, like endogamous marriage more broadly defined, is declining over time, but the rate remains significant. Of the last fifty-eight members of the descent group who have married, eleven married other descendants of Marei Ibrahim Nasr, or about one in five. Considering that all these individuals were residents of Cairo, Alexandria, or European cities, that almost all were educated at least to the university level or were married to a spouse who was, that most are fluent in at least one foreign language and in general can be thought of as members of the highly Westernized Egyptian elite, it seems that modernization in the forms of urbanization, education, and exposure to foreign cultures is by no means incompatible with the traditional practice of cousin marriage, although it may operate to lessen its incidence. Whether the rate of descent group endogamy in the Marei family has now reached a plateau beyond which it will decline no further is impossible to determine from the scanty statistical evidence as yet available for the fifth generation. An inference supporting the conclusion that endogamy will continue at about its present rate can, however, be drawn from the analysis of the most restrictive category of endogamy, that of the patrilineage.

The patrilineage of Marei Ibrahim Nasr consists of himself and all his descendants through males. Table 4 presents the thirty male and female members of the patrilineage in the third and fourth generations by type of marriage. The second generation has been excluded from this analysis because of the impossibility of marriage in that generation within the descent group as here defined. The fifth generation has been omitted because there are as yet insufficient marriages within the patrilineage to merit analysis. From Table 4 it can be seen that the grandchildren (third generation) of Marei Ibrahim Nasr through his four sons had a rate of descent-group endogamy of almost 35 percent. One of the eight endogamous marriages was to a Nasr, or in other words, within the larger

TABLE 4: MEMBERS OF THE PATRILINEAGE OF MAREI IBRAHIM NASR
BY TYPE OF MARRIAGE

| GENERATION | TYPE OF MARRIAGE | | TOTAL INDIVIDUALS MARRIED | % OF INDIVIDUALS WITH EXOGAMOUS MARRIAGES |
	ENDOGAMOUS*	EXOGAMOUS		
Third	8	15	23	34.8
Fourth	7	15	22	31.9
Total	15	30	45	33.3

*Defined as marriage within the descent group of Marei Ibrahim Nasr.

patrilineage of which Marei Ibrahim Nasr was himself a member. The remaining seven marriages were all within the immediate descent group of Marei Ibrahim Nasr. Similarly, of the great-grandchildren (fourth generation) within the patrilineage, seven of the twenty-two who married chose spouses also descended from Marei Ibrahim Nasr, for a rate of endogamous marriage of almost 32 percent. By comparison, the data in Table 3 for the larger kinship category of the descent group reveal a much lower propensity for endogamous marriage. Among all the grandchildren of Marei Ibrahim Nasr, 28.1 percent, as opposed to the 34.8 percent of those within the patrilineage, chose spouses within the descent group. In the succeeding generation the rate of endogamy within the descent group, as provided in Table 3, dropped to 18.9 percent, as compared to the rate of 31.8 percent for the patrilineage.

In other words, while the descent group has a tendency toward fragmentation over time as a result of the decreasing number of endogamous marriages, the patrilineage gives little sign of being dissolved through out-marriage. Within the patrilineage, the overall rate of endogamy for the third and fourth generations has been constant at about the rate of one in three. At the heart of the descent group, then, is a smaller nucleus composed of members of the more exclusive patrilineage who manifest a considerably higher and more constant tendency toward marriage among themselves. This evidence in support of patrilineality reflects the outcome of a combination of individual choices designed, at least in part, to preserve wealth and power within the family. It is not by chance, for example, that the family patriarch and the leader of the family's political fortunes are both within the patrilineage and have married within the descent group.

Further confirmatory evidence of the relative cohesion of the patrilineage is provided by the rate of parallel cousin marriage. Table

5 presents data on the endogamous marriages of males in the patrilineage within the third and fourth generations. Three of the five in the third generation and all of the three in the fourth generation who married chose their father's brother's daughter as their spouse, or the intergenerational functional equivalent, for example, father's brother's son's daughter, father's father's brother's daughter, or father's father's brother's son's daughter's daughter.[24] Only two of the eight male members of the patrilineage in these two generations married their cross cousins, that is, their father's sister's daughter. In that it is patrilateral parallel cousin marriage (i.e., FBD marriage) that acts to encyst the lineage, and cross-cousin marriage that provides the means by which larger kinship groups are united, it is clear that endogamous marriage in the patrilineage manifests a strong tendency (i.e., 75 percent) toward reinforcing the cohesion of the inner core of the family, the patrilineage.

In addition to the six FBD marriages by male members of the patrilineage, there are six more FBD marriages for non-Mareis marrying members of the descent group of Marei Ibrahim Nasr. Thus twelve of the total of ninety-nine marriages made by members of the descent group were FBD marriages or their equivalent, for a rate of 12.2 percent. This places the Marei descent group toward the top end of the range of FBD marriages in those Middle Eastern urban societies which have been analyzed. It suggests, therefore, that patrilateral parallel cousin marriage, the most extreme form of endogamy and that which is exclusive to the Middle Eastern cultural area, continues to be relatively common in a family that is, by the standards of the region, highly Westernized. The tradition of cousin marriage appears to die hard, if it is dying at all, suggesting in turn that it performs a

TABLE 5: MEMBERS OF THE PATRILINEAGE OF MAREI IBRAHIM NASR BY TYPE OF ENDOGAMOUS MARRIAGE

| GENERATION | TYPE OF MARRIAGE | | TOTAL ENDOGAMOUS MARRIAGES | % OF ENDOGAMOUS MARRIAGES THAT ARE FBD OR EQUIVALENT |
	FBD OR EQUIVALENT*	CROSS–COUSIN		
Third	3	2	5	60
Fourth	3	0	3	100
Total	6	2	8	75

*Father's brother's son's daughter, father's father's brother's daughter, or father's father's brother's son's daughter.

vital function for modern Arab families and, indirectly, for society as a whole.

EXOGAMOUS MARRIAGES

The preservation of class, status, and power from one generation to another requires of most families, unless they are very large and well endowed with resources, a judicious mixture of endogamous and exogamous marriages. At the core of the Marei descent group is the patrilineage which, through its propensity for endogamy, maintains its cohesion and to a lesser extent the cohesion of the larger group of descendants of Marei Ibrahim Nasr. But without the addition of well-executed exogamous marriages, the Marei descent group and its patrilineage, having insufficient resources in and of themselves, would lack the access which exogamous marriages provide to further political and economic resources and to the symbolic capital of status. Exogamous marriages therefore represent another aspect of the Marei family strategy for perpetuating its own power and privilege. Most notably, Mareis tend to marry into Sharqawi (i.e., from Sharqiya) families that are (1) both wealthy and politically prominent or (2) just wealthy, or into families from elsewhere in Egypt that are (3) wealthy and politically powerful or (4) just wealthy. Considering types 1 to 4, respectively, the first category includes such politically well-known Sharqawi families as the Shamsi, Qandeel, Ayyoub, Abd al Rahman, al Dib, Farahat, Eid, Muhi al Din,[25] Abaza, and Elwan. All these families have had representatives in parliament in the nineteenth and/or twentieth centuries, and several have provided politicians prominent on the national scene, including Ali Shamsi Pasha, Mursi Farahat, Khaled and Zakariya Muhi al Din, Wagih Abaza, and several others both before and after 1952. Moreover, marriages between Mareis and members of these families have occurred in all the generations descending from Marei Ibrahim Nasr, and although the rate of marriage to members of Sharqawi families of both types, (1) political and (2) nonpolitical, is declining, it nevertheless still accounts for a sizable proportion of all marriages. In the fourth generation, for example, some ten of the fifty-three marriages were to members of Sharqawi families that are still active in at least provincial politics. Other Sharqawi families into which Mareis marry are those of type 2, whose class origins as landowners are identical to the Mareis, but who, for one reason or another, never sought political careers.

Marriages into families of national political prominence from provinces other than Sharqiya (type 3) are likewise common across all the generations, excepting that of the children of Marei Ibrahim Nasr, for at that time the Mareis were still an isolated provincial family in Sharqiya. In the third, fourth, and fifth generations, Mareis married into the Seif al Nasr, al Loba, Foda, Sidqy, Abd al Razzaq, Habashi, Fahmy, Mahmoud, and Sadat families, all of which, except the last, sired more than one at least fairly well-known politician. Families which are of national prominence by virtue of their wealth and status, but not by virtue of political power (type 4), and into which Mareis have married, are typified by the al Lozi,[26] one of Egypt's leading industrialist families, and by the al Dib family of Alexandria.

CONCLUSION

Social units based on kinship and affinity clearly provide the Mareis with a wealth of opportunities to pursue their various interests. United as a family partly through lineage but, more important, through the renewal of kinship ties by endogamous marriage, and enjoying marital connections to a vast array of economically and politically powerful families in Sharqiya and Egypt as a whole, it would be surprising if the Mareis did not capitalize economically and politically on the social network spreading out from their patrilineage. Common sense is, in this case, supported by behavioral evidence. Social, economic, and political interaction within the family is of a type and intensity to suggest that it acts as the home base not only for domestic affairs but also for political and economic activities. And forays out into the larger worlds of economics and politics, while not always made along pathways cleared by marriage connections, do so frequently follow this route that one might surmise that an Egyptian without a large family and numerous strategic exogamous marriages is an Egyptian lacking fundamental political and economic resources. While success in these realms may nevertheless be possible, as other institutions can and do provide substitutes, a man endowed with the resources provided by a family and its connections starts his career on the run.

3 | MAREI FAMILY SOCIAL AND ECONOMIC BEHAVIOR

Do the descendants of Marei Ibrahim Nasr constitute a family in any meaningful behavioral sense, or are they simply a collection of individuals sharing a common ancestor and little else? On first glance the family tree may appear to be simply a curiosity, long since drained of any real life. The descent group is, after all, not a true lineage in the sense that all its members have in their minds a precise map of the maze of genealogical connections by which they are tied together. Moreover, interaction within the descent group is structured within certain channels, many members seeing even their age cohorts only infrequently, and those much older or younger than themselves seldom, if at all. Their homes are scattered throughout the more affluent districts of Cairo, a city in which transport and communications are approaching the impossible, while a few live in Alexandria and at least two as far afield as North America. Not all of those in the descent group still own land in the neighborhood of the ancestral home and, of those who do, many have not ventured out to Sharqiya for years. The descent group itself owns nothing, not even land, in common. Even endogamous marriages, which now account for something like one in five marriages within the descent group and rather more within the patrilineage, may not renew a sufficient proportion of the genealogical links for the descent group

to remain anything more than a vague and distant memory, symbol-
ized by a dusty copy of the family tree locked away in some forgotten
closet. In short, affected as it has been by urbanization, the transformation from rural notability to "new middle class," and modernization in general, the descent group of Marei Ibrahim Nasr might be
thought to have fragmented into its constituent nuclear families, as
have countless such descent groups in the West in previous times.

The truth, however, is different. Nuclear families do of course
exist within the descent group, and they may be in the process of
becoming more self-contained kinship as well as behavioral units.
But there are, in addition to nuclear families, affinal sets linking
nuclear families within the descent group, and they show little sign
of being undermined by the rapid social, economic, and political
changes that have been under way in Egypt and gathering pace for
several generations. Moreover, there is evidence to suggest that the
descent group itself remains intact, constituting a meaningful referent for the social, economic, and political behavior of a large percentage of its members. The Marei family is in a behavioral sense, then,
a three-tiered unit: the largest and most encompassing, although least
compelling unit being the descent group itself; the smallest and most
cohesive being the nuclear families within it. At an intermediate level
are those webs of nuclear families defined as affinal sets, by means
of which a variety of functions, including that of securing suitable
spouses, can more adequately be performed.

THE DESCENT GROUP

That the descent group is more than an empty shell is suggested in
the first instance by the fact that a large number of its members
obviously value it highly. The genealogy of the descent group, and
particularly of the patrilineal backbone within it, is consciously
taught to sons and daughters, and it embarrasses members of the
family to find that their memorization of the family tree is less than
perfect. By the standards of North American and European families,
a surprising level of detail about the family is known by virtually all
its members. Those individuals and sublineages that tend to be most
frequently forgotten in recitations of the family structure, or were
never properly learned, are those that dropped out of the patrilineage
at an early date or are by kinship and affinity relatively distant from
the person concerned. So, for example, Steta, the eldest daughter of

Marei Ibrahim Nasr, married a Qandeel, and while one of their sons married a Nasr, there have been no marriages directly with Mareis since. Many younger Mareis are unaware of their affinal connection in an ascending generation to the Qandeels, and most cannot accurately reconstruct this branch of the family tree. None of the other descent groups of the children of Marei Ibrahim Nasr has become so alienated from and essentially unknown to the Marei family, although for all members of the descent group of Marei Ibrahim Nasr now living, there are areas of the family tree about which only the rough outlines are known. In particular, female offspring and wives of relatives seem to be most easily forgotten.

Physical contact among members of the descent group is intermittent but not all that infrequent, for due to the sheer number of people involved, weddings and funerals are regular occurrences. The former are especially important occasions for renewing family ties, because not only are many marriages contracted within the family, but the act of marriage itself is "a compact entered into by two bodies of kin."[1] Marriage, in other words, implies certain obligations, as well as presenting an opportunity for the relatives of both bride and groom to renew ties. Recognition of this fact through attendance at the wedding ceremony is therefore a socially significant act.

The fact that the descent group constitutes the primary referent for family honor is yet another indication of that collectivity's continuing relevance for the behavior of its members. "While 'ird (family honor) is most evident in the tribal and peasant sectors of society, it also appears in the contemporary urban sector, in all but the most 'modernized' families."[2] 'ird is a complex phenomenon, being an attribute both of the individual male members of a lineage and of the collectivity as a whole. It is concerned primarily with the sexual purity of women but also with the family's reputation more generally.[3] In its collective sense, 'ird among the Mareis takes its most obvious form in a code of conduct encompassing both sexual and status prescriptions. The choice of spouse is first and foremost a reflection of family honor and is therefore a matter in which the family has a legitimate interest. If the family deems that the matrimonial choice of one of its members is inappropriate, by which is normally implied that the intended spouse is not from a "good" family—"good" referring to both class background and honorable behavior—then it withholds approval of the marriage. In this way family honor is preserved, for the family has not sanctioned the match, and the marriage, if it goes ahead, is an aberrant act, by which the person separates himself or herself from his or her kin. As mentioned previously, this is a rare occurrence, due to elaborate family procedures for heading off such a showdown, beginning with arranged marriages or the highly developed patterns of chaperoned intersex socializing, which permit the family an influential role in mate selection from the outset, and concluding with those negotiations which give the family patriarch final approval of the choice. Because the concept of 'ird is so heavily laden with sexual and status implications, it is hardly surprising that the family should intervene to structure the marital choices of its members.

Family honor continues to be involved in the marriage once contracted. It is presumed that since both the individual and the family sanctioned the marriage, it represents an irrevocable choice, an affront to which besmirches both the individual's and the family's honor. Affairs, if they become too well known and too common, can offend in this way, particularly if they involve males with much younger women.[4] Of even greater seriousness is the act of taking a second wife while the first is still alive, for this is a direct affront to the first wife and her family and, in turn, a reflection on the honor of the husband and his entire family. Thus the second marriage of one of Marei Ibrahim Nasr's descendants to Egypt's, and indeed the Arab World's, leading female movie star, Fatin Hamama, is no cause for boasting to most members of the descent group, who refer to it reluctantly if at all. Similarly, Amin, son of Huseyn, having already taken as a wife Aziza Habashi of that prestigious Damanhour family, subsequently married two other women, to whom members of the Marei family simply refer as "those women." With these marriages Amin so alienated himself from his kin that despite having been the only Marei to be elected to the Senate, his relatives prefer not to mention his name at all. Violation of family honor follows one even to the grave. It is registered not only in the rancor one finds between the offspring of different wives but also in the attitudes of members of the descent group affected less directly, for to besmirch the family honor is something no one is inclined to forgive and forget.

The descent group, then, and especially the patrilineage within it, remains the key collective referent for 'ird and as such continues to play a central role in the calculations and behavior of its individual members. Urbanization, according to a leading sociologist of Arab families, "appears to have had relatively little impact on the valuation of honor."[5] 'ird, with its implied strong sanctions on behavior, is a key ingredient in the social adhesive with which descent groups in the Arab world hold together in the face of social change.

Yet another feature of the descent group, and especially of the patrilineage, which reinforces the viability of these institutions is the degree to which they are embedded in a transnational tribal structure. This tribal structure in turn provides both status and the possibility of beneficial personal contacts with other Arabs in related tribes. The Mareis, for example, trace their connections backward through the Nasr not only to an original tribe of the Nagd in Saudi Arabia, from which the Nasr split off, but also to the fragment of the Nasr that broke away during the Muhamed Ali period and fled to Palestine, where it is still to be found. The Mareis are proud to boast that one of their kinsmen has served under King Hussein in the Jordanian parliament. Furthermore, the Nasr themselves, while generally not as successful as the Mareis, have produced some notably influential persons with whom the Mareis have remained in contact. Taha Sayed Nasr, for example, onetime chairman of the Coca Cola Company in Egypt, recruited his relative Omar Marei into the company in the early 1950s. Taha's son, Ali Nasr, became a well-known military doctor in Egypt, parachuting in behind Israeli lines in the Sinai Peninsula and eventually marrying a cousin of Queen Dunya, a relative of the Nasr and the former wife of King Hussein. These distant affinal and kin connections are of more than simply passing interest. Sayed Marei has for years had important contacts with the Palestinians and the Jordanian government, and the fact that he has blood connections in that area provides a degree of legitimacy for his role, as well as providing his relations with important Jordanians and Palestinians with an aura of social intimacy.

Similar transnational tribal connections link the Nosseir to Arabs of wealth and power, and the Mareis invoke these connections when possible. Nosseir family legend maintains that the Nosseir are one of the five branches of a large tribe, of which the remaining four are the Sabah, now the ruling tribe of Kuwait; the Aneza of the northeastern Arabian Peninsula; the Shammar of the Syrian-Iraqi border area of the Great Syrian Desert; and the Saudi tribe itself. On more than one occasion these distant tribal connections have been the topic of conversation among the Mareis, who in these instances can define themselves through their matrilineages as Nosseirs, and important Arabs, including the Sabahs in Kuwait and members of the ruling Saudi dynasty. This distant connection has helped pave the way for the Mareis, and especially Sayed and Omar, when dealing with the Sabahs and the Saudis, and in the case of Omar it contributed to his securing Saudi backing for his appointment as chairman of the Feysal Islamic Bank, incorporated in Egypt in 1975, but funded largely by the Saudis. Since these tribal connections span several Arab countries, they can be invoked in many different situations. In 1958, following the union of Egypt and Syria, for example, the Mareis invited to Cairo some seventy-five members of the very distantly related Shammar tribe of Syria to celebrate the event. The descent group thus provides one of the links in a lengthy chain by which individual Mareis are connected with other Arabs. In that such kinship, whether real or imaginary, is valued throughout the Arab World, it is a useful resource for the Mareis at times when they are involved in political and economic negotiations in the region.

The descent group may in fact be more relevant in economic and political dealings than in everyday social interaction. Evidence to be discussed below suggests that while members of the descent group may not socialize regularly with one another, and may indeed be quite distant genealogically speaking, they have no compunction about asking their kin and affines for economic and political favors. This seems to suggest that the descent group as a cohesive unit commanding the loyalty of its members is so much taken for granted as to obviate the necessity of cultivating relationships within it on a continuous basis. If one is in need, one can count on one's relatives, as long as the general prescriptions regarding behavior and protection of family honor are followed. There is of course an even greater density of political and economic transactions within the subunits of the descent group, which are socially more tightly knit, but one-off favors with distant relatives are more common than one might expect. The descent group is a flexible unit with numerous lines of communication, which may lie dormant or be activated, as the external situation requires. While inactivity must cause some erosion of these personal networks, the bonds of kinship and affinity are surprisingly durable, especially when compared to more secular units of human interaction in Egypt.

Finally, the descent group is equivalent to a federal sovereign entity in providing both the territory and the constitutional structure within which its member, partially sovereign, units interact. These units are the affinal sets composed of those groupings of individuals and nuclear families drawn together primarily by virtue of the closest links of kinship and affinity. To varying degrees members of an affinal set are aware of and involved in transactions with other members of the descent group enmeshed in different affinal sets. The relationships of the parts to each other and between the parts and the whole are similar to those characteristic of federal political systems, involving bargaining, negotiation, compromise and a pervasive sense of common identity.

The reference groups in terms of which each individual member defines his own identity are therefore three: the nuclear family, the affinal set, and the descent group. While the former two set the boundaries for the greater part of an individual's social life within the family—such social life accounting for a very large share of the social activity for any given individual—the descent group as such not only is the appropriate referent for some behavior, but also remains the overall structure within which the other units fit and without which they could not otherwise subsist.

AFFINAL SETS

Affinal sets tend to be based on the sublineages descended from the male children of Marei Ibrahim Nasr, with the addition of individuals drawn in directly through their own marriages or indirectly through the marriages of close kin. At the core of affinal sets are to be found, then, brothers, sisters, and their spouses and children and, in addition, other individuals attracted through a combination of genealogical or affinal proximity. At present the largest and most influential affinal set in the descent group, and the only one to be discussed in detail here, is that composed of the nucleus of Marei Ibrahim Nasr's son Ahmad's three sons through Ahmad's first wife, Zeynab. Each of these sons married within the family. The eldest, Hassan-41, married his father's sister Fatma's daughter, while Sayed-42 and Marei-43 married their father's brother Hassanein's son Hassan's daughters. A further linkage between the sublineages of Ahmad and Hassanein, and thus a strengthening of the affinal set, was provided by the marriage of Aziza-44, a full sister of Hassan, Sayed, and Marei, to Hassanein's eldest grandson Ahmad-48 through his eldest son Sayed-11. The importance of this match lay in the fact that Aziza's husband Ahmad, as the first son of the first son of the first son of Marei Ibrahim Nasr, has a genealogical claim to be leader of the entire descent group. Lest a possible rivalry split the family, as the conflict between Ahmad-48's uncle Hassan-17 and his wife's uncle Ahmad-10 had done from the 1920s to the 1940s, it was important that the leading members of these two sublineages be united in the same affinal set. Ahmad-48, outnumbered by his wife's brothers, was clearly in a secondary position in such an arrangement. Hassan-62, grandson of Hassanein through his daughter Muntaha-17, was another member at the core of this affinal set. Hassan, who died suddenly of a heart attack in 1977 at some forty-five years of age, had been raised in part by his mother's brother's daughter Suad-53 and her husband Sayed-42, for his own mother had died in childbirth. Hassan's marriage to his father's brother's daughter, Jehan Hussein Ayyoub of the powerful Ayyoub family of Sharqiya, had brought into the affinal set this potentially useful outsider. The other family member closest to the center of the affinal set is Samira-55, sister of Suad-53 and Samiha-54. Samira, the youngest of the three sisters, married Aziz Qadry, a close friend of her sisters' husbands.

These various couples and their children constitute an affinal set, and a sociogram would reveal a very dense network of social, economic, and political interactions among them. They see one another several times a week, while their children grow up together, going to the same schools, sharing the same friendships, accompanying one another on trips to Alexandria and to Europe, and frequently obtaining jobs in the same institutions. In short, they may be thought of as a laterally extended family, some of them even sharing residences.

On the periphery of this affinal set are several other families which also have close connections to other members of the descent group, thereby serving further to anchor the affinal set based on Hassan, Sayed, and Marei within the larger collectivity. The other full sister of these three brothers and her husband, Mursi Farahat, represent one of these peripheral families, as do the families of Saad-47 and Ali-49, brothers of Ahmad-48, the husband of Aziza-44. Amr-67, son of Aida-24, the daughter of Huseyn-3, is another peripheral member of this affinal set. Amr is included because of his close friendship with Hassan-62, who was raised by Sayed-42 and Suad-53, and because his aunt Amina-13 married Hassan-12, the father of Suad, Samiha, and Samira. In sum, the affinal set comprises six husbands and wives and their children, plus four more couples and their children on the periphery. Although the four families in the latter group do not interact with one another or with the members of the core group of the affinal set as regularly as do the six in the former, they are relatively close and depend heavily on the affinal set for social, economic, and political contacts.

The three affinal sets in the descent group may be conceptualized as overlapping circles, some members in each having affinal and/or extensive social, political, and economic contacts with members of one or both of the others. Those individuals found within the area of overlap tend either to be those on the periphery of the affinal sets or the male heads of families that provide their leadership. In the case of the peripheral members, interaction within two affinal sets is the consequence of dual webs of affinity and friendship that draw them in both directions. So, for example, Amr-67, grandson of Huseyn through his daughter Aida-24, is a member of both an affinal set centered on Huseyn's grandsons Huseyn-19a and Ibrahim-19b, sons of Amin-19, and another centered on Hassan, Sayed, and Marei. He is a member of the latter because his cousin and close friend Hassan-62 was raised by Sayed and Suad, which places him firmly within the confines of that affinal set.

The motivation for dominant males within each affinal set to maintain close contact with at least the leaders of other sets grows out of their roles as the chief protector of the family's overall interest. As members of the patrilineage, they consider it their duty to maintain the cohesion of the descent group to the highest degree possible, and while, like other members of the respective affinal sets, their social interaction is mostly confined to their own set, they nevertheless keep family lines of communication open for economic and political purposes. It is accepted as natural that the descent group should be divided into smaller units for social purposes, but it is also believed that such divisions should not hinder the natural economic and political functionings of the family as a whole.

NUCLEAR FAMILIES

Nuclear families within the descent group are of two types. The first are those in which a single set of parents and their children live under one roof, with the possible addition of grandparents, aunts, or uncles. Egyptian nuclear families differ from those in the West in that they are embedded in affinal sets, so that daily interaction for all members is less circumscribed by the borders of the nuclear family itself. Fathers tend to work in the same business, university, or ministry as their brothers or cousins; mothers spend their days socializing with their sisters, cousins, and sisters-in-law; and children grow up with a cluster of cousins.

It is not surprising, therefore, that the borders between nuclear families disappear altogether in some cases and the families become bi- or tri-modal clusters consisting of two or three nuclear families living permanently in the same household. This is especially the case when sets of brothers and sisters marry. It is a practice which originated in the countryside, where the father and all his sons and their wives and children traditionally lived in the same house or compound, and which has now been brought into Egypt's urban centers, where it occurs among Egyptians of various social classes.

Midway between uni-modal and multi-modal families are those that share accommodations with other nuclear families for part of the year, normally the summer months. Hassan, for example, the patriarch of the family, has for years spent the summers in a flat in Alexandria, where he lives with his family and the family of his sister, who is married to their father's brother (Hassanein's) grandson Ahmad-48. In this case and in the cases of permanently shared domiciles, the premises are jointly owned, these being virtually the only examples of communal economic ownership within the family.

ECONOMIC BEHAVIOR—LANDHOLDINGS

An analysis of landownership and land management can disclose, in fact, the dynamics of social interaction within and among nuclear families. Most important, land is owned by individuals, not by nuclear families, affinal sets, or the descent group. Women as well as men own land, the former retaining their right of ownership after marriage. Moslem inheritance laws, under which men take full shares and women half shares of estates, have been followed by the Mareis throughout this century. Thus all living members of the patrilineage of Marei Ibrahim Nasr, as well as a large percentage of those in the descent group only, own land or will own land on the death of their parents. But although they are landowners, very few Mareis personally manage their agricultural properties. They do not, if they can avoid it, however, rent out the land directly to peasants, for once such a rental contract is signed the peasant and his descendants have the right of usufruct to that land in perpetuity for the nominal rent of some £E25 per year. A feddan owned free and clear can earn up to £E600 per year and is therefore worth on the open market several times more than the equivalent feddan encumbered with a rental contract. The family provides the means through which this problem is circumvented, some members of the family managing land for others; and it is in the very intricacies of who manages land for whom that indications of family trust and intimacy are to be found.

In general, brothers pool their land, to be worked jointly under the supervision of one of the brothers if at all possible, or under a hired manager as very much a second-best choice—nonfamily members not being trusted. Such a pool may include in addition the land

of one or more of the wives of the brothers, or the land of one or more
of their sisters, depending on such objective factors as the amount of
land, its location, and the ability of other husbands or brothers to
manage the land, as well as the subjective factor of trust. One such
family land pool comprises the land of the brothers Hassan, Sayed,
and Marei; that of their wives, who are also of the descent group; the
land of their sister Amina, who is married to Mursi Farahat; and that
of one of the descendants of Huseyn. The latter's land is included by
virtue of his affiliation with the affinal set. The youngest brother,
Marei, manages the land, making the one- to one-and-a-half hour
trip from Cairo to Sharqiya a couple of times a week to make the
necessary arrangements for agricultural operations to be conducted.
At the end of each harvest the proceeds are divided among members
of the pool according to the yields of their respective plots of land,
detailed figures being kept on the productivity of each and every
feddan. Similar pools are operated by Ahmad-48 for his land, the
land of his wife, and the land of his brothers, and by numerous other
family members for little clusters of their relatives. Land management tends to be handled by affinal sets and closely connected nuclear families within them. This pattern of mutually exploiting
individually owned economic assets reinforces interpersonal linkages
within the family and provides an additional illustration of the plas-
ticity of the boundaries between one nuclear family and another as
well as between nuclear families and affinal sets.

For most members of the family, landholdings provide only a
secondary source of income, but the value of land transcends its sheer
immediate economic return. It is a symbol of the family patrimony,
an ongoing focus of family activity, and virtually the only reliable
form of insurance available in an economy characterized by rapid and
extreme fluctuations between public and private sector dominance
and beset by ever-increasing inflation. It is essential, moreover, that
the family continue to own land in Sharqiya to maintain its rural
political base. Finally, landownership is closely associated with social
status in many areas of the Middle East and particularly in Egypt. The
family therefore tenaciously holds on to its land, expands its holdings
if possible, and looks upon the loss of even a feddan as a family
tragedy. If land is sold or traded, every possible attempt is made to
complete the transaction within the family.

Land transactions within the family are based on the guiding
principle that the holdings of those members of the family who wish
to pool their land for the sake of collective management be concentrated geographically. The death of a family member may result in

the ownership of various plots of land being reshuffled to ensure that each individual's holdings are in an area of Sharqiya, Qalyubiya, or Menoufiya, conveniently close to those of other family members with whom management is pooled. The only land sold outright by the family out of choice, and not under duress, was a parcel of 170 feddans in Abu Firqas, which is situated in Minya Province in Upper Egypt. This land had been acquired by Ahmad Marei, son of Marei Ibrahim Nasr. His heirs, preferring to concentrate their landholdings as close to the Sharqiya side of Cairo as possible, sold the land and with the proceeds bought a parcel in Menoufiya Province situated immediately to the north of Cairo and within a thirty-minute drive of their Sharqiya estates. As a consequence of fragmentation and the continual reshuffling of ownership within the family, Marei rural landholdings clump together along the lines of nuclear families and are situated in locations in Sharqiya and the immediately adjoining provinces of Qalyubiya and Menoufiya. The sites of the largest land parcels are in Azizeha, Kafr al Arbain, Hiyar, Saadin, Saadiya, Bilbeis, and near Zagazig in Sharqiya; Orman, adjacent to Benha in Qalyubiya; and Baranya, adjacent to Ashmoun in Menoufiya Province.

Fragmentation of landholdings as a result of Moslem laws of inheritance spared the Mareis the fate of the biggest landowners, who lost extensive holdings in the 1952, 1961, and 1969 agrarian reforms. While Sayed Marei himself was in charge of the organizations responsible for supervising the 1952 and 1969 reforms, it was probably unnecessary for him to take any particular measures to protect the interests of his family members. It should, however, be noted that it was only in the 1961 agrarian reform, implemented after Sayed Marei was dismissed from office in disgrace, that any Mareis had land confiscated. But the Mareis had never been among the country's tiny stratum of landowners whose holdings were well up in the four figures, and by 1952 the estates of Marei Ibrahim Nasr's children had already been divided among the thirty-six grandchildren, so very few could have owned much in excess of the 200 feddans permitted an individual or 300 for a family.

Following the announcement in September 1952 of the agrarian reform, a list naming all those landowners whose holdings might exceed the legal maximum was compiled from tax registers by the Higher Committee for Agrarian Reform. Only two Marei names appeared on the list, those of Amin-19, son of Huseyn, and Ali-31, son of Fawzi, and in neither case did their holdings actually exceed the legal maximum, although Amin's parcels of 150 feddans in Zagazig and 50 in Bilbeis placed him right at the limit. It is clear from information supplied by the family itself and from the list of names and holdings drawn up after the declaration of the 1961 agrarian reform, a list which Sayed Marei was not in a position to influence, that most Marei holdings were just within the specified maximum. Seven Mareis and one Nasr appeared on the 1961 list, suggesting that their holdings were close to the new legal maximum of 100 feddans per individual plus 100 feddans for dependent children. Sayed's father-in-law, Hassan, and his daughters, Samira-55 and Samiha-54, were among the seven Mareis named, but his third daughter, Suad, who is also Sayed's wife, did not appear on the list. Her name may have been omitted because she had transferred ownership to her children, whereas her sisters had not, or because Sayed, politically vulnerable in his post as minister of agrarian reform, had taken steps to ensure that his nuclear family would not be in violation of land-ownership laws. Suad's uncle Abd al Aziz-15 was one of the Mareis to lose land in the 1961 reform—some 57 feddans—as was her father, Hassan, who lost 39 feddans. The third Marei to lose land was Amin-19, whose name had also appeared on the 1952 list and who should have heeded the warning at that time. Neither Amin, Hassan, nor Abd al Aziz forgave Sayed for not forewarning them of the impending reform. Hassan felt particularly aggrieved because, according to Sayed's account, a few hours before the reform was announced on Radio Cairo, Hassan had asked him to confirm or deny the rumor of an impending reform law. Sayed, having been informed of the measure shortly before, evaded his father-in-law's question.[6]

The Marei family had weathered the first two drastic agrarian reforms under Nasser with the loss of not more than 125 feddans, and such a loss, although causing some rancor within the family, was by no means a catastrophe. But other threats loomed on the horizon. A gradual shift to the left in Egyptian politics from mid-1965, knowledge that the family's main protector Sayed was "on the shelf" as a result of having lost a round in political infighting within the elite, and finally, in May 1966, the creation of the Committee for the Liquidation of Feudalists, empowered as it was to sequester land,[7] caused panic in the family. Meeting late at night over survey maps of Sharqiya, Qalyubiya, and Menoufiya, Sayed and other of the family's leaders decided which parcels should be sold off before they could be seized by the committee. As it transpired, the June War intervened and the Committee for the Liquidation of Feudalists, its chairman, Abd al Hakim Amer, having been disgraced and subsequently purged, was adjourned sine die.[8] In the meantime, however, the Mareis had sold some of their holdings, concentrating especially on those held by the individuals whose names had appeared on the 1961 agrarian reform list. Sayed's sisters-in-law Samira and Samiha, whose landholdings had probably been the largest of the group threatened by the reform, now joined their uncle Abd al Aziz in ruining their fate and cursing the luck that had caused their brother-in-law to lose his influence over agrarian reform and give them what turned out to be bad advice.

Some years later, however, Sayed redeemed himself in the eyes of at least those family members who own land on the outskirts of Zagazig. Threatened by the loss of land in the early 1970s because of the right of eminent domain exercised by the newly founded Zagazig University, these Mareis benefited from the cancellation of some of the proceedings, the delay of others, and vastly increased prices for the land that was eventually taken. Those Mareis concerned are full of praise for their cousin Sayed, who was then as he is now a member of the board of trustees of Zagazig University, for aiding their cause.

Land transactions clearly evoke the deepest feelings among family members, serving to unite the family through shared interest, as well as threatening to fragment it into feuding factions. The sheer intensity of emotion related to the whole issue of landownership suggests a complex intermixture of associated motives involving status, economic gain, security, political power, and power within the family itself. The most crucial ingredient in this mixture is probably economic, however, for shorn of their landholdings the Mareis would have little insurance against the vicissitudes of the Egyptian economic system, dependent as it is on the political substructure.[9] The great significance of that insurance is suggested by the estimate of the size, capital value, and annual return of Marei holdings of rural real estate as provided in Appendix D. With Sayed Marei's nuclear family alone possessing at least $1 million worth of farmland, it is hardly surprising that land transactions are a matter of great concern and interest to the family's members.[10]

ECONOMIC BEHAVIOR—
THE MODERN SECTOR

The family is not a corporation in the sense of being a unified structure engaged in a single activity. The pooling of individually owned agricultural land for the purpose of joint management is as close as units of the family come to acting as a proprietary firm. But even in this case, nuclear family clusters rather than the patrilineage or the descent group as a whole constitute the units engaged in joint economic activity. Moreover, while family norms clearly specify that any member of the descent group who is in a position to protect any other member's landholdings should do so, that situation arises only intermittently even in the case of the Mareis, represented as they are by Sayed, "the Father of the Egyptian Agrarian Reform."[11] Family membership thus imposes obligations on each of its members to assist in whatever way possible in financial dealings, but the family itself is not a cohesive economic unit. It is rather a network through which its members grant and obtain financial favors, and, as such, only one of several networks, albeit generally the most important, within which each member is enmeshed.

In those modern nonagricultural sectors of the economy in which the Mareis have direct interests either through their own personal careers or through investments, there are relatively few opportunities for unmediated transactions between one member of the family and another. The family does not, for example, own jointly a large company that could provide employment for many of its members, although Sayed himself owns several small enterprises in addition to his highly successful Arabian horse stud.[12] Family members have a propensity to concentrate in certain areas of economic and professional activity—especially agriculture and medicine —which facilitate mutually advantageous exchanges, but such dealings typically take the form of one member of the family acting as a *wasit* (middleman) for another, making a connection to a third party who is in a position to provide employment or needed goods and services.

The occasions on which one member of the family is in a position to service the interests of another directly, without involving a nonfamily member, are less frequent, but they do occur. Abd al Aziz Marei-15, for example, chairman of the commerce faculty at Ain Shams University, appointed his father's sister's daughter Bahiya's husband, Amin Abdilla, nephew of Ahmad Abdilla, husband of Fatma-9, to a professorial post in the same department. The career of Aziz Qadry, high school and university classmate, close friend and brother-in-law of Sayed Marei, also illustrates how direct exchanges can and do work over time. A year after graduation from the faculty of agriculture of Cairo University in 1937, Qadry obtained a job with the landscaping department of the Cairo municipality through the good offices of his close friend, fellow agricultural graduate and employee in the municipality, Hussein Murad. Qadry's big chance came several years later when his brother-in-law Sayed Marei was made chairman of the Higher Committee for Agrarian Reform, which was personally endowed by President Nasser with the right to circumvent public service personnel regulations. Qadry was hired by Marei as director of research for the Higher Committee, and shortly thereafter promoted to the post of secretary-general of the committee. In 1956, when the Higher Committee was transformed into a full-fledged ministry and thereby lost the right to circumvent civil service regulations and pay exceptionally high salaries, Qadry obtained the post of managing director of the largest jute company in Egypt, established with capital provided by the Mareis and several close friends. The company rapidly became the main supplier of packing bags to the agrarian reform cooperative societies of which Sayed Marei was the general director. One year later, Qadry shifted the jute company's operations from Shubra al Kheima, an industrial suburb of Cairo, to Bilbeis in Sharqiya, where the Mareis, including Qadry's wife, own considerable land.

Up to this stage in his career, Aziz Qadry had benefited from his brother-in-law Sayed Marei's direct control over jobs, first in his capacity as super civil servant and second as a financier behind a private capitalist business venture. But as the Egyptian economy grew more complex as a result of Nasser's industrialization drive, and as the state began to nationalize the commanding and not-so-commanding heights of the economy, it became less and less possible for one man to control single-handedly any sizable area of economic activity. As a result, interpersonal connections involving three or more parties began to replace a single individual's authority as the basis on which jobs and favors were arranged. So in 1961, when the jute company was nationalized, the then minister of industry, Aziz Sidqy, at that time friend and political ally of Sayed Marei, kept Qadry on as manager of the firm, a post which he held until his retirement in the early 1970s.

Other examples of Mareis servicing one another's interests directly cluster in two time periods. The first was before the Nasser government began to socialize the economy and to create a byzantine and overgrown bureaucracy, a time at which the Mareis were in positions to act more or less autonomously. Being chairman of the Higher Committee for Agrarian Reform did not, for example, preclude Sayed Marei from holding membership on the boards of numerous private enterprises, including several concerned mainly with agricultural inputs, such as fertilizers, pesticides, and credit. Board membership of such companies as the Egyptian branch of Shell, the Abu Zaabal Agricultural Company, and Bank Misr not only earned Sayed Marei some £E15,000 per year while he was also drawing his salary as chairman of the Higher Committee, but also placed him in a position to effect the hiring of his relatives. His sister Aziza's husband, Ahmad, the grandson of Hassanein, for example, was given a job with the Abu Zaabal Company, where he remained throughout his working life; Sayed's brother Hassan, after losing his job in 1954 as minister of commerce and industry, set up a private consulting firm which did extensive work for the jute company owned in part by members of the family and managed by Aziz Qadry.

The Mareis, who truly flourish in a free enterprise economy, did not do all that poorly in the much more restrictive atmosphere of Arab Socialism. They did, however, pursue a strategy based much more heavily on the principle of *wasta* or mediation, than on direct control of employment opportunities and goods and services. The case of Aziz Qadry's job as general manager of the jute company being protected through the good offices of his brother-in-law Sayed Marei's onetime political ally Aziz Sidqy has already been mentioned. Sidqy and the other prominent minister of industry in the Nasser period, Mustafa Khalil, who was also a political ally of Sayed Marei, joined together to protect Sayed's brother Marei's position in the public sector. First he was kept on as general manager of the National Paper Company of Alexandria after it was nationalized in 1961, and then five years later he was placed in charge of the Chemical Mouassassat, the state organization responsible for overseeing all public sector firms active in that branch of industry.

Another example of the process of securing employment during the Nasser era is similarly illustrative of the role played by the family. Dr. Amr Abd al Rahman-67, son of Aida Marei and a peripheral member of the affinal set based on the three brothers Hassan, Sayed, and Marei, returned from England in 1968 having completed specialist training and obtaining his F.R.C.S. (Fellow of the Royal College of Surgeons). Informed by his mother's sister's son Muhamed-63, another doctor and Amr's closest friend in the family, that the position of staff doctor at the newspaper *al Ahram* had become available, Amr contacted his cousin Sayed Marei, whom he knew had excellent relations with the newspaper's editor, Muhamed Hassanein Heykal. Sayed accompanied his cousin Amr to his friend Heykal's office, and Amr was immediately given the job as staff doctor, a post which he still holds. Ever-mindful of family obligations, and thankful for its role in obtaining his permanent employment, Dr. Amr refers his patients who require special-ist treatment to Dr. Muhamed, his mother's sister's son, and to Dr. Qasdi Madwar, his sister's husband.

In short, whether the job in question was that of managing Egypt's chemical industry or looking after the health of its journal-ists, these jobs were in the latter years of the Nasser era similar in that they were located within the public sector. *Wasta,* rather than direct control over the means of production, therefore became the key ingredient to financial success, and the Mareis, like many other well-placed Egyptian families, were able to convert family influence into this new currency. As a result they, like numerous other respectable members of the class of large landowners who had played such an important role in the pre-1952 economic and political life of the country, continued to enjoy successful economic and political careers in Nasser's new Egypt.

It was not until the *infitah* (opening) policy declared by Sadat in the wake of the October War, a policy designed in part to stimulate private enterprise generally at the expense of the public sector, that conditions resembling those prevailing in the early and mid-1950s returned. Having adjusted their strategy to cope with Nasserism, the Mareis quickly readjusted to take advantage of the reemergence of significant private economic activity. Omar Marei, for example, ben-efited from the *infitah* and his excellent connections with the Saudis by becoming the managing director of the Feysal Islamic Bank. The nucleus of the staff hired immediately by Omar to process the rush of job applicants for the various remaining positions and to otherwise get the operation off the ground included as consultant the seventy-two-year-old Ahmad Nosseir-28, the grandson of Marei Ibrahim Nasr, who had been raised along with Omar in the household of Ahmad Marei and his second wife Nabawiya, Omar's mother. A further sprinkling of distant Nasr cousins from Sharqiya and mem-bers of the network centered on the old Liberal Constitutionalist Party elite families rounded out the office staff.

In a similar fashion, Ciba-Geigy, one of the largest producers of agricultural chemicals and supplies in Egypt, managed locally by a close family friend who owes his job to support from Sayed Marei, hired two of Sayed's sons: Nasr-83, to serve as chief consultant for its expanding and lucrative operations in the gulf area; and the younger son, Hassan-85, to supervise the production and marketing in Egypt of a new brand of Ciba-Geigy toothpaste. In the meantime Sayed's brother Marei was in 1974 placed in charge of Egyptian-Iranian economic relations, a post from which he arranged the importation of a fleet of Mercedes buses assembled in Iran for the Cairo Municipal Transport Authority. This deal became the subject of allegations of fraud, the specific charge being that the price of each bus exceeded that at which superior German-assembled Mercedes buses could have been purchased, suggesting therefore the likelihood that bribes had been paid. The attempt by opposition M.P.s, especially Hilmy Murad and Mahmoud al Qadi, to raise the matter in parliament was headed off by allies of the speaker of the assembly, Sayed Marei.

MAREIS AS BANKERS

As suggested in the discussion above, the Mareis have tended to concentrate either in the agricultural sector of the economy, because they are themselves landowners and agronomists, or in medicine, the most prestigious of the professions. Several other members of the descent group have made careers as businessmen, and many of them have been civil servants. It is also interesting to note that since the early 1930s the Mareis have had a sustained interest and involvement in the banking sector, suggesting not only the ease with which influential individuals may move from one sector of the economy to another—and hence the relative lack of structural differentiation within the Egyptian economy—but also the astuteness of the Mareis in appreciating the ever-growing importance of finance capital within the Egyptian economy.

The first penetration by the Mareis of the emergent banking sector was made in 1932 when Ahmad Nosseir-28, cousin of Hassan, Sayed, and Marei and raised by their father Ahmad, obtained a managerial job in the Agricultural Credit Bank, which had been created by the new prime minister, Ismail Sidqy, in 1931 to ease the plight of Egypt's landowners as a result of the Great Depression. Sidqy's daughter, it will be recalled, had in 1931 married Ahmad Nosseir's virtual brother, Ali Marei-31. The more important connection for the Mareis, however, was through Ali Shamsi Pasha, brother of Huseyn Marei's wife and the longest serving director of Bank Misr (the Egyptian National Bank) in parliamentary Egypt. Thus Sayed Marei could draw on either or both the Shamsi and Sidqy connections in order to penetrate the banking sector.

He did so in April 1949, being elected to the board of the same bank in which Ahmad Nosseir was now a manager, which had been renamed the Agricultural Cooperative Bank. This bank was later to be transferred from the authority of the Ministry of Finance to the Ministry of Agrarian Reform, where it was placed directly under the control of Sayed Marei, the holder of that portfolio. While Sayed was supervisor of the Agricultural Cooperative Bank from his post as director of the agrarian reform, his brother Omar had become the managing director of the Arab-Egyptian Bank, a post which he was to lose within months of his brother's dismissal from the ministry in 1961. In March 1963, after having been in disgrace for some eighteen months following his ejection from the cabinet, Sayed made his comeback to public life in the form of an appointment by presidential decree to the post of third managing director of Bank Misr, Ali Shamsi's old fiefdom. Sayed and Omar were not the only family members in the Nasser and Sadat eras to have gained access to Egypt's main financial institutions. In 1957, Ali Muhamed al Loba, brother of Ahmad Marei-18's wife, became the managing director of the Cairo Bank.

It was after Sadat replaced Nasser, however, that the door to Egypt's banking sector was swung wide open. Sayed's son Hassan-85's first job after graduation from the American University in Cairo in the early 1970s was at the Arab-American Bank, while his son-in-law Muhamed al Dib-76 was likewise ensconced at the Egyptian International Bank. Sayed's brother Omar nailed down the plum job in the rapidly expanding area of joint venture Arab banks when in 1975 he became managing director of the Feysal Islamic Bank.

For almost half a century, then, the Mareis have had a foothold in Egypt's banking industry, either directly or through affines. Their degree of penetration was greatest in the 1930s and 1940s, when they could count on the Shamsi and Sidqy connections, and in the 1970s, when they have been in a position to cash in on the personal connection to Sadat and on the more freewheeling system over which he presides. But even during the latter Nasser era, when the Mareis were in danger of being dirtied by mud being slung at suspected "feudalists" and when military officers and various other parvenus were able, because of their personal ties to members of the inner core of the elite, to compete successfully for top jobs in all sectors of the economy, the Mareis still kept a toehold in the Egyptian financial world. It is all the more a testament to the varied skills of members of the family, and to the enormous degree of personalism within even the banking sector, that Sayed and Omar, both with only B.Sc.'s in agronomy, should end up as bank managers at a time when Egypt's universities had already produced tens of thousands of commerce graduates, a fair proportion of whom have gone on to complete Ph.D.'s in finance and commerce overseas.

SUMMARY OF ECONOMIC BEHAVIOR

Evidence on the behavior of family members within the economic system suggests in the first instance that the family is of extreme importance for each of its members. Many of them have obtained their jobs directly from kin or affines, or indirectly through them serving as *wasits.* The tendency is, moreover, for these to be relatively long-term commitments so that a family member's vocational career is made possible almost entirely through efforts exerted on his behalf by other members of the descent group. Thus, while the family is not a tightly knit corporate unit whose profits and losses are totalled on a common balance sheet, it is the preeminent network to which almost all its members turn when seeking economic opportunities. The relative stability of the economic system, as compared at least to the political system, is probably the underlying factor reinforcing the economic role of the family. In the ever-changing world of politics, virtually no arrangements are as permanent as those in the economic sector. Political jobs generally are not protected by claims to professional expertise, by civil service regulations, or by sheer market conditions. Political success requires that an individual make innumerable personal contacts so that in a rapidly changing situation he will not be left without at least one ally whose star is ascending. In such volatile conditions, the family is a necessary but not a sufficient condition for success. In the much more stable economic system, however, the family comes much closer to providing the necessary and sufficient preconditions for an individual's financial upward mobility.

Within the family itself, economic pathways tend to follow social ones, but this is not invariably the case. Invoking the assistance of a fairly distant cousin outside the affinal set to obtain employment is not seen as being presumptuous. Moreover, direct intervention by one relative on behalf of another is not always necessary, and some members of the family can simply cash in on the family name if others are ensuring its prominence. So, for example, Omar and Marei, the brothers of Sayed who had been down home on the farm since completing their B.Sc.'s in 1938 and in 1942 respectively, suddenly, once their brother was catapulted to fame as supervisor of the agrarian reform, were sought after to serve on the boards of various agricultural companies. Marei accepted invitations to serve on the boards of three different cotton-ginning and processing companies, while Omar became a member of the board of the Misr Cotton Export Company, the Misr Dairy Company, and several other firms engaged in food-processing. Thus by obtaining active direct or indirect support, or by simply riding the coattails of another more influential member of the family, members of the descent group depend heavily on their family when pursuing economic goals.

4 | MAREI FAMILY POLITICAL BEHAVIOR

THE FAMILY AS A POLITICAL ORGANIZATION

During the Nasser period, political influence was a prerequisite for significant financial success, and although this relationship is not as strong in Sadat's Egypt, politics and economics remain intimately related. Their interconnection, however, should not obscure the fact that behavior in the economic and political systems is quite dissimilar, at least as far as the family unit is concerned. Ownership is simply not possible in politics, so family business firms have no equivalent in the political arena. Politics is much more an individual affair, and while a family may provide the beginnings for a political career, it cannot guarantee a successful end. While one can pull strings for one's relatives so that they obtain jobs, promotions, and other economic benefits, it is unusual for one member of a family to single-handedly bring about the recruitment to high political office of another.

This was not always the case. When land was the major and indeed virtually the only important source of capital, and when its ownership became, after the mid-nineteenth century, increasingly concentrated in the hands of some two thousand families,[1] Egyptian politics had been little more than a summation of the interaction at the provincial and national levels of these locally predominant families. Rural politics were stifled by landlord control, since very few villages were centers for competing interests and most were owned lock, stock, and barrel by one extended family. In this relatively primitive political system, the family was naturally of much greater importance. Each family determined which of its members were to enter politics, and the families were themselves clustered into groups by virtue of intermarriage. These groups in turn tended to adopt similar political positions, the most important family clusters providing the national-level leadership of the various contending political parties, such as the Wafd, the Liberal Constitutionalists, and the Saadists. In other words, the model of the family firm is not all that misleading when applied to ancien régime politics, especially in the early days.

The Mareis, as we have seen, first united their fortunes locally with the Nosseir and Abdilla families and then, spreading their geographical compass, intermarried with other powerful families, including the Shamsis, Sidqys, and Habashis. But as the ancien régime drew to a close and new social forces were mobilized into politics and old alliances began to fragment, the Marei family too began to resemble more a communications network than a family dynasty. Various of its members made contacts through marriage or friendship with politically prominent individuals, and by the 1940s the Mareis had close personal contacts with the leading members of the Wafd, Saadist, Liberal Constitutionalist, and Shaab parties, as well as with the radical movements, Misr al Fatat (Young Egypt) and the Moslem Brotherhood.[2] While the family was still the major point of reference for each of its members, it was not as a unit locked into a fixed position vis-à-vis other families or easily typecast within the political arena more generally. The Mareis were thus spared the fate of politically more prominent families that were identified with, and in some cases virtually coterminous with, the leadership of specific political parties.

The successful exogamous marriages of the Mareis, and the fact that they were not in the first rank of nationally prominent and politically powerful families, facilitated a flexibility that was essential to success in the drastically new conditions of Nasserist Egypt. Since that time there has been no reason for the family to revert to a more rigid and structured political organization, and it has not done so. The vestigial remains of the family as a clan, in the sense of most of its members uniting behind its leadership for the attainment of a shared political goal, are to be seen in election campaigning. Campaigns are still occasions on which most family members will turn out to support the family candidate, in the case of the Mareis, Sayed Bey. All members of the affinal set, male and female, as well as more distant members of the descent group, journey to Sharqiya to serve as campaign workers during elections, and festive open houses are established in various of the family's villas in the provinces. Those members of the family who for one reason or another are on good terms with locally influential individuals approach them on Sayed's behalf.

Having more or less abandoned Sharqiya as a permanent home by the 1930s, the Mareis have had to ensure that the position of *umdah* in key villages, and especially their own, would not pass into the hands of potential rivals and thus undermine their electoral base. This transition was secured in Azizeha by handing the position of *umdah* from Hassan Marei in the 1930s to a relative in the Nasr clan, within which it has remained since that time.[3] The Nosseirs who have continued to live in Kafr al Arbain still control the position of *umdah* there, while the Abdilla do the same in Sanafen. The Marei/ Nasr, Nosseir, and Abdilla alliance remains an ingredient in the continuation of the Mareis' political prominence in western Sharqiya, although the relative importance of the local base itself has declined. If clout in Sharqiya were the only political resource the Mareis disposed of, they would long ago have passed into obscurity.

FAMILY NESTS

What may be thought of as a relic of the alliances of well-known families during the heyday of the ancien régime is a phenomenon best described as family nesting. Family nesting occurs when two families, tied together through marriage, reinforce that connection through a series of social, economic, and political exchanges. Mindful of the fate of large and sprawling family networks when Nasser seized power, members of family nests do not go out of their way to publicize their extensive interconnections. While some members of the political elite are aware that the Mareis and the Muhi al Dins, for example, are tied together by a series of marriages, economic and political favors, and alliances, not by any means all of Egypt's prominent politicians over the past twenty years have known this. Semi-clandestine and small-scale, these nests have replaced larger alliances of families, the composition of which was common knowledge not only within the political elite of the day but also virtually throughout society. These alliances in fact became targets for opponents of the regime from the 1930s on and a symbol of its elitist nature, so it is not surprising that in today's Egypt the more limited nests of united families are slightly secretive affairs.

The family histories of the Mareis and Muhi al Dins so closely parallel one another that one has only to change a few names and the story will remain the same, except for the fact that the Muhi al Dins were not Arabs. Of obscure origins, although probably Turkish-Macedonian, the Muhi al Dins settled in Kafr Shukr, a village in Qalyubiya just across the border from Sharqiya, at about the same time the Nasrs settled in Azizeha. They eventually became *umad* (plural of *umdah*) of Barqata, a small village on the outskirts of Kafr Shukr, and in the late nineteenth and early twentieth centuries they, like so many other *umdah* families, made their move into politics. The Muhi al Dins were not as large or as powerful a family as the Mareis, though, and it was not until 1938 that one of their members, Kholi Muhi al Din, brother of the father of Zakariya Muhi al Din, was elected to parliament as an independent, joining the Wafd upon taking his seat in the Chamber of Deputies. The family as a whole was not strongly committed to the Wafd, however, and Kholi himself eventually left it for the *Kutla* (Bloc) of Makram Obeid. Zakariya's father supported the Liberal Constitutionalists, although as a friend of the Mareis, and particularly of Ahmad Marei, he occasionally supported Marei candidacies for parliament, under the aegis of the Wafd in the case of Hassan, or the Saadists in the case of Ahmad. Like the Mareis, the Muhi al Dins had moved to Abbasiya in Cairo for the education of their children, who in fact became classmates at Fuad I secondary school. The elder brother of Zakariya, Abd al Aziz Muhi al Din, graduated in the same class as Marei Ahmad Marei, before going on to the Cairo University faculty of agriculture, from which he graduated once again in the same class as Marei. Zakariya graduated from Fuad I in 1936, the very year that military academy enrollment was expanded from twenty to two hundred members, so along with Hussein Shafei and Anwar Sadat he joined the ranks. Essentially apolitical and having no deep commitment to the military, Zakariya was simply seeking a path of upward mobility in a newly expanding profession. His eventual involvement in the Free Officer conspiracy, and his subsequent rise to the highest echelons of Egyptian politics, first as minister of the interior during the 1950s and then as prime minister in 1965, were the result of his having become close friends with the prime mover of that conspiracy, Gamal Abd al Nasser. Nasser and Muhi al Din served together at Falluga, the pocket surrounded by Israeli troops in the 1948 war and made famous by Nasser's reminiscences.[4] The other Muhi al Din member of the Free Officers, Khaled, was, unlike his first cousin Zakariya, intensely political and has long been associated with the Egyptian left —possibly because his father was the most conservative of the Muhi al Dins. His leftist inclinations and his cousin Zakariya's generally conservative outlook have not, however, led to any family difficulties, and all members of the Muhi al Din family campaign for whichever of the two runs for the Kafr Shukr parliamentary seat. The first loyalty of the Muhi al Dins, like the Mareis and most other Egyptians, is to the family itself, and political ideology is not sufficiently compelling to undermine primordial family ties.

Prior to World War II, the Mareis and Muhi al Dins had not intermarried, for the latter traditionally married either among themselves or with the Hindi family, who inhabit a small village which lies just beyond the Nosseir village of Gamgara. But during the war a series of three marriages between the Mareis and the Muhi al Dins linked the families much more closely. Ibrahim-60, son of Fatma-16, the eldest daughter of Hassanein, married a cousin of Zakariya Muhi al Din. Ibrahim's brother Gamal-61 then married Samia Muhi al Din, sister of Zakariya. Within a few months Mumtaha-59, a sister of Ibrahim and Gamal, married Sayed Muhi al Din, the brother of Ibrahim's wife. These marriages consecrated an increasingly intimate relationship and paved the way to more extensive contacts between various members of the two families.

Following the overthrow of the monarchy in July 1952, Sayed Marei was chosen to negotiate with the new military rulers on behalf of his party, the Saadists. Called to the Revolutionary Command Council's headquarters in a villa on the Nile, Sayed began to address his plea for consideration of the Saadist cause to the revolution's ostensible leader, Muhamed Neguib. Frequently interrupted by a hawk-nosed young colonel, Sayed Marei was finally moved to remark with exasperation that unless the young colonel would let him speak his piece to General Neguib there was no point in his being there. At that point, Zakariya Muhi al Din called a temporary adjournment of the meeting, drawing his friend Sayed Marei out into the corridor to inform him that it was the hawk-nosed young colonel, Gamal Abd al Nasser, who was the real force behind the dramatic events of July 23–26 and that General Neguib was but a figurehead. From that time on, Zakariya, one of the most powerful members of the political elite, was to prove useful to Sayed Marei as one of his several links to the inner core of officers grouped around Nasser.

This connection was reinforced by a parallel connection between Sayed and Zakariya's elder brother Abd al Aziz, who upon graduation from Cairo University had gone directly into the Ministry of Agriculture. Following Sayed Marei's appointment as minister of agriculture in 1957, Abd al Aziz Muhi al Din was rapidly promoted, and in 1959 he was appointed one of the five under secretaries in the ministry. Ten years later, Sayed Marei, on his return to that same ministry, offered the post of deputy minister of agriculture to Abd al Aziz, who out of fear of the impermanent nature of the position and mindful of the traumatic events in the ministry in the 1960s, opted instead for the newly created sinecure of first under secretary. On his retirement eight years later, Abd al Aziz was taken on by the Ciba-Geigy Agricultural Chemicals Division as consultant, a job arranged by Sayed Marei.

The Mareis and the Muhi al Dins, originally drawn together by living in close geographical proximity in the provinces, and then by intermarriage, have evolved a mutually beneficial relationship based on a series of exchanges of political and economic favors. They have been careful, however, not to demonstrate ostentatiously their intermarriages or tactical alliances within the bureaucratic and political elites—which are at any rate so honeycombed with nested families that one tie more or less may easily go unnoticed.

The Sabrys are another family nested with the Mareis. While there are no direct marriages between Sabrys and Mareis, Huseyn Marei, son of Marei Ibrahim Nasr, married Nemet Shamsi, sister of Ali Shamsi Pasha. One of Shamsi Pasha's other sisters, Dawlat, married a Sabry, and they in turn had four sons, Ali, Ismaen, Muhamed Zulfikar, and Omar, and one daughter, Nadya. Thus the Sabrys, a landowning family in Sharqiya of rather less account than the Mareis, were tied to the Mareis through their mutual connection to the Shamsis, who at the time of the marriage, around the turn of the century, were among the most prominent of Sharqiya's families. This mutual connection to the Shamsis had both positive and negative aspects. On the one hand, it smoothed the way for mutual cooperation between the Mareis and the Sabrys, but on the other hand, it placed them in competition for the favor of the Shamsis, who were in a position to secure party endorsements for potential Wafdist parliamentary candidates. This duality manifested itself most clearly in relations between Dawlat Shamsi's son Ali and Sayed Marei, for both were politically ambitious and therefore vied for the favor of Ali

Shamsi Pasha. Sayed and Marei Ahmad Marei and Ali Sabry's three brothers Ismaen, Zulfikar, and Omar and their wives have socialized regularly together for some forty years, but Ali Sabry tended to remain aloof from these gatherings, presumably in part because Ali Shamsi Pasha was attracted to Sayed Marei rather than to him. But when Nasser and his colleagues seized power and Ali Sabry's name was catapulted into prominence as a Free Officer and the Revolutionary Command Council's first emissary to Washington, Sayed Marei set about the task of trying to overcome this mutual hostility. On excellent terms with Ali's older brother Ismaen, a businessman employed by a sugar company, and also on relatively good terms with Ali's fellow air force officer Zulfikar Sabry, who on occasion enjoyed prominence as one of Nasser's officer-diplomats,[5] Sayed managed to restore amicable relations between himself and Ali. On his appointment as chairman of the Higher Committee for Agrarian Reform, facilitated in part by Ali Sabry himself, Sayed Marei further reinforced his ties to the Sabrys by hiring Omar Sabry, the fourth brother, as his secretary.

The strain between Sayed and Ali was never completely overcome, however. When in 1961 Sayed Marei was dropped from the cabinet and placed under semi-house arrest as a result of intrigues by former Revolutionary Command Council members Kemal al Din Hussein and Abd al Hakim Amer, Omar Sabry resigned in protest and demanded that his brother Ali come to Sayed's defense. While Ali, acceding to his brother's request, was at least partly responsible for the resuscitation of Sayed Marei's career in March 1963, when he was appointed to the board of Bank Misr, Sayed and Ali's political outlooks and career interests eventually led to irreconcilable differences. Later in 1963, Ali Sabry and the new minister of agriculture and agrarian reform, Abd al Mohsen Abu al Nour, began experiments in Kafr al Sheikh and Beni Suef governorates, designed to lead to the eventual collectivization of land.[6] Ali Sabry, sensing the drift to the left in foreign and domestic policy and intent on riding that trend to the top, became one of the leading spokesmen in the regime for socialism and alliance with the Soviets, eventually being placed in charge of the single party in Egypt, the Arab Socialist Union.

Sayed Marei, while opposed tooth and nail to the collectivization of land, to socialism generally, and to the Soviets, although he too was later to serve as first secretary of the Arab Socialist Union, began a behind-the-scenes struggle with Sabry from that time, although their personal and political differences did not preclude occasional truces. Had Sabry, for example, emerged victorious from his conflict with Sadat in the spring of 1971, there is reason to believe that Marei would have cooperated with him and cut his tie to Sadat. In any case, the Mareis and the other Sabrys remained on close terms throughout the period, and Sayed eventually arranged a job for Omar Sabry with the Food and Agriculture Organization (FAO) of the U.N.

Yet another example of the Mareis forging an alliance based primarily on affinity with a prominent Sharqiya family involves the Abazas, who have long been the province's leading family and one of the largest and most prominent families in the country. The Abazas, like the Muhi al Dins and the Sabrys, lived at a greater distance from the Mareis than did the Nosseirs and Abdillas, and the Abazas intermarried to such an extraordinary degree that it was not until well into this century that a marriage linking the two families took place. This marriage, however, between Leyla-19d, daughter of Amin-19, and one Ahmad Abaza, coach of the National Football Club, was of no greater importance than another but an indirect affinal connection through Bahiya Sidqy. Daughter of Prime Minister Ismail Sidqy, Bahiya Sidqy had married Ali Marei-31 in 1931, while her sister Amina married Aziz Pasha Abaza, a well-known poet, M.P. from Sharqiya, and the half brother of Ahmad Abaza, the current patriarch of that sprawling family. Ali and Sayed Marei, raised by the same father, were sufficiently close for Sayed to take advantage of the Sidqy connection to the Abazas, and he and Ahmad Abaza eventually became close friends and political allies.

As head of the dominant branch of the largest family in Sharqiya, Ahmad Abaza disposes of more votes than any other man in the province. Since a large portion of the votes are cast in the Minya al Qamh constituency, from which Sayed Marei runs for parliament, it behooves Marei to work closely with Ahmad Abaza, and he does. For more than a decade, Sayed has run in tandem with Ahmad's nephew Sami Abaza from the Minya al Qamh constituency, Sami offering his candidacy as a "worker," and Marei running in the "other" category—it being mandatory for one of the two candidates from each constituency to be either a worker or a peasant. Sami Abaza is a "worker" by virtue of his onetime employment in the Sharqiya branch of the Agricultural Cooperative Bank, which at the time of his employment was under the control of Sayed Marei in the Ministry of Agriculture and Agrarian Reform. Sayed, as speaker of the parliament in 1976, backed Sami Abaza in his successful candidacy to become the youngest committee chairman in recent parliamentary history, and Sami Abaza in turn acted as Speaker Marei's informal whip. Another Abaza who won election from Sharqiya in 1976, and who works closely with his cousin Sami and with Sayed Marei, is Dr. Shamil Abaza, son of the famous Liberal Constitutionalist M.P. and frequent cabinet minister of the 1930s and 1940s, Ibrahim Disuqi Abaza, whose other son is Tharwat Abaza, one of Egypt's leading editorialists. Tharwat and Shamil's cousin, Fikry Abaza, is the main force behind one of Egypt's leading weekly journals, *al Musawwar.*

Thus Sayed Marei, as affine, close friend, political associate, and neighbor of the family patriarch, Ahmad Abaza, in both Sharqiya and Cairo, has opened the door to the enormously influential Abaza family. This connection has been useful for a variety of political purposes going back to the late 1940s, when Ahmad Abaza and Sayed Marei were both members of the Sharqiya parliamentary delegation. Since that time, access to the press through the Abazas has on occasion been crucial to Sayed Marei's political career. In addition, during the Nasser era Sayed was friendly with Free Officer Wagih Abaza, who was first the public relations director for the Revolutionary Command Council and later a powerful governor, but who, following Nasser's death, made the mistake of supporting Ali Sabry against Anwar Sadat and paid for it with a brief prison term. In the 1970s, as the People's Assembly has emerged as a moderately influential political institution, Sayed Marei has found it useful to work closely with Sami, and to a lesser extent, Shamil Abaza. During this entire period the Mareis and the Abazas have socialized together regularly, both in their villas in Sharqiya, which are some ten minutes distant by car, and in their flats and villas in Cairo. Always mindful of his friends' interests, Sayed hired two Abaza women as secretaries in the speaker's office of parliament when serving in that capacity between 1974 and 1978.

Yet another Sharqiya family with which the Mareis are nested is that of the Mashour. Nabawiya Nosseir, wife of Fawzi and then Ahmad Marei, had a sister, Nefissa Nosseir, who married Salem Mashour, whose daughter in turn was married to her father's brother's son, Mashour Ahmad Mashour. This Mashour has become one of the more powerful men in Sadat's Egypt, having first been appointed to the prestigious post of chairman of the Suez Canal Authority and having then broadened the scope of his influence into various other technical and political areas. He, along with Osman Ahmad Osman, Egypt's leading building contractor, Sayed Marei, and various other individuals from time to time, including from 1978 Mansour Hassan, another Sharqawi, have been the most prominent members of the entourage around President Sadat. Mashour Ahmad

Mashour's brother, Abdulla Ahmad Mashour, was elected to parliament in 1976 from the family constituency of Mashtul al Suq and became a figure of some prominence in the newly created Center Party of the president. In Sharqiya provincial politics, the Mashour, unlike many other landowning families, have retained considerable influence, because they have continued to maintain a presence on the land, actively managing their own estates. Their main connection to the Mareis is through Nabawiya's son Omar by her second husband Ahmad, for not only are Omar and Mashour Ahmad Mashour's wife first cousins, but Omar, having gone to primary school in Minya al Qamh and having actively farmed his land lying in that vicinity, has long been a neighbor of the Mashour family. Thus, while Sayed Marei and his distant relatives the Mashours are political allies within the elite, their connection is mediated by Sayed's brother Omar. Like other family interests, this one is advertised by neither the Mareis nor the Mashours, and they are not seen together conspicuously in public. They tend to communicate and to socialize with one another discreetly, and the Mareis clearly prefer that their kinship and friendship ties with the Mashours not attract public attention.

The Mareis are also intimately connected with at least one other prominent Sharqiya family—the Elwans. From the Bilbeis area, the Elwans have long been one of the most powerful families in the province by virtue of their control of the Shaziliya, a large Sufi order in Sharqiya. Descended from the founder of the order, the Elwans are landowners and businessmen as well as Sufi sheikhs, but it is in their latter capacity that they have most successfully penetrated the political arena. Sheikh Muhamed Elwan, first elected to parliament as a Saadist in 1945 and reelected in 1950 in the face of the Wafdist purge of Saadists, clearly demonstrated by his victory the political strength of religion.

This moral was not lost on the Free Officers, and when they seized power they immediately took steps to undermine the influence of religious figures in the countryside, including that of Sheikh Muhamed Elwan. Known as a high-living man with a reputation for drinking whiskey from a tea glass in order to mislead the faithful, Sheikh Elwan was attacked as "a decadent hashishi" (i.e., smoker of hashish) by the special revolutionary court set up by the Free Officers. But the tables were turned shortly thereafter when Nasser, locked into his struggle against General Neguib for control of the country, desperately needed a public relations success to shore up his position. Since Nasser and the Revolutionary Command Council had as yet accomplished little in the way of dramatic success except for agrarian reform, Nasser had to use that in the attempt to legitimate his position, inquiring of Sayed Marei where the maximum public relations value from distributing title deeds to peasants could be derived. Marei cautioned him against several areas on the grounds of continuing support for the Moslem Brotherhood but suggested that he visit the village of Minshiya, adjacent to Bilbeis.

Minshiya is the home of Sheikh Elwan, and Sayed Marei proceeded to convince Elwan to let bygones be bygones and to assist Nasser's mission. Agreeing reluctantly, Sheikh Elwan turned his energies to mobilizing support among the peasants for Nasser's public-relations gesture, which was in fact an enormous success and widely reported as such in the Egyptian media.[7] In return, Nasser appointed Sheikh Elwan as Sheikh al Musheyikh (sheikh of sheikhs), or the leader of the Council of Egyptian Sufi Brotherhoods, an appointment which Nasser's Minister of the Interior, Zakariya Muhi al Din, opposed, in the fear that Sheikh Elwan might further consolidate his position, partly at the expense of the revolution and partly at the expense of the Muhi al Dins, who are neighbors of the Elwans. But the Mareis and the Elwans, despite the conflicting connection between the Mareis and the Muhi al Dins, were to continue to grow closer together, and Sayed's brother Hassan then married his daughter Hoda to Dr. Hussama Elwan, Sheikh Elwan's nephew.

In 1961–62 disaster struck both the Elwan and the Marei families. In the fall of 1961, Sayed Marei was evicted from the cabinet and placed under virtual house arrest, and in early 1962 Omar Marei and Sheikh Elwan were arrested for "plotting against the state." As it transpired, Omar had apparently been meeting with numerous other religiously inclined individuals opposed to Arab Socialism in the Sayedna Hussein mosque in old Cairo. They exchanged views on the current state of affairs and went so far as to assign to themselves, half-jokingly, various cabinet portfolios in a government which they would constitute on the demise of Nasser and Co. The leader of the group was a *darwish* (mystic) well known in the area for his opposition to the regime, but who in the end proved to be an officer in the Moukhabarat (secret police) acting as an agent provocateur. Omar Marei was placed on trial by a military court held in camera and was convicted and sentenced to death. At this point, Sheikh Elwan, who was under semi-house arrest on suspicion of being disloyal to Nasser, used his connection to Field

Marshal Abd al Hakim Amer to free himself and get Omar off the hook.

Known for his free and easy life-style, and reputed to be fond of hashish, Amer had become acquainted with Elwan, because the Air Academy is situated in Bilbeis, a town in which the Elwans are of considerable account. Personally attracted to Sheikh Elwan and sufficiently politically ambitious to court locally prominent individuals, Amer spent long hours at the Elwan home. Amer was, moreover, not fond of socialism himself and was thus perfectly willing to intervene on Sheikh Elwan's behalf. But Amer, as we shall see below, was not close to Sayed Marei, primarily because of conflicting interests in the agricultural sector, so he was unwilling to push too hard for Sayed's half brother Omar. He did, however, succeed in having Omar's death sentence commuted to twenty-five years in prison plus sequestration of all his property. Omar served two years before being sent home under house arrest, and in 1971 he was completely freed, with his property restored.

The Mareis and the Elwans have been through good and bad times together, and as might be expected they are very close, spending long evenings together at the Marei villas adjacent to the pyramids. In Sharqiya the Elwans assist Marei election campaigns, while the Elwans and Omar Marei are once again intimately involved in the politics of religion at the highest level, moving in a circle that includes Egypt's best-known religious figures, who are therefore also of political importance. Sheikh Abd al Halim Mahmoud, Sheikh al Azhar and minister of *awqaf* until his death in 1978; Outa Wasfi, director of the Maglis al Dawla (Council of State); and several others number among this circle. Thus Sayed Marei, one of the leading representatives of technocracy and secularism in the Egyptian elite, is caught up in a nest that unites the Marei and Elwan families. This in turn opens doors to organized and popular Islam in Egypt, a world which has very obvious political overtones and which offers numerous political opportunities.

Family nests are built on a combination of kinship and/or affinity, geographical proximity in the countryside, a shared interest in attaining national political prominence for at least one member of each family, and the mutual desire to perpetuate local political standing. The whole mixture is leavened by the possibilities of mutual economic advantage to be derived from the relationship. In that these nests are based on interactions among families rather than among individuals, they provide scope for large-scale and complex mutual assistance, facilitating transactions across a broad front and assisting concealment. So, for example, while there was relatively little Sayed Marei could do directly for Zakariya Muhi al Din or for Ali Sabry to repay various political services rendered at the highest level of the political elite, he could repay them indirectly by granting favors, in this case jobs, to their brothers. Since nepotism can be a delicate issue in Egyptian politics,[8] it is clearly advantageous even for top members of the elite to have arrangements made for their family members through third parties, rather than to do it directly themselves.

Family nests represent an adaptation of the much larger, more cohesive and politically institutionalized family alliances of the ancien régime to the more flexible and fluid situation that has prevailed since World War II and especially since 1952. As such they suit their environment admirably and have survived even the stresses and strains imposed by the period of political radicalization in the 1960s. While the falling out between Ali Sabry and Sayed Marei was a symptom of those strains, the remarkable feature of Marei family nests is that, though one connection within them may have withered in the face of external political threats and opportunities, as a whole they remained almost completely intact throughout the period of Nasser's experiments in the mobilization and transformation of Egyptian society.

Families and alliances of families clearly continue to take precedence over commitment to the larger and impersonal social, economic, and political organizations that have grown up in modern Egypt. The major difference between the ancien régime and the post-1952 period is that, while in the former such family alliances were made and conducted openly, in the latter a variety of factors—including negative public attitudes toward wealthy families, Nasser's hostility toward powerful families individually and collectively, and the very nature of the socialized economy and highly centralized political system—have all suggested that a wise strategy would be one based on a low profile. Nasser and Sadat have not demanded that individuals transform their allegiances to their families and to those families with which they are nested. But these leaders, and particularly Nasser, have demanded that at least lip service be accorded the notion of the regime and its institutions meriting the primary loyalty of Egyptian citizens. While by no means all members of prominent families in the ancien régime were willing to grant even this concession, those who were and did could then proceed with an almost business-as-usual attitude, albeit with the understanding that they were jockeying for the spoils of the system and not for control over it.

THE FAMILY AS A COMMUNICATIONS NETWORK

The family is a useful political resource to the Mareis, individually and collectively, in one further way. It provides innumerable and frequently indirect connections to politically prominent individuals who otherwise could not easily be approached. These connections may result in temporary political alliances on one or more issues, or they may serve merely to facilitate the mutual exchange of favors. These relatively less intense personal ties, usually restricted to one or a few issue areas, illustrate very clearly the importance of the descent group as a collective entity. Connections made through affinity, friendship, or even shared economic interest by any member of the descent group are generally considered to belong to the joint domain of the entire descent group. While such connections may be thought of as latent, for they are by no means always brought to life, they constitute part of the family's political capital available to any individual members who care to draw on it. Whether that capital is redeemed depends on the larger political situation. The turning of fortune's political wheel may place someone to whom a member of the family has a tie in a crucial position, in which case the tie will be activated.

Examples of these short-term political alliances resulting from indirect contacts through third parties within the descent group span the ancien régime and the Nasser and Sadat eras. In the 1940s, for example, following the marriage in 1943 of Ahmad Marei-18, son of Huseyn, to Rawhiya al Loba, a communication channel was opened up between Rawhiya's brother Ali Muhamed al Loba, who at that time was in the cotton section of the Ministry of Finance, and Ahmad Marei's first cousin, Sayed Marei, who was then a first-term deputy from Sharqiya. Cotton, on which the Egyptian economy depended for more than half of its export earnings, was a frequent and sharply contested subject of parliamentary debates. Sayed Marei, a young deputy and agronomist attempting to develop and demonstrate a competence on agricultural issues, when dealing with questions related to the growing and marketing of cotton, relied heavily on information and statistics provided surreptitiously from the Ministry of Finance by his affine Ali Muhamed al Loba. After Sayed Marei's defeat in the 1950 election, he no longer had a compelling political motivation to maintain contact with Ali Muhamed al Loba, and the connection lapsed, never to be reestablished in this form again.

During his only term in parliament prior to the Nasser era, Sayed Marei advanced his standing within the Sharqiya parliamentary delegation and parliament generally, at least in part through the skillful use of distant family relations, sometimes reinforced by other ties. One of the leaders of the 1945–50 parliament was Ali Shishini, a prominent agronomist at the time and as such well known to Sayed Marei. Their political alliance within parliament was sealed through shared professional interests, a similar political outlook, and the marriage of Ali Shishini's son to a woman whose sister married Muhamed Abu Nosseir, who after the death of his parents had been raised in Sayed Marei's household. Another leading political figure who exercised considerable power in parliament during the 1940s was the Liberal Constitutionalist Mahmoud Muhamed al Alfi Bey, a wealthy Sharqiya landowner who married the third sister of Ali Shamsi Pasha, the first two having married Huseyn Marei and the father of Ali Sabry, respectively. Sayed Marei, a member of the Saadist Party, was therefore on excellent terms with two of the most prominent Liberal Constitutionalists in the 1945–50 Sharqiya parliamentary delegation, al Alfi Bey and, as discussed above, Ibrahim Disuqi Abaza.

The sheer range of Marei family connections was such that, when the Free Officers seized power in 1952, members of the family were in a position to let drop suddenly useless connections to prominent ancien régime politicians and simultaneously begin to nurture connections to individuals just catapulted into positions of power. In addition to affinal ties to the two Muhi al Din Free Officers, to Ali Sabry, Zulfikar Sabry, and to Wagih Abaza, also Free Officers, the Mareis had a connection to Kemal al Din Hussein, another of the most powerful members of the Revolutionary Command Council. The Hussein family estates are situated in Benha, close to the Marei and to the Nosseir properties. Kemal al Din Hussein's father, a Wafdist, was a prominent local landowner whom the Nosseirs and Mareis usually approached for electoral support in their frequent parliamentary campaigns. Kemal al Din Hussein's brother married a Nosseir, possibly a niece of Nabawiya Nosseir, Ahmad Marei's second wife. Immediately after the seizure of power in 1952, Kemal al Din Hussein became a major figure in the new government, choosing as his personal secretary a member of the Shawarby family, with whom the Mareis were close. Yet another connection for the Mareis to the original members of the Revolutionary Command Council was established in the early 1960s, when Muhamed Nosseir, son of Ibrahim Nosseir, the brother of Nabawiya, married the daughter of Abd al

Latif Baghdady, one of the revolution's leading figures. If the marriage of Sayed Marei's son Hassan to Anwar Sadat's daughter Noha is also included, by 1975 the Mareis had established affinal ties with the families of four of the original thirteen members of the Revolutionary Command Council, plus affinal ties to the families of several Free Officers, some of whom, including Ali Sabry, Khaled Muhi al Din, and Wagih Abaza, were to become prominent national figures.

The Mareis also appreciated the power of the media and used kinship and affinity, among other ties, to gain access to it. In addition to the affinal connections to the Abazas at *al Ahram* and *al Musawwar,* the Mareis also established a personal relationship with Muhamed Sid Ahmed, a leading journalist at *al Ahram* and one of Egypt's most prominent Marxists.[9] The connection to Muhamed Sid Ahmed was through Bahiya Sidqy, wife of Ali Marei-31. Bahiya's mother, the wife of Ismail Sidqy, was the daughter of Amin Pasha Sid Ahmed, and her brother's son is Muhamed Sid Ahmed of *al Ahram.* The Sidqys and Sid Ahmeds, both very wealthy Gharbiya families, included the Mareis in their social circle, and in this way Sayed Marei and Muhamed Sid Ahmed became acquainted. As we shall see below, access to the pages of *al Ahram,* which has throughout Sayed Marei's career been crucial for his political success, was gained in part through distant affinal ties. There are, finally, numerous distant affinal connections between the Mareis and other civilians who played important political roles after 1952. Omar Marei's full sister Aisha, for example, married Muhamed Eid, who is a cousin of Osman Ahmad Osman, Egypt's leading building contractor and an important member of the Nasser and later of the Sadat entourages.

The affinal linkages to Osman Ahmad Osman and to Kemal al Din Hussein illustrate the precarious nature of these distant connections. They are by no means binding on either party, serving merely to bring the two parties together, making further relationships possible. This is in itself a vital function in the Egyptian political elite, which is sufficiently large and heterogeneous that all its members are not personally known to one another. Thus kinship and affinity provide one of many arenas within which personal contacts are established that may subsequently take on economic and political importance. These connections certainly do not, however, prevent the two parties from becoming bitter enemies, as the protracted conflict between Kemal al Din Hussein and Sayed Marei suggests. Nor are affinal ties of greater importance than situational factors in determining individual's attitudes toward one another. Osman Ahmad Osman and Sayed Marei, for example, although sharing an affinal kinship connection through Muhamed Eid, Sayed Marei's brother-in-law and father of his nephew's wife, have been in competitive positions as members of the presidential entourage. Vying for the favor of Nasser and especially of Sadat—for both have been more successful under the latter—they have become neither personally close nor politically allied beyond a general shared support for the regime. Were something to happen which would bring about a change in their structural positions so that cooperation rather than competition would be advantageous to both, the affinal-kinship connection would likely facilitate a warming of relations.

Distant affinal-kinship connections are of value largely because they may pave the way for social, economic, and political interactions. They are generally not of sufficient intensity to lead to a close personal association which might have significant political consequences. On the other hand, the kind of close relations established between members of nested families, like that between Ali Sabry and Sayed Marei, can go sour and lead to personal bitterness played out in the public sphere. This is also the case within the even more intimate setting of the family itself, as the relationship between Muhamed Abu Nosseir and the Mareis suggests. Grandson of the most profligate of the Nosseirs, Muhamed Abu Nosseir lived with his parents in increasingly straightened circumstances in a house adjacent to Ahmad Marei's in the Cairo quarter of Abbasiya. While Muhamed was an adolescent, the house caught fire and burned to the ground, killing everyone within but Muhamed, who was then raised in the Ahmad Marei household. Resentful of his poor-cousin status, Muhamed Abu Nosseir remained an outsider in the Marei household, apparently nursing his grudge and waiting for an opportunity to get even with his wealthier relatives. In 1954 his opportunity came. Hassan Marei, riding the coattails of his brother Sayed, had just been appointed minister of commerce and industry, and he immediately arranged for Muhamed Abu Nosseir to become undersecretary of the ministry. From that post, Muhamed Abu Nosseir began a rumor campaign against his benefactor, Hassan Marei, which eventually became so scurrilous that Hassan Marei simply resigned the portfolio and Muhamed Abu Nosseir took his place. Some years later Muhamed Abu Nosseir joined forces with Ali Sabry, who likewise ground an axe at the Mareis' expense. It is hardly surprising that the Mareis remain bitter about their Nosseir relative to this day. Rifts of this sort can be costly, for they render the family vulnerable to attack by political opponents. But personal animosities of this intensity are presumably an inevitable side effect of family intimacy.

In conclusion, the relevance of the family for the political behavior of the Mareis is considerable, providing as it does the staff for electoral campaigns and, through linkage with the Nasrs, Nosseirs, and Abdillas, guaranteeing control over various villages through the post of *umdah.* But it is by nesting with other families that the descent group of the Mareis performs the greatest services for its members. The sheer number of family members involved in these nests, and the scope of their various economic and political activities, provide a complex of opportunities for the exchange of economic and political favors. At least one kinship or affinal tie appears to be associated with the formation of these alliances, thereby suggesting that kinship and/or affinity serve as crucial symbols of trust. But given that nests are limited to two families and are of a semisecret nature, they are clearly not the exact equivalent of the coalitions of landed families that dominated ancien régime politics. They represent instead a rational adaptation to a changed environment in which sprawling networks of intermarried and wealthy families render themselves all too vulnerable to attack.

Finally, the Marei descent group provides for each of its members numerous individual contacts that may or may not take on importance, depending on where those individuals are placed within the political and/or economic systems. While functional substitutes for the family as campaign machine, protector of the rural interest, and the basis for alliances with other families would be difficult to find, numerous contending units of social organization can provide functional substitutes for the role of the family in making available useful individual contacts. The various social units which act as functional substitutes for the family as a source of personal contacts are the subject of Chapter 5.

5 | NONFAMILIAL UNITS OF POLITICAL SOLIDARITY AND INTERACTION

PROVINCIAL LOYALTIES

For most Egyptians, the distinction is blurred between kinship, at least in its extended forms, and shared village or regional origins. Kinship is calculated to relatively distant degrees, and marriages, at least until recently, have tended to unite men and women of the same locales. The probability of villagers, or those in the same district, being related is therefore high, and one study reports virtually all the inhabitants of a sample village as being members of the same extended family or clan.[1]

The Mareis, a typical notable family, are enmeshed in a network of kinship and affinal connections in the Minya al Qamh district of Sharqiya Province. In their home village of Azizeha, the majority of the twenty thousand residents are, like the Mareis, members of the Nasr lineage, and they think of one another as relatives. The Mareis are also related to the Nosseirs and Abdillas, hence to the majority of inhabitants of the Nosseir villages of Kafr al Arbain and Gamgara as well as those of the Abdilla village of Sanafen. For the Mareis and others, the effect of kinship overlapping regional origins is to reinforce both as meaningful units of collective behavior.

Interlinking kinship and regional ties were in the past, and are to a lesser extent today, pulled together even more tightly by provincial social stratification based on landownership. A cadastral survey map of Sharqiya Province for the first half of this century would reveal it as having been carved into three types of farming units. The first type constituted the few large estates of some 5,000 to 10,000 feddans, owned by the royal family but managed by agricultural supervisors, and serving not as homes for their owners but as sources of income. The second type of units, and those covering the largest total area in the province, were the *ezab* (singular, *ezba*) of the nonaristocratic but wealthy landowners, who numbered some two thousand families in Egypt and around one hundred families in Sharqiya.[2] The typical *ezba* consisted of several hundred feddans on which were frequently situated the family home and one or more villages of peasant retainers. Remaining land in Sharqiya was owned by peasants in small plots, some of which were insufficient to provide their owners a livable income. Such poor landowning peasants, and those completely landless, worked on the estates of the royal family or on the *ezab* of the wealthy landowners.

The one hundred or so wealthy landowning families dominated the social, economic, and political life of Sharqiya. They composed a cohesive social universe in which most were personally known to one another and were in many cases intermarried. As the twentieth century wore on and they urbanized, usually leaving one member of each succeeding generation to manage the family estate, these families nevertheless tended to retain their self-identifications as Sharqawis as well as the personal connections established within that locus. Thus Sayed Marei, despite having moved in his early childhood to Cairo for a modern education, was well acquainted with the leading families of Sharqiya long before he reestablished his residence there in 1937. Growing up in Abbasiya, a Cairo suburb favored in the first third of the century by Sharqiya migrants to the city, he was surrounded by youths who hailed from his home province. Far from blotting from memory their rural origins, these families took pride in them. Fathers instructed sons in the political sociology of the province as if it were an integral part of the family genealogy. Sons learned which families held sway in what areas, what their ethnic origins were, how much land they owned, with whom they intermarried, which political parties they favored, and what vocations they tended to favor on coming to Cairo. Transplanted to an urban environment, provincial society remained surprisingly cohesive throughout the first half of the century. To this day it retains some of that cohesiveness.

It is hardly surprising then that Sharqiya's landed families, and especially those active in politics, should have provided Sayed Marei useful contacts at the outset of his career and as a whole, a reference group. More intriguing is the fact that this connection has continued to be of great importance throughout his political life, although not in an invariable or uniform fashion. At the outset, regional ties were crucial for him politically, but with the abrogation of parliament in 1952 and increasing concentration of power in the hands of the officer members of the elite, the utility of Sharqiya connections declined. In the Sadat era, the revival of parliament, the diffusion of political power more widely across the elite, the redistribution of power away from the lower and toward the upper classes, and possibly even the president's infatuation with rural life have caused provincial ties to reemerge as political resources of considerable importance. An indication of the fluctuating significance for Sayed Marei of the Sharqiya society of large landowners, and of his central role within it, is suggested by the changing composition of Sharqiya parliamentary delegations since 1945.

When Sayed Marei first entered the parliamentary delegation of 1944–45, it was as if he were entering a familiar club, made up of acquaintances, long-standing friends, and affines. The Mareis were already married, or were eventually to marry, into the families of seven of the sixteen deputies. These included the Abazas, of whom there were four in the delegation; the al Dibs, one of whom was already married to Marei's first cousin Nabiha-38; the Ayyoubs, who were tied to the Mareis through the marriage of the brother of M.P. Ali Sayed Ayyoub to Sayed Marei's first cousin Muntaha-17; and the Elwans, whose leader, M.P. Sheikh Muhamed Elwan, arranged a marriage between his nephew and Sayed Marei's niece Hoda-82. The Mareis were on intimate social terms with other families represented in the delegation, including, for example, the Salems from Abu Kabir. Wealthy landowners and dominant in the district still, the Salems had succeeded in electing to parliament one of their kinsmen in five of the eight parliaments that preceded that of 1944–45. In the parliament of 1944–45 they were represented by Ahmad al Sayed Salem, a Saadist under whose aegis Sayed Marei became closely acquainted with Abd al Aziz Abdulla Salem, then an under secretary in the Ministry of Agriculture who later, as we shall see, played an instrumental role in Sayed Marei's rise to power in the early Nasser period.

The Saadist Ali Mansour, whose family was also friendly with the Mareis, won the 1944 election in the Qanayat district. Mansour defeated Cordi Radwan, husband of an Abaza woman and nephew of the industrialist Abd al Aziz Radwan, who had lost a bitterly contested Senate election to Sayed Marei's cousin Amin in 1938. Ali Mansour was eventually to resign from parliament and go on to pursue a career in law, which took him to Libya, where he became chief justice under King Idris. In 1974, however, he was expelled by Qadaffi as a result of a dispute over the drafting of the new Libyan legal code. Mansour thereupon returned to Cairo, where he was immediately offered a consulting position by Omar Marei, Sayed's half brother, in the newly created Feysal Islamic Bank. The Mansours and the Mareis had, throughout the intervening years, remained in contact.

In similar fashion a working alliance between the Turkish-descended Bilegh family of Hihiya and the Mareis has, from the ancien régime to the Sadat era, been faithfully maintained. Muhamed Hilmy Bilegh, a Saadist, won the family seat in the 1944 elections, while his kinsman Amr Allah Bilegh, first elected to parliament in 1957, has represented Hihiya throughout the Sadat era. As leader of the Sharqiya parliamentary delegation, a post he gained by virtue of Sayed Marei's assistance, Amr Allah Bilegh has become an influential deputy and a useful supporter of his colleague Marei.

Political alliances based on regional origins in Sharqiya and suggested by evidence of affinity and long-term association have been forged by Sayed Marei exclusively within the confines of this class of wealthy landowners. These same provincial notables completely dominated Sharqiya politics under the ancien régime, a fact demonstrated by the appearance of the names of many of the members of the 1944–45 parliamentary delegation on the agrarian reform registers compiled in 1952 and again in 1961. Two of the four Abaza members of the 1944–45 delegation had land confiscated in the 1952 reform, as did several other members of the extended family. In the 1961 reform, eight more Abazas lost land. (In that virtually all of the some eight thousand Abazas in Egypt are originally Sharqawis descended through Suliman or Said Abaza, who were nineteenth-century descendants of Hassan Abaza, the Arab founder of the Egyptian line, they may be considered as constituting one family.)

Of the remaining twelve members of the 1944–45 delegation the names of seven, or the names of members of their family, can be positively identified on the agrarian reform registers. Muhamed al Dib, for example, a Wafdist M.P. from Zagazig and a Marei affine, had to surrender 102 feddans of his property in Bilbeis. Ali Sayed Ayyoub, a perennial Sharqiya M.P. and sometime Saadist cabinet member, whose brother was married to Muntaha Marei, was listed on the 1952 register as owning 219 feddans, and one of his female relatives was shown as having 107 feddans of her land taken by the government. The other deputies whose names, or names of their family members, appeared were Mahmoud Muhamed al Alfi, a Liberal Constitutionalist from Sanhour; National Party M.P. Imam Abd al Latif Wakid; Muhamed Fathi al Muslimani, another Liberal Constitutionalist; Muhamed Hilmy Bilegh; and Sayed Marei.

Of the five remaining members of the 1944 delegation, all were from wealthy landowning families but cannot be positively identified on the agrarian reform registers, their family names, except that of Elwan, being simply too common. Other evidence confirms their class origins, however. Ahmad Mukhtar was a Liberal Constitutionalist—the preeminent political grouping of large landowners—and a secretary to King Farouk. Amin Yussef Amer was a socially and politically prominent Sharqawi who enjoyed the honorific title of Bey and had served in the 1930, 1936, and 1938 parliaments. The Salem family were then, as now, the largest landowners in Abu Kabir, and the Mansour family owned several hundred feddans in Beni Shibli, outside Qanayat. The Elwans, owners of relatively small estates, were toward the bottom end of the landowning class, and their political success is due more to their religious influence as leaders of a Sufi order than to their status as landowners.

By contrast, the composition of Sharqiya delegations in the various parliaments of the Nasser era suggests that prominent landowning families were, especially after 1957, increasingly either unable or unwilling to enter parliament. In the first elections following Nasser's seizure of power, held in July 1957, well before the socialist phase of Nasserism set in, numerous Sharqiya notables contested the elections, and several won seats. Hussein Muhamed Salem carried the banner for the prominent Salem family of Abu Kabir, but lost to a lesser-known candidate by the narrow margin of 420 votes out of more than 14,000 votes cast.[3] In Bilbeis, Sheikh Muhamed Elwan lost in a runoff election to a doctor by some 750 votes out of more than 16,800 total. Even the Tahawi family, of whom eight were listed in the 1952 agrarian reform register as owning at least 200 feddans each in the Husseiniya district, and of whom eleven were listed in the 1961 register, were insufficiently intimidated by Nasserism at this stage to withhold candidacy, to which the fact that three offered themselves as contenders, although none successfully, attests. Ahmad al Alfi, of that prominent family which had sent deputies to the 1931 and 1938 parliaments, was also defeated.

Other prominent families fared better in the 1957 elections. The

Abazas elected two of their number, including Wagih Abaza, virtually the only family member in the military and one who had been
sufficiently astute to join the Free Officer organization. The Wakid
family also managed to elect two of their number, although only one
from Sharqiya. Imam Abd al Latif Wakid, who had land seized in
1952 and again in 1961, and who had first been elected to parliament
in 1925 as a member of the National Party, had also won in the 1938,
1944, and 1950 elections and won again in 1957. A younger member
of the family, Lutfi Wakid, like Wagih Abaza a military officer and
a member of the Free Officer conspiracy, who held leftist views
similar to those of Khaled Muhi al Din, was elected too, but from a
Cairo constituency.[4] The Idarous and the al Hout, two prominent
intermarried families, sent a product of their liaison, Muhamed Mustafa Idarous al Hout, to parliament from Sahiya. Muhamed Mustafa
Khalil won election from Faqoos, a seat which had been held by his
titled kinsmen (pashas and beys) in the 1925, 1931, 1936, and 1942
parliaments. The Bilegh family elected Amr Allah Bilegh, and the
Sabrys, "a frankly aristocratic family related to the queen but
through a ruined branch,"[5] were represented by Ali Sabry, another
Free Officer. The Mashour family, related to the Mareis through the
Nosseirs, elected Abdulla Ahmad Mashour. Sayed Marei, by this
time a cabinet member, won election from Azizeha.

In sum, while the 1957 election did provide an opportunity for
nonnotables to gain access to parliament, still more than one-third of
the twenty-one members were from prominent landowning families
that had previously been represented in the Sharqiya delegation.
Nasser's revolution, if that was what it was, clearly had not yet
excluded the rural notability from positions of political influence. But
in the 1960s that was almost to be accomplished.

The Socialist Decrees of July 1961, the creation of the Arab
Socialist Union, the requirement that 50 percent of deputies be workers or peasants, and other features of the general drift to the left
greatly influenced the composition of Sharqiya parliamentary delegations. In the parliament elected in March 1964, eight of the
twenty-four deputies had served in previous parliaments, but of
those eight, six had first begun their parliamentary careers only with
the Nasser parliament of 1957. Of the remaining two, Ahmad Sayed
Shurbagi had served in the 1942 Wafdist parliament, and Sayed
Marei had been in all parliaments since that of 1944–45 except for
the Wafdist parliament of 1950–52. Apart from Sayed Marei, the
only scion of a formerly notable family in the 1964 delegation was
Ismail Muhamed Abdoun, whose relatives had served in the 1926,

1930, and 1950 parliaments. Ahmad Abd al Meguid Negm, M.P. for Abu Hamad, owned, according to the 1952 agrarian reform register, 187 feddans in Faqoos, but the Negm had never been of great prominence, and in any case, in the Faqoos district, part of which is desert, land is cheap and holdings tend to be large. Candidates defeated in the March 1964 elections were from origins as obscure as those of most of the victors.

The parliament elected in October 1968 reveals a similar lack of deputies from notable Sharqiya families. Eighteen of the twenty-four members of the delegation were new to the Assembly. Of the six holdovers, none had been elected to any other than the 1964 parliament. Four of these six were workers or peasants. Of the two re-elected in the "other" category, Ismail Muhamed Abdoun was the sole representative of a previously notable family. Only two other members of the delegation, Abd al Rahman Amer and Sami Abaza, were from landowning families which had been prominent in Sharqiya during the ancien régime. Sayed Marei, having been placed on political probation by the Arab Socialist Union, could not run for reelection in 1968. In short, the Sharqiya notability had by 1968 just about been completely squeezed out of parliament and, while they had other bases from which to defend their interests, their inability to maintain a significant position within the Assembly indicated the broad decline of their power within the system. This in turn meant that the Sharqiya connection was of little use to Marei, who during this period pursued his political ambitions virtually without regard to Sharqiya and its society of notables.

The election held in October 1971, the first following Sadat's ascension to the presidency, reversed the downward trend of representation by notable families in the Sharqiya delegation. Of the twenty-four successful candidates, seven, all running in the "other" category, were from such families. Only one of them, Sami Abaza, had been in the preceding parliament. Sayed Marei, running unopposed in his Minya al Qamh constituency, and Hussein ali Hamdy Salem of the Abu Kabir Salem family, were elected. Amr Allah Bilegh, an engineer who manages a successful private business in Alexandria but who in conjunction with his family continues to dominate the Hihiya district of Sharqiya, was also returned to parliament. And Salah Tarhuti, a lawyer with a lucrative Cairo practice whose family has been prominent for three generations, was elected to represent Faqoos.[6]

Abdulla Ahmad Mashour of that large family related to the Mareis won the seat of Mashtul al Suq, while his brother, Mashour

Ahmad Mashour, director of the Suez Canal Authority, won the seat of Ismailiya. Muhamed Amin Amer, of the large Amer family of the Faqoos area, won the Abu Hamad seat, while Mansour al Ahmad Mansour, patriarch of the Mansour family that has long provided the head sheikh of the Ahmadiya Sufi order in Sharqiya, won the seat of Kafr Saqr. Mansour's grandfather had served in the 1926 and 1930 parliaments, and his father had represented Telrak in the 1936 parliament.

All those Sharqawis from notable families elected to parliament in 1971 were reelected in 1976, greatly exceeding thereby the overall reelection rate of 42.6 percent for all incumbents.[7] Sami Abaza, running in 1976 in tandem with Sayed Marei from the Minya al Qamh constituency, won reelection as a "worker," having switched from the "other" category. Joining the Sharqiya delegation for the first time was Sami Abaza's cousin, Dr. Shamil Abaza, the brother of prominent *al Ahram* editorialist Tharwat Abaza and the son of the perennial leader of the ancien régime Sharqiya delegation and prominent Liberal Constitutionalist, Ibrahim Disuqi Abaza. Altogether, seven of the twenty-four deputies in the 1976 Sharqiya delegation were from prominent landowning families, a ratio equivalent to that which obtained in the parliament elected in 1957 before Nasser embarked on his experiment in Arab Socialism.

But the 1976 Sharqiya parliamentary delegation was, in one crucial respect, not the exact political equivalent of its predecessor in 1957. Landowner deputies, who had not played an important role in the 1957 parliament, for it had been dominated by military officers, did emerge following Sadat's rise to power as a potent force within the Sharqiya delegation and within the parliament itself. The chairman and vice-chairman of the Sharqiya delegation since 1971 have been Amr Allah Bilegh and Salah Tarhuti, respectively, both of whom are influential figures in parliament, a fact suggested by their frequent inclusion in parliamentary delegations traveling overseas. The Abaza cousins are also leading members of the Sharqiya delegation, and both acted as informal whips for Speaker Marei during the 1976–78 parliamentary sessions. Sami Abaza was one of the main organizers within Sadat's Center Party and subsequently his National Democratic Party, and he is in addition chairman of the Assembly's Youth Committee. Another committee chairman drawn from this group of prominent Sharqawis is one Hussein Ali Hamdi Salem, who was in the 1976 parliament chairman of the Agriculture and Irrigation Committee, whose deputy chairman was Amr Allah Bilegh. Abdulla Ahmad Mashour is among the informal leaders of the Sharqiya delegation. His position is due in part to the fact that his family has remained centered in Sharqiya and now numbers among the three or four most powerful Sharqawi families, and in part to the fact that his brother Mashour Ahmad Mashour is a member of Sadat's entourage. Not unrelated is the fact that the Mashours and the Mareis are close political allies. It should be noted that Sayed Marei, who in the 1957 parliament played no conspicuous role, had emerged in 1974 as speaker of the Assembly and the favorite son of Sharqiya Province.

To conclude, the group of half a dozen or so deputies within the Sharqiya delegation who hail from ancien régime landowning families dominate that delegation and, in some instances, play key roles at higher levels. None of the remaining Sharqiya deputies, whether of worker, peasant, or "other" backgrounds, occupies a formal role in the delegation or in the Assembly, or is conspicuous for his informal influence in parliament or elsewhere. Although the clock has not been turned back to the pre-1952 period—for the majority of deputies are of comparatively modest origins and the entire context of political debate has shifted—it is nevertheless true that a small coterie of individuals from Sharqiya landowning families did manage to survive Nasser's socialist phase to reemerge as leading politicians in the Sadat era.

The importance of regional ties for Sayed Marei's political career has fluctuated in accordance both with the importance of landowners within the Sharqiya delegation and with the importance of parliament in the political system. During the ancien régime and the Sadat era, his connections in the Sharqiya elite have been useful resources within parliament and the political arena more generally, but during the Nasser period, when power was much more centralized and parliament little more than window dressing, the Sharqiya connection was of scant use to Marei and he devoted little attention to it.

It is also important to note that, while being well-connected in Sharqiya has at times been a valuable asset for Marei, in cases where kinship and affinity are isolated from shared regional origins as the basis for social and political cohesion, as they can be, regional ties have always been secondary. Sayed Marei has relied much more heavily on contacts with members of families with whom the Mareis are intermarried than with those to whom there are no such parallel bonds. Regional ties not reinforced by kinship and/or affinity have never served Marei as bases for more intimate associations that would combine affective and instrumental goals. Marei interacts with Sharqiya politicians like Amr Allah Bilegh and Salah Tarhuti on a limited, tactical basis. Such alliances have never developed into the more intimate groupings known as *shillal*[8] in the way that family-based contacts and associations first formed at university and reinforced by career contacts have. In other words, the family, on one hand, and orientation toward modern professions, on the other, have been more compelling to Marei than has the traditional social milieu of his home province. Although class, status, and power in Sharqiya have been of political importance to him, the fact that when the family base is not serviceable, education and profession rather than region provide the frameworks within which durable affective and instrumental ties are established, suggests that Marei is essentially a modern rather than traditional figure. For the Mareis of preceding generations, including Sayed's father and his cousins Amin and Hassan, all of whom served in parliament, Sharqiya provided virtually all the social, political, and economic contacts necessary to pursue successful political careers. Sayed Marei, by contrast, might never have survived his 1950 election defeat had he not developed modern skills and the resources, both professional and political, associated with those skills.

SOLIDARITIES BASED ON EDUCATION AND PROFESSION (ORGANIC *SHILLAL*)

Our *shilla* of students at the college included Aziz Qadry, the deceased Abd al Qadar al Abd, Hussein Murad, Hafiz Awad, Mustafa Far, Abd al Azim Shahata, and others.[9]

—Sayed Marei

Every Thursday since I graduated from the faculty of agriculture until now, I get together with all my college friends in my house at the Pyramids, no matter how different their social class. We have a family gathering discussing matters in the true spirit of the Egyptian family.[10]

—Sayed Marei

Sayed Marei began his education at the Azizeha *kuttab*, where for two years he was instructed in reading, writing, and Quranic recitation. At the age of seven, he and his family moved to Abbasiya, where he was enrolled in the Sayeda Nefissa primary school and subsequently the Husseiniya primary school, graduating from the latter at the top of his class in 1928. Both primary schools were then private, but fees were nominal, whereas Fuad I High School, from which he graduated in 1933, demanded a yearly tuition of some £E100. Marei's high school classmates tended to be from families which could afford such relatively sizable sums, but the willingness of parents to make financial sacrifices to obtain educations for their sons meant that students of lower-middle-class backgrounds were also among the 250 graduates of the class of 1933. Anwar Sadat, for example, whose father was a government clerk, attended Fuad I in 1930–31 before transferring to another school.

Nevertheless, the high school classmates with whom Sayed Marei associated at the time, and with whom he has kept in touch over the years, were on the whole from backgrounds similar to his own. Fikry Makram Obeid, for example, a younger brother of Makram Obeid, the Coptic Wafdist leader who had split from the party in 1942 and formed his own rival *Kutla* (Bloc), became a close friend of Marei's at Fuad I. In 1978 Fikry Makram Obeid became the leader of Sadat's National Democratic Party. The deputy leader of this party, Mahmoud Abu Zeid, like his classmate Fikry Makram Obeid, had been an active Wafdist and political leader among the students of Fuad I High School. Sidqy Mahmoud, the air force commander cashiered and imprisoned following the debacle of June 6, 1967, army general Abd al Rahman Amin, and Ahmad al Tuni, a parliamentarian in the Sadat era, were other schoolboy friends of Sayed Marei who attended Fuad I and who hailed from the provincial landowning class.[11] So too were Abd al Aziz Muhi al Din and his younger brother Zakariya, who like the Mareis had moved into Abbasiya from their family estates.

With the exception of the Muhi al Dins, who were anyway tied to the Mareis through marriage and, in the case of Abd al Aziz, through membership in the same university class as Marei Ahmad Marei, none of Sayed Marei's old high school friends have been as closely associated with him over the years as the group of his classmates from the 1937 graduating class of the Cairo University faculty of agriculture. The comparative intensity and durability of ties formed among these university students attests not only to the more mature age at which they were formed, but also to the fact that faculty of agriculture students were yet more homogeneous in their social origins, predominantly being from the provincial notability. Furthermore, as agronomists they were to pursue careers in related fields and hence would interact over the years in professional and other settings. While friendships formed with other students enrolled in the faculty, but not in the same class, were in a few cases to be permanent, the intensity of relationships formed within a given class was much greater, and such relationships have generally lasted longer. Natural intimacy resulting from four years of shared experience was reinforced, for students of agronomy, by a mandatory thirty-day field trip prior to graduation. For Sayed Marei, as no doubt for others, this was a profound experience, being the first protracted time spent away from comfortable and reassuring family surroundings.[12] Such shared educational experiences have led to the formation of units which do in fact serve as functional substitutes for the family and which are known as *shillal* (singular, *shilla*).

Intimate groupings of half a dozen or so individuals who socialize regularly and work together to achieve a wide range of goals, *shillal* tend to be formed as a result of acquaintanceships made in larger formal or informal settings, such as schools and universities, social clubs, political organizations, or the bureaucracy, or they may be formed through family contacts. Their relative cohesiveness, durability, and ubiquity cause Egyptians to evaluate them normatively, much as they do the family. On the one hand, they extol the virtues of intimacy and loyalty that are to be found in *shillal* as in families, while on the other hand they bemoan the inner-directed selfishness of these cliques and their tendency to undercut loyalties to society as a whole. Thus Anwar Sadat, reminiscing about some of the happier moments in his life, referred to the formation of *shillal* among the members of the military academy and the pleasure they afforded their members.[13] Gamal Abd al Nasser, having been on the receiving end of some of those same *shilla* loyalties, condemned them in the wake of the June 1967 war. Arguing that Field Marshall Abd al Hakim Amer was a competent officer of good character, Nasser pinned the blame for Amer's failures in the 1967 war and his subsequent disloyalty on the evil influence of members of his *shilla*.[14] Prime Minister Mahmoud Fawzy, speaking in parliament on November 25, 1970, in the wake of Nasser's death, attributed the ills of the Egyptian political system to the proliferation of *shillal,* playing on the word in saying that, "the *shilla* (small group) and the *shilla* (paralysis) are two words in agreement, written with the same letters and describing the same disease."[15] The Marei *shilla,* formed from among graduates of the 1937 faculty of agriculture, provides supportive evidence for the observations of each of these prominent Egyptians.

The behavioral intensity of the Marei *shilla* is suggested by the fact that Egyptians who are personally acquainted with but not necessarily close friends of Sayed Marei are as likely to know the names of those in his *shilla* as they are the names of members of his family. There is, moreover, virtually 100 percent agreement by observers on the membership of the *shilla*, although there are varying interpretations, even by the members themselves, of who in the *shilla* is closer to whom. As Marei's own comment cited at the beginning of this section suggests, the *shilla* has been remarkably durable over the years. The causes of this cohesion and durability may be seen through an examination of the connections uniting some of the members.

Since many of the Cairo University faculty of agriculture students in the 1930s were from notable provincial families, some were already familiar with one another or had heard their names, prior to enrolling in the faculty. The father of Sayed Marei's fellow student Mustafa Far, for example, was a Kafr al Sheikh landowner who was acquainted with Ahmad Marei, Sayed's father, and who, like Marei Ibrahim Nasr, had attended Al Azhar. Thus Mustafa Far was aware of the Mareis before he first met Sayed at Cairo University. During their four years as students they, along with a handful of others, became very close friends, so that following graduation they remained in constant contact. They met once a week in Cairo, Alexandria, or on their provincial estates, most frequently on that of the Mareis in Kafr al Arbain.

While friendly social contact in pleasant surroundings was one purpose of these gatherings, they also had political overtones. Mustafa Far, for example, had family contacts that were of use to Sayed Marei once he embarked on his political career in 1944. Four members of the Far family were active in politics, two serving in the Maglis al Shuyukh (Senate) and two others in the Chamber of Deputies. Most prominent among the Fars was Muhamed Disuqi Far, Mustafa Far's uncle, who like his relatives was a Saadist. He was elected to parliament in 1938, 1944, and again in 1950. Mustafa Far introduced Sayed Marei to his politically prominent uncle, whose degree from the agricultural secondary school in Damanhour and standing within the Saadist Party paved the way for him to serve as chairman of the parliamentary agricultural committee when the Saadists formed governments between 1945 and 1949. This was a vital contact for Marei, who as a young graduate in agronomy and member of the agricultural committee was trying to establish his reputation as a technical specialist in that area, a goal which Muhamed Disuqi Far happily helped to further. From his post as chairman of the agricultural committee, Muhamed Disuqi Far had also pushed along his nephew Mustafa's career in the Ministry of Agriculture. Having taken his first job in the Survey Department by virtue of the good offices of the brother of his *shilla* partner, Hafiz Awad, who was director of that department, Mustafa Far, following his uncle's rise to prominence in parliament, enjoyed meteoric success, becoming in 1947 the youngest under secretary in the history of the Ministry of Agriculture.

The politically active Fars encountered great difficulty, however, in making the transition to Nasserite politics. Two were investigated by the agrarian reform authorities following the declaration of the 1952 agrarian reform law, and no less than 323 feddans in Kafr al Sheikh were confiscated from them. One of their kinswomen, Zeynab Far, was also listed on the 1961 agrarian reform register, which suggests that she too may have had land taken from her. Muhamed Disuqi Far tried to salvage the family's political fortunes in 1957 when he ran for parliament, but the regime, anxious to have as many loyalists as possible elected, backed a relative of Muhamed Giyar, Nasser's secretary and interpreter, who won the election. It was not until 1976 that another Far, this time Sayed Marei's *shilla* partner Mustafa Far, gave a thought to running for parliament, but by then the influence of the Far family in the Disuq area of Kafr al Sheikh had declined so much that he gave up the cause as lost.

The political and economic misfortunes of the Far family following Nasser's rise to power were cushioned for Mustafa Far, however, by his presence in the *shilla* of agricultural graduates around Sayed Marei, which ensured him a successful career in the agricultural bureaucracy. In 1958, Far was hired as a consultant by Marei's Ministry of Agrarian Reform, while continuing to be promoted within his own Ministry of Agriculture during the period that Marei served as minister. Far's career culminated, in fact, with his appointment by Marei to the directorship of the Agricultural Credit Bank, and on Far's retirement in 1972, Marei arranged a position for him as consultant to the FAO. In 1974, when Marei became speaker of the Assembly, Mustafa Far was hired as a consultant to the Agricultural Committee of the Assembly.[16]

Other members of the *shilla* enjoyed similar career success. Hafiz Awad, from a landowning Daqhaliya family whose patriarch was also acquainted with Sayed Marei's father, joined the Survey Department of the Ministry of Agriculture upon graduation, the director of which was his brother. In 1951 he transferred to the Ministry of Social Affairs and two years later became inspector general of the Higher Committee for Agrarian Reform, whose director was Sayed Marei. In 1957 he was promoted to director general of the cabinet of the Ministry of Agrarian Reform, and a year later, to director general of agrarian reform. Closely identified with Marei, Hafiz Awad was purged from the Ministry of Agrarian Reform on January 1, 1962, following Marei's expulsion from the cabinet in October of the preceding year. A job for Awad as under secretary was then arranged in the Ministry of Supply by its minister, Kemal Ramzy Stino, a graduate of the 1934 class of the faculty of agriculture. In the fall of 1967, Sayed Marei, newly reappointed to his old posts as minister of agriculture and agrarian reform, offered Awad his old job back at the Ministry of Agrarian Reform, but Awad, fearing that Marei's tenure as minister might be cut short again, declined, preferring the security of the Ministry of Supply until his retirement in 1975.[17]

While most members of the *shilla* made their careers in the bureaucracy, at least two, Muhamed Salmawi and Hussein Murad, became businessmen. Salmawi, also from a large landowning family from the Disuq area of Kafr al Sheikh Province, set himself up as an importer, bringing into Egypt, among other things, airplanes for spraying pesticides, which were sold to the Ministries of Agriculture and Agrarian Reform.[18] Hussein Murad, the only member of the *shilla* from a Cairo rather than a provincial family, had become acquainted with Sayed Marei at Fuad I secondary school. In 1937 Murad went to work for the Royal Agricultural Society, and following that he was employed by several agricultural companies before joining Giancles, the Greek-Egyptian owned agricultural company founded at the turn of the century and known primarily for its reclamation of land lying to the west of the Delta and the production of wine from grapes grown there. Murad became vice-president of Giancles after it was nationalized in the late 1960s and brought under the control of the minister of agriculture, who was at that time Sayed Marei. In 1961, following Marei's ejection from the cabinet, Murad was jailed briefly on charges of misappropriation of funds belonging to the Ministries of Agriculture and Agrarian Reform—funds which were allegedly illegally transferred with the connivance of Murad and Marei. Hussein Murad came through that ordeal more or less unscathed, however, partly due to the efforts of his brother Ahmad Murad, a military officer with excellent connections in the officer-dominated elite, who was well known during this period as the president of the Gezira Sporting Club, a favorite gathering place for new and old members of Cairo's high society.[19]

The hobbies of Hussein Murad and other members of the *shilla*, and the organizational memberships that grew out of these pastimes, have also served to reinforce the cohesiveness of the group. Hussein

Murad assumed the presidency of the Egyptian Jockey Club in the early 1970s, while his close friend Amin Zaher was still director of the Egyptian Agricultural Organization, the government agency responsible for breeding and certifying the bloodlines of Arabian horses. Zaher, a veterinarian specializing in horses and the only nonagronomist member of the *shilla,* was drawn into contact with Marei by virtue of his professional expertise and shared interest in horses. Murad, Zaher, and Marei also own stables, and Murad, prior to his assumption of the post of president of the Jockey Club, which controls Egypt's four racetracks, ran one of the largest strings of racehorses in the country. These three lovers of horses also pass time at the Egyptian Automobile Club, formerly the Royal Automobile Club, the president of which is Mustafa Far. On occasion, members of the *shilla* drop in at the Culture Club, a favorite watering hole and literary salon during the ancien régime, which paid for its fame by losing the major part of its Nile-side villa as a consequence of the Revolutionary Command Council's animosity toward such symbols of ancien régime decadence. *Shilla* partner Hafiz Awad is the long-serving president of the Cairo Culture Club.

A *shilla* as cohesive and enduring as this one does not go unnoticed in the political elite, as the dislocation to its members caused by Marei's fall from power in 1961 serves to confirm. Bent on destroying Marei's influence, several officers in the elite, including Abd al Hakim Amer, Kemal al Din Hussein, Abd al Mohsen Abu al Nour, and others, set about to dislodge Marei's *shilla* partners from their various sinecures. As mentioned above, Hussein Murad actually went to jail, while Hafiz Awad was thrown out of the Ministry of Agrarian Reform, eventually landing in the Ministry of Supply. Amin Zaher, who Marei had appointed as an under secretary in the Ministry of Agrarian Reform, was sacked from that post, later also to be picked up by Kemal Ramzy Stino in the Ministry of Supply. Mustafa Far, entrenched as an under secretary in the older, more institutionalized, politically less sensitive, and technically more complex Ministry of Agriculture, was left to his fate—and that was miserable enough under the new and intimidating minister, Abd al Mohsen Abu al Nour. Aziz Qadry, another member of the *shilla* and Sayed Marei's brother-in-law and manager of the Bilbeis Jute Company, partly owned by the Mareis, had some anxious moments before the storm blew over and his future as plant manager of that newly nationalized company was assured. This *shilla,* then, although shaken by the political upheavals of the radical phase of Egyptian politics in the early and mid-1960s, actually proved more durable than the forces buffeting it, thereby testifying to its functional significance. From the point of view of its members, who had embarked upon their careers as young provincial notables, the passage to urbanized professional life was facilitated—instrumentally and psychologically—by the loyalties afforded through membership in the *shilla*. It became a functional substitute for the extended family as a vehicle with which to pursue affective and instrumental goals. In seeking these goals through the *shilla*, individual members became involved, indirectly and directly, in infighting within the political elite, an involvement which was very much intensified by the fact of Sayed Marei's political preeminence and by his utilization of resources provided by *shilla* loyalties in the pursuit of his career—a matter to be discussed in greater detail in Part Two.

POLITICAL *SHILLAL*

The *shilla* composed of Sayed Marei and several of his fellow graduates in the class of 1937 has been durable, intense, and multiplex, that is, encompassing a wide range of activities. While no other social unit of which Sayed Marei is a member, except his family, so compels his loyalty, cliques within the political elite of which he has been a member, and which are referred to as *shillal* by other Egyptians but not by Marei himself,[20] constitute watered-down versions of the type of *shilla* discussed above. Marei's hesitance to identify these groupings in the political elite as *shillal* suggests the slightly negative connotations that the phenomenon takes on when directly engaged in politics. It also points to the fact that such groupings are less durable, intense, and multiplex than the more organic *shillal* formed earlier in life by individuals who share more in common than just tactical political interests. Nevertheless, because the Egyptian vocabulary does not make the distinction between what might be considered as two different types of small groups, and since they are similar, they will be referred to here collectively as *shillal*.

The relatively transitory nature of more overtly political *shillal*, and the fact that they tend to be more instrumental and less affective than lower-level or nonpolitical *shillal*, attests to the structural context of the political system within which they are embedded. That context is more fluid and changeable than the bureaucratic setting within which the latter function. It should likewise be noted that political *shillal* are significantly more cohesive and durable than single-issue, temporary coalitions of politicians. While such coalitions may over time give rise to *shillal,* that transformation requires a qualitative change in the level of commitment to the relationship by all parties concerned.

Another semantic distinction needs to be clarified. In the lexicon of political clientelism, we have the patron and his cluster of clients.[21] A useful reconceptualization of patron-client dyadic relationships has referred to them as lopsided friendships, thus implying greater fluidity and less inequality of resources than is typically found in patron-client relationships as such.[22] The notion of lopsided friendships also suggests placement of the individuals concerned within the modern rather than the traditional sector. It might then reasonably be asked if the *shilla* is simply a specific manifestation of the more general phenomenon of lopsided friendships. With regard to *shillal* within the political elite, the answer appears to be in the affirmative, for these groupings seem to congrue to the lopsided friendship model of moderately unequal exchange relationships. One member of the *shilla* usually does have greater influence and status than the others. The mutual expectation is that he will use these resources to aid his cohorts, and they in turn will use their more limited resources to assist him. The easy informality characteristic of *shilla* relationships, even those obtaining in the political elite, attests more to the style of Egyptian interpersonal relations than to the absence of inequality between members.

On the other hand, organic *shilla,* as one may term them, or those found outside the political elite, tend to be much more enduring and more likely to be composed of members of equal status and influence. In the case of Marei's *shilla,* even had he not been so successful in politics, it is probable that the *shilla* would have remained intact. All its members would have assisted one another, as they are supposed to do in such relationships, but none would necessarily have possessed sufficiently greater status and power to be thought of as a patron, as Marei in this case, due to his unmatched success, clearly was. In short, the highly competitive, unequal world of politics gives rise to the patron-client or, more accurately, lopsided friendship configurations within *shillal.*

Egyptians frequently observe that the nature of their elite politics is such that it abhors equality between individual participants. In this simple truism may lie a clue to understanding the effect of politics on *shillal.* Intense competition within the same hierarchical system is not conducive to warm personal relationships between those of more or less equal standing, struggling to achieve the same goal. Such competition is inversely related to the degree of inequality in relationships, so the more unequal relationships are less competitive and hence more durable. Thus, the numerous dyadic relationships between the patron and his clients, or the more and less powerful friends, constitute the backbone of *shillal.* Relationships between the clients themselves are secondary features, for membership in *shillal* is motivated for clients primarily by the benefits each obtains through attachment to an effective patron (or, stated differently, through the lopsided friendship) and only secondarily by whatever further benefits may derive from being enmeshed within a cluster of similarly placed individuals. It may therefore be anticipated that some *shillal* will disintegrate as a consequence of heightened competition between their client members for the favor of the patron, or as a result of their being placed into directly competitive positions in the political elite. A *shilla* of which Sayed Marei was a member during the Nasser and early Sadat eras illustrates just this consequence of competition among the less important members of the group.

Marei first met Muhamed Hassanein Heykal in 1953 through a mutual Coptic friend, Abd al Nour, who like Heykal was on the staff at *Akhar Sa'a,* which in the late 1940s had been a virtual organ of the Saadist government.[23] Heykal and Marei were drawn to each other by mutual admiration for one another's intelligence and dynamism, by their similar landowner backgrounds, and by their shared ambitions as civilians to make it in the new military-dominated government. A consummate political operator, Heykal saw in Marei and other young civilians like him, all of whom could more or less convincingly be labeled as technocrats, a key resource for high-level political combat. By bringing them together and acting as their spokesman, Heykal, well aware of the technical orientation of the officers-turned-politicians, could place himself in a visible and strategic position. For their part, Marei and the other "technocrats" needed Heykal as a channel into the elite. This tactical alliance, preceded by mutual exploratory contacts, was eventually consummated in 1956 with the formation in July of that year of a new cabinet, which four of Heykal's technocrats entered for the first time. Sayed Marei became minister of state for agrarian reform, Aziz Sidqy minister of industry, Mustafa Khalil minister of communications, and Abd al Moneim Qaissouny minister of finance. They became the core of a *shilla* which at various times included on the fringe other members of the elite, such as Anwar Sadat, Mahmoud Fawzy, and Ismail Fahmy.

This *shilla* was more than a tactical political coalition, as the fact that its members socialized regularly over the years suggests. Sidqy, Marei, and Khalil had known one another as students at Cairo University, and Sidqy and Marei's wives were good friends. Weekends would find the members of the *shilla,* their families, and other guests at Heykal's or Marei's farms adjacent to the pyramids, where entertainment would be provided by Egypt's preeminent vocalist, Um Kalthoum, or by other leading singers and musicians. In the summers they would adjourn to Alexandria, where they rented adjoining beach cabanas. Favors of various sorts were also exchanged. Marei arranged for his close friend Adil Serafy, a wealthy agronomist whom Marei had put in charge of the Egyptian Agricultural Organization, to supervise the development of Heykal's two farms in Mansouriya. Political favors took the form of Heykal giving prominent coverage in *al Ahram* to the activities of Marei and Sidqy and putting its pages at their disposal even when they did not hold cabinet portfolios. With unrivaled access to Nasser, Heykal provided his *shilla* partners with inside information and advice which they could turn to good advantage, and they conferred among themselves on matters of political strategy and tactics.[24]

But ambition, competition, and conflicting loyalties were eventually to destroy the *shilla.* Khalil and Sidqy, both engineers, had from the outset been somewhat reserved toward one another, and in 1964 Khalil, then a deputy prime minister and minister of transport and communications, broke ranks and issued a report highly critical of Sidqy's crash industrialization program. Later a parting of the ways, to be described in detail in Chapter 9, occurred between Sidqy and Marei as a result of their being placed in competitive positions by Sadat. Marei and Qaissouny then fell out over economic policy matters. The Marei-Heykal connection, which had remained intact while the *shilla* was disintegrating, was eventually strained to the breaking point as a result of the Sadat-Heykal clash and the consequent conflict of loyalties that it caused Marei. Unable to bring the two men together despite repeated efforts at mediation, Marei was eventually forced to cast his lot with Sadat. Discretion required that he cut communication with his old friend Heykal, so by the summer of 1977 Marei's dealings with the former editor of *al Ahram* were reduced to chance meetings on the beach at Alexandria, where they would chat pleasantly but briefly. The last remnant of the *shilla* formed in the mid-1950s had fallen victim to the changing political circumstances of the Sadat era.

The stakes at the pinnacle of the elite are too high to permit the formation of a precisely delineated *shilla* around the president. The requirement that he divide his underlings in order to rule them, the necessity of his maintaining contact with various groupings within the system, and the ambitions of those close to the top all militate against a presidential *shilla.* Sadat's entourage has therefore changed in composition and internal relations rather more quickly than typical *shillal,* especially those at some distance from the inner core of the elite. And Sayed Marei, like other members of the entourage such as Osman Ahmad Osman, Mustafa Khalil, Mashour Ahmad Mashour, and Mansour Hassan, enjoys more or less access to the president, and greater or lesser prominence, as politics take its course and personal power requirements, stances on salient issues, and so on, dictate changes.

In conclusion, *shillal* are an integral aspect of elite politics, but they are not the entirety of it. There is no presidential *shilla* at the top, and at the lower levels other loyalties and considerations, such as those which grow out of family ties and bureaucratic politics, are of considerable importance. Thus *shillal* are not hegemonic, but they are one of the most durable units, if not the most durable, within the political elite. As such they are crucial to the political careers of their members, and it is a rare politician who succeeds in the absence of close *shilla* loyalties.

POLITICAL CLIENTELISM

As I have suggested, the political clientelism model is probably too rigid accurately to depict Egyptian elite politics, which may more appropriately be thought of as a system composed at least in part of *shillal,* which group a handful of equals around a more influential (lopsided) friend. But political clientelism clearly prevails at lower levels on the fringe of the political elite, and during the Nasser era it was particularly pronounced. The bureaucratic enclaves which resulted from the concentration of power under Nasser were breeding grounds for patron-client relationships. Magdi Hassanein, for example, created a government within a government in Liberation Province, and one in which he, as sole dispenser of patronage, was the undisputed patron. Abd al Hakim Amer did the same in the officer corps, while Ali Sabry worked assiduously to convert the Arab Socialist Union into his own fiefdom, stocked with his loyal clients. Marei did the same in the bureaucratic organizations in the agricultural sector over which he presided. On being appointed chairman of the Higher Committee for Agrarian Reform, Sayed Marei immediately recruited several members of his *shilla* from the class of 1937. He also hired numerous individuals with whom he did not have intimate social relations. Many of these employees were to become loyal clients, although none were to establish relationships with their boss as close as those which bound him to his *shilla* partners.

One such client was Saad Hagrass. The Wafdist government that had come to power in 1950 had initiated a program for the distribution of some 6,000 feddans to landless peasants in the Kafr Sa'a area in the northern Delta under the jurisdiction of the Ministry of Social Affairs. Saad Hagrass, having benefited from a U.N. fellowship for the study of land distribution in Europe, was the chief technical advisor for this project. Through inquiries at the Syndicate of Agricultural Engineers, Marei learned of Hagrass and offered him a position with the Higher Committee. But Minister of Social Affairs Abbas Ammar, attempting to carve out a role for himself and his ministry in the agrarian reform, tried to block the transfer. Possessed of better ties than Ammar to the military elite, Marei was able to pry Hagrass and two other vital technicians, Mahmoud Fawzy and Ezzat Saqr, away from the Land Distribution Department of the Ministry of Social Affairs. All three were to become dependable clients whose promotions closely paralleled Marei's own rise within the elite.

The Marei-Hagrass relationship and the latter's career illustrate the difference between patron-client and *shilla* relationships. Hagrass served as deputy director of the Land Distribution Department of the Higher Committee for Agrarian Reform from 1953 to 1956, when he was promoted to technical secretary of the Ministry of Agrarian Reform. In 1960 he was made director general of the Agrarian Reform Organization, a post from which he was dismissed immediately after Marei was dropped from the cabinet in October 1961. Twelve months later, Marei used his contacts with the FAO to obtain for Hagrass a job as consultant to that organization in Nigeria.

In 1963, Marei brought Hagrass back to Egypt to participate in the land improvement project in Menoufiya and Minya provinces that Nasser had assigned to Marei, an indication that he was to be rehabilitated as an instrument in Nasser's attempt to counterbalance the growing power of Ali Sabry and Abd al Mohsen Abu al Nour in the field of agriculture. That project, however, was subverted by Sabry and Minister of Agriculture Abu al Nour, who quietly withheld funds from it. Marei then brought Hagrass's plight as an unemployed technocrat to Nasser's attention, who appointed Hagrass under secretary for agriculture in the Ministry of Planning. This appointment enabled Nasser to keep an eye on Ali Sabry's client Labib Shuqair, who was then minister of planning. From this position, Hagrass sniped away at the minister of agriculture, Agrarian Reform and Land Reclamation, Abd al Mohsen Abu al Nour, and particularly at his extravagant schemes for reclaiming the desert.

Finally, on June 20, 1967, with Nasser's political system reeling from defeat in the June War, Marei was brought back into the cabinet. He in turn immediately offered the post of chairman of the board of directors of the Agrarian Reform Organization to his *shilla* partner Hafiz Awad, who turned it down because he thought the position too risky, and then to Hagrass, who leapt at the chance of returning to work in his old fiefdom. Subsequently Hagrass, under Marei's guardianship, made the switch to the Ministry of Agriculture, where he has for several years been deputy minister.

This long-standing and mutually beneficial patron-client relationship was eventually destroyed by Hagrass's ambition, fostered in part by Marei's enemies. In 1976 Hagrass ran for parliament from his family's home district of Bilkheis in Daqhaliya and won a resounding majority. Despite being a first-termer, Hagrass, with the backing of Prime Minister Salem and opponents of Marei in the Center Party, became chairman of the Agricultural Committee, the largest committee in the Assembly. During 1976 and 1977, Hagrass, always backed by Salem, made progress on other fronts, becoming one of the vice-presidents of the Center Party while also being elected president of the Syndicate of Agricultural Engineers and president of the Syndicate of Arab Agricultural Engineers. In the fall of 1977, Hagrass launched a campaign to win election as deputy speaker of parliament, but Speaker Marei, leery of Hagrass's growing influence and his new alliance with Prime Minister Mamdouh Salem, threw his support behind Dr. Gamal Oteify, who won the election. During the subsequent parliamentary session, opposition to Hagrass, at least tolerated and probably stimulated by Marei, arose within the ranks of the members of the Agricultural Committee. It was argued that, as deputy minister of agriculture, Hagrass could not be chairman of the assembly's Agriculture Committee, which, it was protested, was to be the watchdog over that very ministry.

That Hagrass and Marei drifted apart is, in many respects, due to the nature of patron-client relationships and structural features of the system in which they are embedded. The Hagrass-Marei relationship was, over the years, almost entirely an instrumental one, in which Marei protected Hagrass and promoted him when possible, in return for Hagrass's professional and political support. The relationship lacked those affective ties that are so much a part of *shilla* loyalties. Hagrass was, for example, never a participant in the weekend sessions at the Marei farm in Mansouriya. So the relationship remained operational just as long as both men needed one another, a condition which eventually changed as a result of two factors that emerged in the later 1970s.

First, Hagrass had risen to about the highest possible level at which a patron-client relationship with Marei could be of use, both because Marei's power was itself declining and because at that level more than one such connection is mandatory for further success. A second factor was the changing structure of the political elite itself, and developments in the political economy of the country as a whole. The downgrading of the public sector following the 1973 war and the appearance of new opportunities in the private sector have been accompanied by an expansion of the political elite. The old command economy and rigidly structured elite have given way to a much more freewheeling, loosely structured system in which opportunities are to be had at a variety of levels in both the public and private sectors. Extended patron-client networks, large and unwieldy, were of great value in the highly centralized Nasserite system, as the example of Abd al Hakim Amer and his sprawling network of clients suggests. But now clientage networks are more difficult to construct, because the public sector controls a smaller percentage of the economy, because there are too many opportunities elsewhere, and because there are a great many more potential patrons striving for influence within the elite. For Marei, then, the tie to Hagrass, as well as linkages to other clients, have lost their utility. The agricultural bureaucracy itself is no longer worth expending much effort to control, for it offers few economic or political rewards. So Marei has permitted his tie to Hagrass and other former clients to wither, seeking new relationships and opportunities elsewhere, especially within the network of family and provincial connections which have once again emerged as valuable units within the political and economic elite.

CLIENTELISM ON THE PERIPHERY

Political clientelism, having gradually declined in significance at the center of Sadat's system, had begun to recede on the periphery more than a generation earlier. Capital intensification of agriculture, including mechanization, the expansion of industrial centers, a concomitant decline in the economic and political importance of rural areas, and urbanization, especially of those on the top of the rural pecking order, have all contributed to the erosion of the scope, density, multiplexity, and political significance of rural patron-client relationships. Even prior to 1952, the value of rural clientage networks had begun to decrease. The political changes effected by Nasser, as well as the increasing momentum of socioeconomic change, simply hastened that process. The political and bureaucratic creations of the Nasser regime in rural areas, including agricultural cooperative societies, cells of the Arab Socialist Union, village councils, and combined health and social service units, provided new nuclei around which the peasantry could coalesce in pursuit of political objectives. Not only did landowners therefore confront the problem of maintaining clientage networks with much reduced resource bases (and in the case of absentee landowners, with less knowledge of local events and personalities), but as the Nasser years wore on, the competition from new power sources grew more intense.

During the Sadat era, urbanization, mechanization, and replacement of field crops by orchards—which require less labor—have all continued at a rapid and even accelerating pace, thereby tending further to erode rural clientelism. On the other hand, the political changes of the Sadat era might appear to be supportive of rural clientelism. Parliamentary elections have been hotly contested, and rural notable families, as suggested by the composition of the Sharqiya parliamentary delegation, are regaining the political initiative. It is not clear, however, that political clientelism on the periphery, so eroded by economic transformations, is, or can be, revived through political changes that fail to have profound economic consequences. The Marei case suggests, in fact, that clientelism is probably too far gone to be resuscitated in anything like its previous form in which peasant clients were tied to wealthy landowning patrons. Long ago having converted their estates to orchards and mechanized their operations, the Mareis have little use for peasant labor. The decaying reception shelters in front of the imposing Marei villas, where years ago peasants were given tea as they were issued their instructions for the day, or as they requested favors from their employer or his representatives, have fallen into disuse and decay. Labor is now hired on a casual basis, usually through labor contractors. As a result, Sayed Marei's electoral success rests not on clientelism in the Minya al Qamh district but on a coalition of the Nasr, Nosseir, Abdilla, and Abaza families, reinforced by his national political stature. In short, while the family has survived the socioeconomic and political changes of the twentieth century and remains a unit of political importance in the rural hinterlands and in the political elite, political clientelism, which has had its ups and downs in the elite, has traced a more or less continuous downward path in the countryside.

At press conference showing map of agrarian reform areas, April 1954

Distributing title deeds to peasants in the presence of members of the Revolutionary Command Council. Kemal al Din Hussein seated on Marei's right, May 2, 1954

116

Examining cotton in Menoufiya Province, May 1957

With Yasser Arafat at the headquarters of the Arab Socialist Union, January 20, 1972

With President Sadat at the headquarters of the Arab Socialist Union, July 26, 1972

118

*In the office of the Speaker of
the People's Assembly, July
26, 1975*

PART II

THE POLITICAL CAREER OF SAYED MAREI

6 | SAYED MAREI'S POLITICAL PERSONAE IN THE ANCIEN RÉGIME

RURAL NOTABLE

Like many youths of his generation and class, Sayed Marei was torn between two very different life-styles. Having moved to Cairo at the age of seven and from that time on having grown accustomed to Western dress, cinemas, elegant clubs and salons, and in general becoming Westernized, he nevertheless harbored an attachment for the values and the life-style still prevailing in rural Egypt. For most young Egyptians, the attraction of the city proved so overwhelmingly irresistible that their choice of modern vocations and urban residences gave rise to little if any dissonance, and for many not even twinges of nostalgia. But for Sayed Marei these choices were not so cut and dried. His personal indecision, moreover, was complicated by his father's extreme devotion to agriculture and rural life and his insistence that his sons follow suit. The eldest, Hassan, preferring to avoid paternal pressure and determined to pursue his own interest in engineering rather than his father's commitment to agronomy, abandoned his claim through primogeniture to be the politician among this branch of the Mareis. After graduating from Cairo University, he departed immediately for England, where he was to remain for ten years.

Ahmad Marei's failure to induce his eldest son to follow in his footsteps caused him to redouble his efforts with Sayed, the next in line. The first clash in the inevitable struggle of wills that was to pit father against son occurred after Sayed's commendable performance in the secondary school certificate examination, in which he finished seventeenth among all candidates in Egypt and thus assured himself a place in the prestigious faculty of medicine. Imagining himself wearing the white physician's cloak and basking in the adulation reserved especially for doctors within Egypt's profession-conscious newly Westernized social elite, Sayed was awakened abruptly from his reverie by his father's demand that he enroll in the College of Agriculture. Although attached to Cairo University, the college was only to attain the status of a full-fledged university faculty and the right to grant B.Sc. degrees two years later in 1935. Sayed was aghast, for this choice implied forsaking a prominent place in Cairo's high society, increasingly composed of doctors, lawyers, and financiers, in which practicing farmers were déclassé. As Afaf Lutfi al-Sayyid-Marsot observed:

"Mothers of marriageable daughters turned up their noses at rich landowners who did not have an occupation other than land. Even when land was their main source of income, mothers preferred suitors who also had a profession, because by then the professions had become more prestigious."[1]

But Ahmad Marei was to overcome his son's status ambitions. Cognizant of Sayed's keen interest in animals, he had in the previous year purchased two Arabian horses and a small herd of cattle, to which he guessed accurately Sayed would become devoted. Threatening then to sell the family estate at Kafr al Arbain and auction the livestock if Sayed did not enroll in the College of Agriculture, Ahmad won the battle.

A similar drama was enacted on Sayed's graduation from Cairo University. Having finished fifth, seventeenth, first, and fourth from the top of his classes of some two hundred students during his four years in the faculty of agriculture, Sayed expected to receive one of the scholarships reserved for outstanding students to enable them to continue studies in England or the United States for the Ph.D. Envisioning his escape from rural life, he informed his father that he did not want to put on the *taqiya* and *galabiya* (peasant headwear and garment) and sit on the *mastaba* (bench), by which he meant the farming life was not for him.[2] His father was not to be so easily dissuaded. Whether he intervened with the dean of the faculty to

have the overseas scholarships for that year canceled, as Sayed explained in an interview in 1958,[3] or whether scholarships were for
financial reasons not given in that mid-depression year, as is stated
in his autobiography,[4] the result was the same. Sayed returned to
Kafr al Arbain to begin his new career as a landowner actively engaged in managing the family estate. Implied in this choice was the
promise that as the eldest son dutifully obedient to his father and
resident on the land, he would inherent the right eventually to contest parliamentary elections with the family's support.

This victory of rural traditionalism over urban modernity did
not occur entirely as a result of Ahmad Marei imposing his will on
his son. Sayed was by early manhood already infatuated with provincial life and well disposed toward the society formed of rural
notables, as his behavior, geared to the status norms of that class,
suggests. A popular student at Fuad I secondary school and subsequently in the faculty of agriculture at Cairo University, Sayed refrained from political activity. Like most offspring of prominent rural
notables, he remained aloof from the contending parties and proto-
parties, all of which had student committees in the university and
even in high schools. Partisan activity, including student strikes and
demonstrations, quintessentially urban phenomena, were regarded
with some ambivalence and even distaste by Sayed and most of his
contemporaries of rural origins. For them, politics was and ought to
be a family affair, arranged at home in the provincial constituency
and compelling neither blind loyalty to causes nor participation in
demonstrations. Such anomic political activity, as viewed from the
perspective of the upper strata of the young notability, was simply
not for them. Upwardly mobile offspring of the lower middle class,
including such prototypical examples as Gamal Abd al Nasser and
Anwar Sadat, provided the backbone of the student movement and
the material for the contending parties, roles for which they had little
competition from their contemporaries from the notability.

Had Sayed Marei been pushed to the point of rebellion against
paternal domination, he may well have acted out his frustrations in
student politics on the streets of Cairo. He chose instead to cast his
lot with his family and his peer group of rural notables. But from his
experiences as a student in the politically turbulent decade of the
1930s, he did acquire nationalist tendencies and a commitment to
social reform, beliefs which he did not find then or later to be in
contradiction with his personal status or political position as a representative of the rural notability.

A further indication that Sayed was himself committed to traditional norms and practices was his marriage to his cousin Suad, daughter of his father's nephew and political rival, Hassan Marei. Perceiving that this liaison would heal the wound to family solidarity and simultaneously make him the ideal candidate around whom all members of the Marei Ibrahim Nasr lineage could rally, Sayed proceeded to convince first his father and then Hassan, Suad's father, of the wisdom of the choice. Quick to seize the opportunity to mend the rift in the family, Hassan advised his daughter to accept the proposal for the good of the family, adding that Sayed was to inherit his father's position of leadership of that branch of the family and was reputed to have excellent business sense. Suad consented to the marriage in the spirit of sacrifice, for hers had been an entirely urban upbringing, including an education in a private French school in the prestigious Cairo suburb of Heliopolis. Anticipating his future daughter-in-law's probable discomfort and possible unhappiness as a result of having to leave Heliopolis for Kafr al Arbain, Ahmad Marei commissioned on their engagement the construction of a new villa in the style then popular in the capital. This imposing residence was situated incongruously in the garden of the mid-nineteenth-century Italianate villa that the Nosseirs had constructed and that had been acquired by Ahmad Marei in the early 1920s. On the completion of their new home in January 1941, Suad and Sayed were married. They immediately set up house as a young and by that time slightly anachronistic version of traditional rural notables.

The war was by this time knocking at Egypt's door. Resultant food shortages, the presence of ill-disciplined Allied troops, and general uncertainties gave Sayed little incentive to travel to Cairo. Forced into rural isolation, he turned his hand to the related pursuits of agriculture and provincial politics. Capitalizing on members' disenchantment with the incumbent director of the Benha Agricultural Cooperative, Sayed succeeded in displacing him. He devoted his considerable energies to expanding the cooperative's activities and succeeded in establishing a fruit packing plant for which he secured contracts as far afield as Palestine and Europe. This achievement caused the minister of commerce, Saba Habashi, father-in-law of Sayed Marei's cousin, Amin-19, to publicize Marei's successful endeavors on behalf of the Benha cooperative. Another proto-political move involved him in becoming president of the Egyptian Beekeeping Society, a grouping of agronomists and landowners who greatly enjoyed their periodic visits to Marei's estate in Kafr al Arbain. His growing prominence in provincial agricultural activities caused his name to be mentioned as a possible future president of the

Royal Agricultural Society's annual fair, the big rural-oriented event of the year. Marei bolstered these semipolitical activities by fostering his connections to the provincial elite, regularly entertaining the governor and other prominent Sharqiya notables.

Such pursuits, which resemble those of an ambitious English or American farmer preparing to run for borough or county office, contributed only marginally, however, to Marei's eventual entry into parliamentary politics, the real key to which was family connections. His father had been unable since the mid-1920s to obtain Wafdist endorsement for the family seat in Azizeha, because prominent Wafdist Ali Shamsi Pasha backed Hassan Marei. Consequently, Ahmad Marei had joined the group of seventy notables led by Ahmad Maher and Nuqrashy Pasha, who split from the Wafd in 1937 to form the Saadist Party. Sayed Marei was therefore in a position to invoke either the tie to the Wafd through his father-in-law Hassan, who won the Azizeha constituency for that party in the 1942 elections, or the tie through his father to the Saadists, who had won the previous election in 1938. His father's personal association with Ahmad Maher, though, and his own disenchantment with the Wafd—an attitude widely shared among youths in the 1930s—as well as his hope that the Saadists might provide innovative solutions to the country's problems, pushed him toward that party and away from the Wafd. The deciding factor proved to be Saadist control of the first elections in which Sayed was of legal age to offer his candidacy, accompanied by the inevitable Wafdist boycott. This scotched Sayed's father-in-law's electoral hopes. Nuqrashy Pasha, anxious to gain the backing of as many notables as possible for his party, and eager to secure their mandatory financial contributions, offered Sayed the Saadist endorsement for the Azizeha constituency, which he accepted, going on to win the election.

Over the next five years, Marei worked assiduously to assure his preeminence in the Azizeha constituency by dipping into the pork barrel for the benefit of his district and by looking after the personal interests of his constituents. During his first two years in parliament he introduced and secured the passage of bills calling for the construction of a post office in Azizeha, a toilet in the town's main mosque, and a road between Gamgara and Kafr al Arbain.[5] Lest his constituents somehow miss the message that he was a man willing and able to defend their interests, he also used a more direct approach. While resident in Kafr al Arbain, he received peasants in his duwwar (reception hall) every morning, and in Cairo he did likewise in his improptu duwwar, a table at the "General" Coffee House, at which he sat ready to greet constituents. From the "General," conveniently located adjacent to government offices, Marei would escort his constituents to the relevant branch of the bureaucracy and assist them in securing necessary papers, stamps, information, and so on. The dutiful *wasit* (middleman), Marei would even use his car to ferry constituents between their homes in Sharqiya and the capital in order to cement their loyalties. To further secure his electoral position, he assiduously cultivated the support of the village *shuyukh* (headmen) and guards, who were in vital positions to facilitate or disrupt the voting process.

Fate, however, was to strike Marei a heavy blow in his very first try for reelection in 1949. His careful preparations were rendered meaningless when the new cabinet formed to oversee the elections included as minister of the interior Muhamed Hashem. A neighbor of Marei's in Sharqiya, Hashem had some years earlier attempted to appropriate a parcel of government land and had been prevented from doing so by Marei. In 1949 Hashem was looking for revenge and was in a position to obtain it. To make matters worse, Fuad Serag al Din, who had offered generous terms to Marei to run on the Wafdist ticket and who was miffed by Marei's refusal, threw his hefty weight into the campaign to defeat him. Hashem and Serag al Din were joined in their opposition to Marei by the Moslem Brotherhood, which also fielded a candidate. On election day, Minister of Interior Hashem dispatched a unit of guards from Upper Egypt to Azizeha and the surrounding villages, where they rounded up the village guards and *shuyukh* loyal to Marei, imprisoned them, and took control of the polls themselves. Preventing Marei's supporters from casting their ballots, the ministry's troops ensured the victory of the Wafdist candidate, Zaki Diab, nephew of the prominent writer Tewfiq Diab, who along with Yehia Ibrahim Pasha had lost to Sayed's father in the 1924 elections.

This summary of Marei's political career from 1937 to 1952 suggests that he was simply a younger version of the traditional rural notable who had played such a dominant role in Egyptian politics throughout the century. Resident on the land, prominent in provincial society, well connected in the political elite through his family, member of a landowner-dominated political party, and disposing of a sizable retinue of peasant clients, Marei's political persona appears little different from his father's or even his grandfather's. Given that the structure of political and economic power so favored the resources disposed of by traditional notables, it is hardly surprising that he cast himself in this mold, thereby availing himself of the ready opportunity to become a political, social, and economic success.

This description, however, portrays but one of the several roles which Marei actually played. The political-economic context of the 1930s was so fundamentally different from the environments in which previous generations of rural notables had matured that Marei, unless he had never left the rural estate in Sharqiya, was bound to be a different and more complex political figure than his predecessors. The characteristic posture which he struck within the political elite was highly imitative of that of the familiar landowner politician, suggesting that the political elite was insulated from changes taking place below it. The Whigish politics of the gentry was anachronistic by the time Marei arrived in parliament, but in that setting they continued to flourish, more or less oblivious to the massive socioeconomic changes that were taking place outside in the streets. So for Marei to be a political success in this environment, he had to play the game according to its antiquated rules, which, as his behavior demonstrates, he was perfectly able and willing to do.

Yet Marei, like other of his contemporaries, had been deeply affected by his experiences as a student in the 1930s, a decade which from the point of view of national academic excellence and political vitality had not previously been equaled, and has not, it is fair to say, since been matched. Exposed to a potpourri of new ideas, including radical Egyptian nationalism, agrarian reform, social reform more generally, the possibility of developing indigenous industrial and financial institutions, and the novel notion of vocational professionalism, Marei was keen to put his newly acquired ideas into practice. From the standpoint of the old guard, that is, the notables of an earlier generation whose experience had been almost exclusively rural in orientation, Marei was a dangerous radical, indeed, to some a communist.[6] But from the still more radical perspective of committed members of system-challenging organizations such as the Moslem Brotherhood, Misr al Fatat, or the Communists themselves, or even from the viewpoint of some of Marei's young fellow politicians from landowner backgrounds, he was fundamentally a member and defender of the old order.

That such varied interpretations of Marei coexisted then, as they have throughout his career, is reflective of his remarkable ability to reconcile several different political roles and play them simultaneously, emphasizing certain aspects of his overall political persona and deemphasizing others as the situation required. He was then as now a masterful political performer, an accomplishment made possible through exposure to competing ideas and belief systems and an ability to reconcile ideologies and their component ideas and associated life-styles that to many are fundamentally contradictory and hence irreconcilable. This relatively rare ability, which as much as any other factor accounts for the fact that he, almost alone among Egyptian politicians, succeeded politically during the ancien régime and the Nasser and Sadat eras, can be seen from the early stages of his political career. In addition to the role of traditional landowner-politician, which he was to play more or less effectively during those years, his various other activities likewise defined fairly clear role orientations, including those of professional agronomist, aspiring industrial and financial capitalist, nationalist, and ardent rural reformer.

PROFESSIONAL AGRONOMIST

As a student, Marei shunned political organizations, and strikes and demonstrations organized by them, but he did take a keen interest in issues affecting agronomists and was willing to work to influence decisions regarding at least one such issue. Even on this occasion, though, he rejected intimidation of the government by way of demonstrations, a tactic preferred by many of his fellow students. He chose instead to exert influence through personal connections. The issue in question was that of distributing agricultural land to graduates of the faculty of agriculture and the agricultural intermediate schools. In the 1930s, as the number of graduates from these institutions began to exceed the supply of jobs in the public and private sectors, a proposal was made to alleviate the problem by giving or selling on favorable terms recently reclaimed land to graduates, which they would in turn work, thereby obtaining gainful employment and contributing to national income. This solution had enormous appeal among Marei's fellow students, and as the government dragged its heels on the issue, clamor for direct action to force the issue increased. Marei proposed instead that the students work through established channels and had himself made chairman of a delegation to pursue the issue with government officials, while other students in the meantime took to the streets. Marei approached the minister of agriculture, but more significantly he also made his case to two of his Abaza neighbors from Sharqiya: Fuad Abaza Pasha, who was director of agricultural cooperatives, and Osman Bey Abaza, director of the administration of properties. The demand he presented was for 50 feddans for each graduate of the faculty of agriculture and 25 feddans for their counterparts from the intermediate schools. Eventually the government gave ground and allotted lesser amounts to both. Marei claimed that this success was due to his behind-the-scenes efforts, while other observers contended that the government, already gravely weakened by the charge of having sold out in negotiations with Britain over the 1936 Treaty of Independence, and facing incessant student demonstrations on that account, simply bought off more trouble by giving in to the young agronomists.

Whether success was had through intimidation or negotiation, or a combination of the two, Marei in any case did not drop the matter at that point. Almost a decade later, while a first-term member of parliament, he pressed the government to release more land to the ever-swelling ranks of graduates and to improve the quality of land, facilities, and services so given.[7] In mid-April 1947, in a speech on the floor of parliament, he called for the creation of cooperatives to assist these beneficiaries in developing their farms.[8] Nine months later he returned to the attack, citing the government's failure to provide beneficiaries with sufficient funds to purchase waterwheels or to erect dwellings.[9] In short, Marei was a dogged defender of the interests of his fellow agronomists and was widely known as their main champion in parliament.

Marei's first major legislative success, if the pork barrel bills mentioned above are disregarded, came just prior to the dissolution of parliament in August 1949. Acting as sponsor, he steered successfully through the lower house a bill calling for the creation of a syndicate of agricultural engineers, including a provision for granting them the title of *muhandis* (engineer). Both issues were near and dear to the hearts and pocketbooks of agronomists, for they entailed increments in prestige and pay. Professional syndicates, which were modeled on the Bar Association, providing their members a forum in which to socialize and discuss professional matters, and which paid a small pension, were a measure of the prestige of a profession. They had to be created by an act of parliament, and this civil engineers had succeeded in obtaining seven years earlier. The distinction of having their own professional syndicate, plus the usage by engineers of the title *muhandis,* a title which had begun to occupy a place alongside "doctor" as a modern equivalent of Pasha or Bey, was a constant irritant to agronomists, who wanted to be considered of equal status. In July 1946 Marei had raised in parliament the question of agronomists being granted the right to use the title *muhandis,* but he met a chilly reception. In 1947 a bill designating electrical, mechanical, and irrigation engineers as *muhandisin,* as their counterparts in civil engineering had previously been so designated, passed parliament. In January 1948, Marei had attempted, again unsuccessfully, to have the provisions of that legislation extended to agronomists. When in 1949 he finally succeeded in shepherding through parliament the bill containing the agronomists' demands, he did so only over the strenuous opposition of the Liberal Constitutionalist minister of agriculture, Abd al Ghaffar Pasha, who belittled agronomists as unsuitable recipients of the title *muhandis* and by so doing suggested the gulf that separated traditional landowner politicians from modern young professionals such as Marei.[10]

A series of questions asked by Marei of the various ministers of agriculture who served between 1945 and 1949, as well as his numerous statements on the floor of parliament having to do with the ministry's alleged mismanagement of the agricultural sector,[11] also intimated the tension between Marei as a young, self-confident, professionally trained agronomist and older, nonprofessional politicians holding portfolios in areas in which they had little experience or expertise. By the time parliament was dissolved in 1949, Marei had carved out a role as one of the deputies most expert in agriculture and the main defender of the interests of agronomists. While his attacks on incumbent ministers may have entailed political costs, they also brought gains. By establishing his credentials as a professional agronomist with a modern, scientific outlook, he had rendered himself highly suitable ministerial material in the not too distant future when young technocrats such as himself would come to play a greater role in politics. One factor pushing this development along was the increasing professionalization of the bureaucracy itself, with agronomists and other university-trained specialists chafing under ministers who were professional neither in certification nor in outlook but were of the notability. Marei, while of that class background, also could legitimately proclaim himself to be a professional agronomist, thereby serving as parliamentary champion both for his constituents from Azizeha and for fellow agronomists.

INDUSTRIAL AND FINANCIAL CAPITALIST

In the late 1940s and early 1950s, Sayed Marei and his three brothers became rapidly and deeply involved in Egypt's nascent industrial and financial sectors. A new departure for them, it was presaged by the accumulation of stock in enterprises operating in those sectors by other members of the Marei family[12] and by marriage connections to Ali Shamsi Pasha and Ismail Sidqy, two of the leading spokesmen for the development of industry and banking. Like other wealthy land-owners, the Mareis were in search of new investment opportunities for their surplus capital and energies. Talaat Harb, founder of Bank Misr, which was to provide the nucleus for a substantial conglomer-ate of Egyptian-controlled enterprises, had paved the way for scores of other Egyptian landowners who possessed sufficient foresight to perceive the opportunities for investment in manufacturing, trade, banking, and so on, of capital accumulated for the most part in the agricultural sector. That Sayed Marei, long an admirer of Talaat Harb and of Ismail Sidqy and a protégé of Ali Shamsi Pasha, turned to a career in banking and industry following his defeat in the 1949 elections and moved his permanent residence from Kafr al Arbain to a Nile-side flat in Cairo was neither atypical nor surprising, but it was enterprising.

Marei's entry into the business world came about because as a farmer-agronomist he, like many other Egyptians of similar back-ground, could recognize opportunities that the modernization of ag-riculture and development of backward and forward linkages into the manufacturing and service sectors would create. It was a Euro-pean fertilizer company, with whose directors Marei had come in contact while a member of parliament, that provided him his first business venture. Construction of a superphosphate plant in Egypt was proposed, and Marei leapt at the chance, not only purchasing shares himself but also inducing other members of his family and several of his affines likewise to subscribe capital.

Having thus bought a seat on the board of directors of the Abu Zaabal and Kafr al Zayyat Company, Marei proceeded to take an active interest in its affairs. Such diligence was unusual for Egyptians serving on the boards of mixed companies. In many cases they were but token nationals, whose presence was required by law but who did little more than provide occasional "introductions." Energetic, know-ledgeable, and possessed of excellent political, social, and economic contacts, Marei was one of the few truly desirable partners for for-eigners interested in doing business in Egypt. Directors of the prestigi-ous and well-financed Mahalla Company for Spinning and Weaving soon offered him a place on their board, and he, along with a mixed group of Egyptians and foreigners, proceeded to establish a company for the purpose of reclaiming barren land and then farming it.

Having established his presence in the agriculturally related manufacturing and service sectors, Marei then moved laterally with the assistance of Ahmad Nosseir, who had been raised virtually as his older brother, into Ismail Sidqy's creation, the Agricultural Credit Bank. From there the next step into the heart of Egypt's rapidly expanding financial sector was arranged. Ali Shamsi Pasha, Marei's chief political advisor, affine, and chairman of the board of Bank al Ahali, which functioned as Egypt's central bank, secured Marei's appointment to its board. Before reaching the age of forty, Marei had become a member of Egypt's top banking circles, but his relentless upward climb into the business elite did not so much as pause with even that resounding triumph. He established his own consulting firm for the purpose of obtaining subcontracts for technical and professional services from those companies on whose boards he and his relatives sat. This venture, in addition to director's fees, but not including income from investments or from agriculture, was earning for Marei some £E12,000 annually at the end of the ancien régime and into the Nasser era. With a cash flow of this magnitude, his thoughts of exploiting backward and forward linkages from agriculture to establish a business empire began to take shape. When the ancien régime came tumbling down, he had plans on the drawing board for a canning plant, a milk-processing installation, and a pesticide factory.

Marei's success story as an industrial and financial capitalist is by no means unique among the notability. Landowners had for several decades been committing their capital and skills to the development of the Egyptian economy. This trend was of sufficient magnitude that by the late 1930s a political party, the Saadists, were identified as its political manifestation. But Marei is distinguished by the unusual scope and intensity of his activities. Ali Shamsi Pasha, Ismail Sidqy, and Talaat Harb, for example, were all of the rural notability, but their preoccupation with industrial and financial development gradually displaced their interest in their own rural estates, their home provinces, in agriculture, and in rural Egypt generally. Other Egyptians of Marei's class and generation, having obtained university degrees, were either busy establishing professional careers or, in some cases, content to occupy themselves on their rural estates. Marei, on the other hand, engaged in all these activities simultaneously, to say nothing of his career in politics. While others dabbled in these kindred activities, he dived in boots and all. He was thus highly successful in his numerous pursuits and, at least as important, ideally placed to emphasize one or another of his areas of expertise as circumstances dictated. As it happened, however, his involvement and expertise in agriculture, industrial and financial capitalism, and ancien régime party politics, and even his wide network of personal contacts, would have been insufficient to secure his smooth transition into the Nasserite system. The other attributes which, in addition to the aforementioned activities and assets, enabled him to make the switch were his nationalism, which made him acceptable, and his commitment to and knowledge of agrarian reform, which made him useful.

NATIONALIST

Among Marei's early childhood memories of Cairo is that of being swept along by a chanting crowd converging on Saad Zaghloul's *beit al umma* (house of the nation). Marei, however, was never personally to participate in radical nationalist politics, either as a student or as an active politician. He avoided student demonstrations, and although he admired some of the principles of political organizations beyond the pale, such as Misr al Fatat (Young Egypt) and the Moslem Brotherhood, he nevertheless rejected their tactics. He was in his own mind, though, fervently nationalistic. He had great admiration for Egypt's national heroes such as Zaghloul and Orabi Pasha; he applauded enthusiastically at film festivals when Egyptian productions were screened; he deeply resented the swaggering presence of British and Commonwealth troops; he disliked the terms of the 1936 treaty; and he approved of boycotts of English and even European goods, including tarbooshes, the most popular types of which were manufactured in Austria.

His nationalist activities as a parliamentarian were, however, low-key and infrequent. In June 1946, he asked Prime Minister Ismail Sidqy, "Upon what grounds did Egypt participate in the victory parade in London?" Sidqy explained that the occasion provided good publicity for the Egyptian army and for Egypt's war effort, so "the government did not hesitate in accepting this offer." Marei ended the exchange: "We hope that this participation will be a good omen for Egypt and a victory for the principles of true democracy, complete independence, and unity of the Nile Valley."[13] Six months later, Marei queried the minister of finance about his efforts to have England release Egypt's frozen sterling deposits, indicating his displeasure with the minister's inaction.[14] But at no time during his ancien régime parliamentary career did he launch an attack on the British from the floor of the Chamber of Deputies. A few pointed questions were the sum total of his contribution to the nationalist cause as voiced in parliament.

Marei did play a small and ineffective behind-the-scenes role in the unfolding drama in Palestine. Saadist leader Nuqrashy Pasha, upon assuming the post of prime minister in December 1946, wanted a firsthand assessment of the situation in that British mandate and dispatched Marei, ostensibly as a visiting agronomist, to assess the contending forces. Extremely impressed by Zionist capabilities and greatly disappointed by Arab disorganization and lack of resources, Marei reported to Nuqrashy that Palestine was lost. Not wanting to hear such bad news, Nuqrashy did not again ask Marei his opinion on Palestine, and thus ended Marei's first brief sortie into foreign policy. When Nuqrashy declared to parliament on May 12, 1948, that the Egyptian army would enter Palestine on the outbreak of hostilities, Marei, knowing that Nuqrashy was aware of the lamentable state of Egyptian forces and the likelihood of defeat, nevertheless held his peace in the debate that followed.[15]

An ardent nationalist by his own account, Marei never let his feelings dictate his political behavior. Aware of the power of the British in Egyptian politics, he did not care to earn their antipathy, nor, upon seeing the disarray of Palestinian Arabs, did he try to sound a warning or lobby for support for this cause as some other Egyptian politicians, including Marei's affine Ali Muhamed al Loba, worked so hard to do. Marei's appeal to the new military government was primarily not, therefore, that he had played a leading role in the nationalist struggle, although he was sufficiently nationalistic not to be discredited or barred from Nasserite politics.

SOCIAL REFORMER

Within the ancien régime political elite, several names were associated with the call for limitations on landholdings. Muhamed Khattib Bey, a member of the Senate, campaigned to impose a 50-feddan maximum and introduced a bill to that effect in the Senate in 1945, a bill which eventually was defeated in 1947. Ibrahim Shukry, elected to parliament in 1950 as a member of the Egyptian Socialist Party (formerly Misr al Fatat), introduced legislation in 1950 likewise calling for a 50-feddan ceiling on ownership. Others, such as Mirrit Ghali and Rashed al Barawy, wrote treatises outlining their models for agrarian reform.[16] Marei, on the other hand, despite his close association with fellow agronomist Muhamed Khattib—who was married to the sister of Marei's classmate from the agricultural faculty, Hussein Murad—endorsed neither Khattib's nor any other call for ownership maximums. His reluctance to do so, as he explains it, was predicated not on opposition to the measure in principle but on the belief that the state lacked the means to implement drastic reforms and the fear that agricultural production would plummet if it tried. He claims to have favored a more moderate reform whereby landowners would have been allowed a period of time in which to divest their holdings in excess of a legally defined maximum,[17] but the public record, which documents Khattib's, Shukry's, Ghali's, and Barawy's calls for agrarian reform, is silent with regard to Marei's. His party, the Saadists, "had virtually refrained from making their views on land distribution known."[18]

Despite his unwillingness to be identified with radical proposals for limiting landownership, Marei was one of the more outspoken advocates of reform of rural Egypt, and he called repeatedly for improving the living conditions of peasants. His specific proposals were based on the ideas of English academician Doreen Warriner, whom Ali Shamsi Pasha, as chairman of the board of Bank al Ahali, had invited to Egypt on a lecture tour. Marei had read her landmark book on agrarian reform in the Middle East, which called for placing limits on landownership, setting minimum wages for agricultural workers, and regulating rents charged for agricultural land. His conversations with her further convinced him of the necessity of applying at least the latter two of these three proposals, and he exerted considerable effort in the 1945–49 parliament publicizing the need to adopt these measures. He avoided an unequivocal stance on the issue of limiting landownership, identifying it in early 1947 as a project "which should be thoroughly studied."[19] In comments on the Report of the Committee on Financial Affairs on the proposed budget for the financial year 1948–49, Marei identified concentration of landownership as the major evil in the country, but suggested attacking the problem not by limiting landholdings but by fixing wages for agricultural workers.[20]

Marei's hesitation in backing calls for limitations on landownership was probably due to tactical political considerations, for he was not as cautious with regard to the less controversial but still sensitive issue of regulating agriculture rents. Less than a year after entering parliament, he began to press the minister of social affairs about the government's stated intention of issuing draft legislation for the purpose of "defining relations between landowners and tenants," the code phrase for imposing maximums on rents.[21] In the following year, he chided Minister of Social Affairs Muhamed Abu Samra Pasha and Minister of Commerce and Industry Abd al Magd Badr Pasha about their unfulfilled promises to introduce legislation fixing rents.[22] And finally, in 1948, Marei and other deputies, despairing of governmental action, introduced their own bill calling for the regulation of rents. The response their bill and its supporters met is indicative of prevailing sentiment in parliament at that time. On rising to speak in favor of the proposed legislation, Marei was labeled a communist by one of the many landowner M.P.'s, and during his speech he was heckled by this and other opponents of the bill, which out of almost total lack of support never came to a vote.[23]

Marei was equally unsuccessful with a variety of other proposals for reform, none of which even went so far as to take the form of specific legislation. He questioned the government, again to no avail, about its stated intention of issuing a minimum wage law for agricultural workers.[24] He called on the government to improve the social and health conditions of peasants by upgrading the construction program of social and health units in the countryside, and to stimulate the rural economy by requiring landowners to construct "agro-industrial" projects, such as dairies, looms, and beehives, on their properties. He further demanded that landowners be required to build sanitary facilities and provide basic social services for their tenants and employees.[25] That Marei, shying away from confrontation with powerful political forces, occasionally bordered on being a liberal do-gooder is suggested by his comments lauding the Ministry of Social Affairs for forming a committee to "fight barefootedness among primary school students, [for] it is a shame to see the majority of the people in a state of unbelievable poverty."[26]

But other of his activities in support of reform had substance. He monitored the government's program of distributing small plots of land to peasants, charging the responsible minister with failing adequately to screen beneficiaries so that undesirable or undeserving elements, including criminals, carpenters, barbers, *imams,* and relatives of *umad* obtained land, whereas landless peasants did not.[27] He also invited the Ministry of Social Affairs to facilitate the government's professed goal of "initiating the seeds of small ownership in Egypt" by grouping the beneficiaries of land distribution schemes into agricultural cooperatives so they could benefit from the provision of essential inputs while obviating the negative consequences of fragmentation of landholdings through collective decisions on crop planting and rotation.[28] In the debate on the revenue section of the proposed budget for 1948–49, Marei supported the call for the imposition of a progressive tax on landowners, arguing that it should take the form of the *zakat*, * "because it is a form of progressive tax [which] no owner will dare say is too much or not useful, because it is a *sharia* tax and must be paid."[29]

By the end of his first term in parliament, Marei was on record as having proposed a wide array of measures which, if adopted, would have brought about significant change in rural Egypt. He was among the small group of increasingly prominent politicians to be identified with agrarian reform as conceived in its broadest terms. In hindsight, the evidence suggests that his blueprint for reform was as elaborate and systematic as those of many of his contemporaries, whose chief preoccupation was limiting landholdings and who believed all other problems subsidiary to this.

While this background of interest in and knowledge of agrarian reform qualified Marei to take command of the agrarian reform program following Nasser's rise to power, the directorship of this most sensitive task of the new government was not to be decided as if it were a civil service post requiring specific credentials or expertise compatible with a bureaucratic setting. Agrarian reform was preeminently a political act requiring of its director an acute political sense and great political skill, with the important but nevertheless secondary attribute of knowledge of rural Egypt and ideas of how to change it. On paper and in fact, Marei had the credentials to take charge, but his recruitment to the post was not accomplished through a routine selection process. It came about as a result of the interplay of his technical expertise and reputation for it, his ability to perceive the political character of the reform and the centrality of it to the regime, and last but by no means least, his effective use of the network of personal connections which enabled him at the outset to place his foot in the door to the revolutionary government's inner councils and then to expand his contacts, so that regardless of personnel changes within the regime, he remained in contact with powerful individuals. How this entry was accomplished and his position then consolidated is the subject of the next chapter.

*The zakat is one of the five pillars of Islam. It requires of all believers that they pay a small percentage of their income in tax.

7 | THE EARLY NASSER ERA: SAYED MAREI AS TECHNOCRAT

RECRUITMENT INTO THE HIGHER COMMITTEE FOR AGRARIAN REFORM

On the morning of July 23, 1952, when Sayed Marei heard Anwar Sadat broadcasting over Radio Cairo news of the revolution, his first thought was to wonder who the revolutionaries were. On the following day the Cairo dailies published photographs of the new junta, and Marei was pleased to observe that Zakariya Muhi al Din was among the thirteen officers, but despite the connections linking the two families, "there was not between us," according to Marei, "an intimate friendship or strong tie."[1]

Anxious to determine what place, if any, there might be for him in the new order of things, Marei nevertheless continued to orient his political activity toward the still extant ancien régime political parties. His first concern was that the Wafd might upstage the Saadists. On July 29 the Wafd issued a statement declaring that the party, in accordance with the wish of the new rulers, would purge itself. Wafdist leader Nahhas Pasha had taken the initiative in establishing contact with the officers, arranging through Fuad Serag al Din's cousin, Aissa Serag al Din, a member of the Free Officers, a meeting with General Neguib, Colonel Nasser, and three other prominent members of the movement.[2] Marei feared the officers would respond to these overtures and choose to collaborate with the Wafd, to the detriment of the other parties. He and other younger Saadists, by way of response to the Wafd, asked for and were granted an audience with Neguib et al. Marei and his colleagues in the delegation, like other young leaders of the second rank in the various parties, were optimistic about their futures, for the purge now demanded by the military men might leave the way clear for them to replace the older, more prominent politicians of the first rank.

Marei, having by this time developed a keen political sense, was disabused of notions of political grandeur sooner than most of his colleagues by his very first meeting with the Revolutionary Command Council (RCC). In reply to their inquiry at this meeting as to what the RCC wanted of the parties, the Saadists were informed that they too must purge themselves. Apprehensive lest he and the other members of the delegation be accused by senior Saadists of using this ill-defined threat to oust them for the benefit of the younger men, Marei requested clarification. This the RCC refused, but Marei, through the good offices of Zakariya Muhi al Din, obtained RCC member Hassan Ibrahim's consent to accompany Marei to party headquarters to explain to President Ibrahim al Hadi, vice-president Hamed al Gouda, and others what had been stated to the Saadist delegation. When Lieutenant Colonel Ibrahim simply reiterated the vague injunction "purge yourselves" to the assembled Saadists, Marei drew the accurate conclusion that the end was nigh and the RCC desired the destruction of the parties, attempting to bring it about by unleashing and encouraging the ambitions of party members of the second rank. Marei began to scout around for a new political future independent of the Saadists and the entire ancien régime political apparatus, still alive but already in its death throes.

As it transpired, he did not have to look far or too long. On September 10, the day after the RCC issued the agrarian reform decree, Marei, who until then had been caught up in the internecine struggles within the Saadist Party, was contacted by the new minister of agriculture in Neguib's first cabinet, Abdulla Salem, an old friend from Sharqiya. Salem instructed Marei to study the declaration carefully, for he had nominated him, along with agronomists Yehia al Alaily and Shalabi Saroufin, for membership in the newly formed Higher Committee for Agrarian Reform (HCAR) charged with implementing the measure. The HCAR was to be chaired by wing commander and RCC member Gamal Salem and included as members Minister of Agriculture Salem and his small coterie of agronomists, as well as the ministers of irrigation, economics, finance, *awqaf* (religious endowments), the chairman of the Council of State, and their assistants. But Nasser, recalling Marei's self-assured, pashalike demeanor and dress at their meeting some weeks earlier, where Marei was representing the Saadists, rejected Salem's suggestion that he serve on the HCAR. Ali Sabry and Zakariya Muhi al Din then came to Marei's defense. Presumably desirous of avoiding as much conflict as possible at this sensitive stage, Nasser gave in, and Marei's nomination was approved.

At the third meeting of the HCAR, Marei was appointed delegate member, which made him the main link between Salem, the RCC's representative overseeing agrarian reform, and the HCAR itself. Marei was thus endowed with greater power and influence than the HCAR's nominal chairman, the minister of agriculture. This readjustment of authority in Marei's favor resulted in part from the fact that the RCC wanted to oversee agrarian reform as directly as possible rather than leave it to the ponderous workings of the bureaucracy. In accordance with the HCAR's new status as an organization independent of the Ministry of Agriculture, its headquarters were transferred in February 1953 from that ministry to Abdin Palace, the nerve center of the new military government.

Marei's meteoric rise within the HCAR, which culminated in his appointment as director on January 26, 1953, and involved him passing meanwhile several other candidates for the post, was due to a combination of factors. In the first instance, several other candidates were ruled out on independent grounds. Ibrahim Shukry, who had just two years earlier introduced legislation in parliament calling for a 50-feddan limit on landownership, and who in the autumn of 1952 went on radio endorsing the new government's proposed agrarian reform, was rejected because the RCC did not want to have to share credit for their main accomplishment with anyone else. Shukry and his party, the Egyptian Socialists (formerly Misr al Fatat), were widely known as outspoken advocates of agrarian reform. The same liability disqualified other supporters of the reform. Those who contributed to the drafting of the legislation itself, such as Dr. Rashed al Barawy, an academic economist; Ahmad Fuad, a leftist attorney; and military officers Gamal Salem, Khaled Muhi al Din, and Yussef Sadiq, lacked training in agronomy.

Of those high-ranking officials in the bureaucracy who did possess the relevant expertise and who were actively competing for the post, none had the array of resources, or utilized those that he had, as skillfully as Marei. Abd al Wahhab Ezzat had early in 1952 been appointed head of a fourteen-man interministerial committee responsible for distributing reclaimed state land in blocs of 5 feddans or less. Ezzat could thus truthfully claim to be the ranking civil servant with the appropriate expertise, and he actively sought a leading role in the new agrarian reform.[3] But he lacked political connections and the insight to understand that the RCC conceptualized the reform in a political rather than bureaucratic context, wanting to use it as a vehicle with which to establish its revolutionary credentials. Minister of Agriculture Abdulla Salem, who was brought on board at the time the reform was announced, was too ancien régime oriented for Gamal Salem and other of his officer colleagues. In December 1952 he was jettisoned, and replaced by Abd al Razzaq Sidqy, who was also angling for a key post in the reform but whose only contact with the elite was through his neighbor, Minister of Finance Dr. Gamal al Emary, a civilian economist who lacked the requisite political clout. The incumbent minister of social affairs, Dr. Abbas Ammar, also had ambitions of playing an active role in the reform, but he too lacked high-level contacts to push his cause.

The possibility of a radical leftist, of whom there were several potential candidates, being entrusted with the agrarian reform was diminished by the fact that the majority of the RCC like Nasser, the most influential member, were moderates. Khaled Muhi al Din and Yussef Sadiq, both of whom helped draft the law itself, were too far to the left for them or any of their nominees to be acceptable to Nasser and the majority of the RCC. Magdi Hassanein, who had played an instrumental role in the events of July 23 and who was one of Nasser's main supporters in the army's mechanized division and in the Free Officer movement, was another leftist with an interest in the agrarian question. Despite being close to Ahmad Murad, a classmate in the military academy who was the brother of Marei's close friend Hussein Murad, Hassanein distrusted Marei and disliked his politics.[4] Nasser wisely prevented a potentially dangerous conflict from emerging between Hassanein on the one side and Gamal Salem and Marei on the other by putting Hassanein in charge of his own fiefdom in the desert, Liberation Province. This cleared the way for Marei to assume the dominant role in the agrarian reform.

Marei did not win the position by default, however, as a review of his activity in this period suggests. His first encounter with Gamal Salem at the inaugural meeting of the HCAR did not bode well for the future. Overlooking the fact that the government considered the agrarian reform law as its very own, virtually inviolable creation, and unaware of Gamal Salem's mercurial personality, Marei proceeded to lecture Salem on revisions necessary for the law to be successfully implemented. Salem exploded at this transgression, and Marei fled the meeting angered and in disarray. All was not lost, however, and Salem, once he had cooled down, was apparently impressed by some of Marei's comments. Highly remorseful, he appeared at Marei's front door late that same night to apologize. In the weeks that followed, their relationship was further cemented by various means. One of Gamal Salem's few friends among the Free Officers was Ali Sabry; the friendship had been formed while both were cadets in the air force academy and later reinforced by shared political outlooks. Sabry and Salem were at this stage both pro-American and generally conservative on domestic economic issues. Sabry assured Salem that Marei was just the man to supervise the agrarian reform program. When Salem fell ill, as he was to do with increasing frequency due to a developing brain tumor, Marei visited him regularly, as did his brother Omar, the Marei family specialist in religious matters.

But for several close observers of these events, the crucial factor in Gamal Salem's appointment of Marei as delegate member of the HCAR was an event that occurred the weekend before that appointment was announced.[5] Marei and his wealthy landowner and agronomist colleague, Yehia al Alaily, were traveling to Komombo for the weekend to look into some matters related to the agrarian reform and to pass the weekend at the lovely Komombo guest house. Marei invited Gamal Salem to accompany them on the trip, which the compulsive, lonely officer readily agreed to. Yehia al Alaily brought his attractive wife along, and Salem was immediately enamored of her. Shortly thereafter they were married, the new husband being forever indebted to matchmaker Marei.

By early 1953, Marei had emerged from among the cluster of contestants for the highly visible job of supervising the agrarian reform. Having cemented his relationship with the RCC member designated to oversee the civilians charged with implementing the reform, Marei's chief worry was that Gamal Salem would be replaced and that he, as Salem's client, would immediately be dismissed. Aware that Nasser monitored such relationships closely and had received intelligence reports to the effect that Marei's car was frequently seen in front of Salem's house when the irascible colonel was ill, Marei did not want to place his future entirely in Salem's hands. He sought other useful associations, chief of which was that with another rising young star in Egyptian politics, Muhamed Hassanein Heykal, who curiously enough had in the first months following the military's seizure of power been attempting to cultivate a close relationship with Gamal Salem's brother Salah. Marei's other tactic for survival as a civilian in a military-dominated regime, from which as the months passed an increasing number of central figures were to be sacked, was to set about building an empire out of the HCAR.

CONSOLIDATION OF CONTROL OVER THE HCAR

In the late fall of 1952, even before his nomination as delegate member, Marei was already paving the way for the HCAR to become an organization autonomous from the bureaucracy and therefore one with far more resources, authority, and freedom to act than a normal government body confined by civil service regulations. On October 26, employees of the HCAR were dispatched to the countryside to begin implementing the reform, and they were immediately met by attempts by large landowners to delay or sabotage that reform.[6] Marei reported this to Salem and argued that, in order to accomplish its mission, the HCAR, which was to have been self-financing, immediately be granted £E1,000,000 by the Agricultural Credit Bank and also be accorded autonomous status under the RCC. Salem took these requests to his officer colleagues, and they, fearing the reform would misfire, granted both. Thus, when some weeks later Marei became the director of the HCAR, he was immediately able to recruit his affines, *shilla* partners, and future clients into the organization, paying them salaries well in excess of what they had been earning in their posts in the bureaucracy and private enterprise.

Nevertheless, these were not just sinecures. Marei demanded and received dedication and hard work from his loyal staffers, who responded enthusiastically and competently. Within a relatively short period it became evident that the agrarian reform was both a technical and a financial success. Production levels were maintained, and the HCAR, now the country's largest landowner, was collecting rents that formerly went to private landowners and obtaining further revenues as marketing agent for beneficiaries of the agrarian reform.

Efficiency was a necessary but not sufficient condition for the political success of the HCAR and its chairman. The reform was designed to destroy the regime's enemies and to win for it mass support and legitimacy. Realizing this, Marei took steps to ensure that the reform would be the showcase project of the new government. As public relations director for the HCAR, he appointed Muhamed Sobieh, who had begun his political career as an editor of the Misr al Fatat paper *al Usbu'a*. Tiring of perennial opposition, Sobieh had shifted to the then-in-government Saadist Party in 1946–47, becoming editor of its paper, *al Asas*. Immediately after the military seized power, he, like other former members of Misr al Fatat, was thrown in jail. Undeterred by Sobieh's misfortune, Marei recruited him as director of public relations for the HCAR. Sobieh in turn hired his brother and two other former members of Misr al Fatat, Ezz al Din Kamel and Ismaen Amer, as his assistants.

In the spring of 1953, a veritable torrent of publicity began to flow from the public relations department of the HCAR. The Egyptian press was saturated with reports of land acquisition and distribution, replete with photographs of ecstatic peasants receiving title deeds from the regime's luminaries, with Marei himself occasionally featured prominently. Sobieh's slogan, "The land for the peasants, not the peasants for the land," was given wide circulation. A deluge of pamphlets, booklets, and press releases issued from the public relations department. Foreign journalists and authors were invited to observe the HCAR and its activities at first hand and were escorted to agrarian reform areas by Marei's closest advisors, including his brother-in-law Aziz Qadry.[7] Partly due to these efforts, the first widely circulated works in European languages on post-Farouk Egypt cataloged one after another the triumphs of Marei and agrarian reform.[8] One such work, Keith Wheelock's *Nasser's New Egypt*, praised the reform but also pointed out discrepancies and contradictions in figures published by the HCAR, and its reticence after 1955 to release statistics on land distribution.[9] Wheelock had in fact stumbled on a contentious issue among Egyptian agronomists, for many were convinced that Sobieh, with Marei's tacit approval or even active support, was playing fast and loose with the figures. While the HCAR's extravagant claims and budgetary juggling were in 1956 and again in 1961 to cause Marei considerable embarrassment and political discomfort, in the early stages of the reform impressive statistics contributed to buying legitimacy for the measure, for Marei, and for the regime as a whole, considerations of no small importance.

By early 1954, Marei and his public relations expert Sobieh had succeeded in making the agrarian reform so attractive that virtually no politically ambitious officer or civilian could afford even obliquely to criticize it. Neguib and Nasser had celebrated the first anniversary of the revolution by visiting agrarian reform areas in the Delta and distributing title deeds to peasants.[10] September 9, 1953, the first anniversary of the issuing of the agrarian reform law, was designated the Day of the Peasant and celebrated by the distribution of yet more title deeds with a host of RCC members in attendance.[11] So by March 1954, when the confrontation between Neguib and Nasser came to a head, the former, along with his conservative supporters, dared not attempt to undo the reform. Nasser and his supporters were not to know that until after the fact, however, and in March they busied themselves with the task of preserving the agrarian reform from an anticipated backlash.

On March 22, Nasser announced that the RCC would be disbanded and parliamentary elections held. This appeared to signal a victory for Neguib, but in fact it was a tactic within a carefully worked out strategy to draw out Neguib and his backers for the purpose of then overwhelming them. Just before Nasser began playing out the line to Neguib, he instructed Marei, through Gamal Salem, to sit tight at the HCAR, protect the reform, and await the RCC's return. Marei called in his staff, and informed them that Neguib, now unfettered from RCC control, might move suddenly to undermine the reform. The staff agreed to work overtime to distribute as much land as possible, making it virtually impossible for that land to be returned to its original owners if the political status quo ante should be restored.

Having thus assured to the fullest possible extent the fate of the reform in the case of a Neguib victory, Marei put the public relations resources of the HCAR at Nasser's disposal. As journalists, students, attorneys, and others began to clamour for a return to parliamentary life in the wake of Nasser's March 22 announcement, it appeared as if Nasser would lose control of the Egyptian "street" to Neguib. Disturbed by the deteriorating situation, Marei accompanied Gamal Salem to a meeting with Nasser, where he offered the services of the HCAR for the purpose of demonstrating the popularity of the revolution in the countryside. Losing ground in urban Egypt and desperately in need of a public relations triumph, Nasser agreed. Marei enlisted the assistance of his former Saadist M.P. colleague and future affine Sheikh Muhamed Elwan, who mobilized his followers to give Nasser a tumultuous welcome on Farouk's old estate in Bilbeis. Sobieh ensured that the Cairo dailies gave the event wide coverage. Not the deciding factor in Nasser's eventual victory over Neguib, it nevertheless contributed significantly to it and in so doing ingratiated Marei with Nasser.

BUILDING A BUREAUCRATIC EMPIRE

Now firmly entrenched in power, Nasser took steps to ensure that the political drama involving him and Neguib would not be replayed with a reversal of roles. One after another he jettisoned potential challengers, Gamal Salem's turn coming in 1956 when the confrontation with the West provided justification for sacking the pro-Western former air force officer. Within days of Salem's dismissal, Marei received a summons to front and center before the president. Shorn of his patron Salem and fearing the worst, Marei went to confront Nasser. But the *ra'is* had something other than demotion or dismissal in mind. Before recounting this tête-à-tête, however, it is necessary first to describe the dynamics of the political elite in this period and Marei's position within it.

By the summer of 1956, Marei had become the most prominent civilian in a government dominated by the military. As the director of the HCAR, he had been lionized by the energetic Sobieh. This personal visibility was not without cost, however, for to many of Nasser's colleagues it was a sore point, aggravated by Marei's background, which was in class and profession antithetical to most of theirs. None wanted to take a back seat, especially not to someone more representative of the ancien régime than of the revolution. Marei's success in completely dominating his own broad field of activity and even expanding it only served to exacerbate these jealousies and rivalries. Several of the Free Officers had hoped to have a hand in the agrarian reform, but in order to avoid overlapping responsibilities and conflicts arising from them, they had agreed to give Gamal Salem a free rein. In return they had enjoyed similar arrangements in their own spheres of competence. But when the agrarian reform came to overshadow all other programs, and when Marei appeared intent on broadening the scope of his activities, they felt the time had come to rid themselves of this troublesome civilian outsider.

Had Marei contented himself with a narrow definition of his responsibilities as director of the HCAR, he may never have become a target of the animosity of those more powerful than himself. But ambition frequently does not listen to reason. He looked upon the HCAR as an excellent base from which to strike out on a broader front, and not as a bureaucratic sinecure in which to languish. Having succeeded in consolidating his power and that of the HCAR, Marei, once the early stages of land reform were completed, began to push for the vertical integration of agricultural activities related to the reform. His strategy was to utilize agricultural cooperative societies in agrarian reform areas as agents to distribute seeds, fertilizers, and other inputs. Peasants had therefore to pledge their crops as collateral to the HCAR, enabling it, in turn, to become the largest buyer and seller of commodities in the country. The one input that remained beyond his control was that of credit, which was extended through the Agricultural Credit and Cooperative Bank, but even that twenty-five-year-old institution was unable to withstand Marei's assault. In November 1955 he secured appointment as chairman of the board of directors of the bank, thus closing the circle so that he oversaw all phases of production and marketing in the vast agrarian reform areas. In that very substantial amounts of money were changing hands at numerous points in these related and complex activities, and in that the HCAR was racking up annual profits in the millions of pounds, Marei's opponents had ample motivation, and possibly just cause, to try to replace him.

The issue which more than any other caused powerful members of the elite to coalesce in bringing about Marei's downfall was that of Liberation Province. From its inception in the spring of 1953, this extravagant reclamation project in the desert west of the Delta was a competitor for funds, personnel, and prestige with agrarian reform. The project's director, Magdi Hassanein, was from a wealthy land-owning family whose father had been a governor and whose brothers were successful and politically conservative businessmen. But Hassanein himself was a committed leftist, later to marry a Russian citizen, and he hoped to transform class relations in rural Egypt, beginning in his very own Liberation Province.[12] Indebted to Hassanein for his support in the military, and needing to balance Gamal Salem's and Marei's control of agrarian reform, Nasser had given Hassanein virtually a blank check with which to pursue his ambitions in the desert. The head-to-head competition between the HCAR and the Liberation Province Organization, and hence between Marei and Hassanein, took various forms. Able to pay salaries double or triple those paid in ministries, the two directors vied with one another to hire the best available talent, and in so doing split the ranks of agronomists and other professionals between those who cast their lot with Marei and those who went with Hassanein.[13] Like Marei, Hassanein had his own connections with the Egyptian press, and he utilized them in widely publicizing Liberation Province. He also charmed foreign visitors, providing guided tours of the province, for which he was rewarded by features in the international press and by chapters in books on Egypt.[14]

But the most deadly combat between Marei and Hassanein took place over land tenure. The agrarian reform had been designed to create a kulak class of small holders, and Marei vigorously defended the social, economic, and political benefits of landownership. Hassanein, on the other hand, saw termination of the misery of poor peasants and a breakthrough to development, as well as justice and equality, coming through communal ownership of land and communalism more generally. As a result, he did not copy the small-holder model provided by agrarian reform but designed Liberation Province as a collective farm, further propagating communalism by forcing peasants to wear identical shirts and pants and having them sing ballads in praise of nationalism and socialism.

All this was too much for Marei. Looking for some way to throw a spanner in Hassanein's works, he settled on the issue of land tenure. Aware that the majority of influential members in the elite, and Nasser himself, favored the small-holder model and opposed collectivism, Marei worked to bring Hassanein's activities in Liberation Province, which had been semisecretive to that time, out into the open. In March 1955 he summoned Hassanein to testify before the Committee for Ownership and Exploitation of Reformed Land, which was under the jurisdiction of the HCAR. Hassanein, cleverly buying time so that he could eventually present the Liberation Province collective farm as a fait accompli, and possibly in the meantime unseat Marei, testified that the agrarian reform model would soon be implemented and settlers assigned specific plots.[15] But Hassanein never delivered on his promise, devoting his energy instead to undermining Marei, whom he referred to openly as a feudalist reactionary.

Marei's two weak points were, first, his success and the jealousy that success stimulated in the officer-dominated elite, and second, his tendency to be cavalier with facts and figures, be they statistics on agrarian reform or financial statements. Hassanein correctly judged the latter weakness as the key with which to release the former. A rumor campaign, presumably started by Hassanein, began to indict Marei as an embezzler of funds from agrarian reform operations. Nasser, ultrasensitive about corruption, took steps to deal with the situation. Thus in June 1956, when Marei received the summons to appear before Nasser, the matter at hand was not demotion or dismissal as a consequence of Gamal Salem's misfortune, but suspected embezzlement.

Nasser had carefully planned his strategy. He did not accuse Marei of pocketing funds or of committing other misdeeds. He simply demanded of him an explanation of his idiosyncratic accounting procedures, which deviated substantially from those required of governmental bodies under civil service regulations and, indeed, virtually any standard accounting practices. Marei explained his bookkeeping eccentricity as being necessary to facilitate flexibility of operations in the HCAR and to avoid bureaucratization, a disease which Marei knew Nasser greatly feared. But Nasser was not to be so easily sidetracked. Nor was he willing on the basis of a rumor campaign to abandon Marei, who had in the past proved his technical competence and political loyalty. Unable to make head or tail of Marei's fast-talking explanation, yet reluctant to resort to an outside auditor, Nasser resolved his dilemma by "promoting" Marei to minister of state for agrarian reform. This made Marei a member of the cabinet without converting the HCAR into a ministry. Thus the HCAR remained beyond the jurisdiction of the civil service, exactly where its employees and director wanted it. But in exchange, Nasser demanded of Marei that he henceforth follow normal accounting procedures. This resolution, and indeed the entire episode, was unpleasant for Marei, indicating as it did Nasser's suspicions and a desire to put him under closer supervision, and it meant that the HCAR was now just one short step away from losing its standing as an autonomous organization. In that Liberation Province was sailing on full steam ahead, it seemed that Hassanein had won a decisive round.[16]

Marei, however, was not long in regaining the initiative. While many of the top members of the elite had little time for him, several had even less for Hassanein and his extravagant scheme. As rumors of flagrant excesses in Liberation Province began to circulate, no doubt helped along by Marei, those in the elite who had formerly shied away from attacking Hassanein and his project for fear of Nasser's reaction overcame their hesitancy. The 1957 parliament, the first to be convened following the revolution, provided the setting in which they could embarrass Hassanein and thus force Nasser to sack him. An omen of what was to come was provided in late August when the minister of agriculture, Abd al Razzaq Sidqy, provided a thorough review of the operations and financial accounts of Hassanein's organization and was then questioned from the floor about various expenses.[17] But the real trouble was to come some weeks later when former RCC member and speaker of the Assembly Abd al Latif Baghdady, announced his intention of stepping down from the speaker's chair in order to speak against Liberation Province. Informed of Baghdady's intention by his supporters in parliament, Nasser instructed the deputy speaker, Anwar Sadat, to adjourn the session as soon as Baghdady vacated the chair. Sadat did as instructed in the midst of loud and indignant protests, which were in turn shouted down by several former officers loyal to Nasser and now serving in parliament. But the matter was not to end here. Former RCC member Kemal al Din Hussein, who did not like Marei or Baghdady but who positively detested Magdi Hassanein, went immediately to Nasser and presented his resignation, and Baghdady joined suit. Confronted thus with the resignations of the speaker of his new parliament and the head of his recently created single party, the National Union, Nasser had little choice but to concede. A presidential order was issued relieving Hassanein of his command over Liberation Province.[18]

Shortly before Hassanein met his Waterloo, Marei had been approached by Ali Sabry acting on Nasser's behalf, who wanted to sound out Marei about a possible appointment as minister of agriculture. Aware of the danger of becoming Magdi Hassanein's nominal superior—for the Liberation Province Organization was in theory within the Ministry of Agriculture—Marei demurred. Nasser was not to be fobbed off so lightly. He invited Marei to his home, where he and Abd al Hakim Amer queried Marei about his reluctance to become minister. Upon hearing the reason for Marei's reluctance, Nasser agreed to transfer the Liberation Province Organization to the presidency. Marei forthwith consented to the appointment, which was announced on November 3, 1957. But before the end of the month, Hassanein was out and Nasser was on the telephone to Marei, explaining that Liberation Province Organization was being transferred from the presidency back to the Ministry of Agriculture.

Although Marei was apprehensive about inheriting the favorite project of many officers active in the political elite, he did not shy away from exerting his influence over the scheme once it was under his jurisdiction. He dispatched two of his chief lieutenants, Mahmoud Fawzy and Saad Hagrass, to the province, which had been off limits to Marei and his colleagues prior to that time. Fawzy and Hagrass reported back to Marei that the settlers were in incipient rebellion, egged on, according to their interpretation, by Hassanein's supporters still in the employ of the organization. Marei immediately traveled out to the province, where he defused the situation by promising to distribute land to those who wanted it and to continue to employ others who preferred to work for wages. Marei was as good as his word. In July 1958, he announced that four hundred peasant families would receive land in Liberation Province, and over the next three years he distributed some 6,000 feddans.[19] Finally, in the spring of 1961, he announced that all agricultural land in Liberation Province would be distributed to peasants.[20] Marei was clearly intent upon undoing the only experiment in collectively held land in Egypt and nearly succeeded in doing so. But before he was able to hand this land over to individual proprietors, his enemies, some angered by this step and some by other of Marei's activities, were to coalesce in bringing about his downfall.

In the late autumn of 1957, though, Marei was riding high and about to go even higher. New to the Ministry of Agriculture, he set about consolidating his personal hold over that sprawling domain by installing his clients and *shilla* partners in key under secretary and various other positions. With this additional bureaucratic empire at his disposal, he was prepared to do battle to expand his domain yet further. His first target was Hussein Shafei, a conservative, devoutly religious original member of the RCC whose personal fiefdom had become the Ministry of Social Affairs, over which he presided as minister for eight years from September 1954. Shafei became Marei's target for no other reason than the fact that the Ministry of Social Affairs was responsible for all cooperative societies other than those in agrarian reform areas, and Marei wanted to gain control over them. That he was willing to test his strength against a former member of the RCC suggests just how powerful he had become by the late 1950s.

The assault on Shafei was not a frontal one. Marei sought instead to isolate him by making Shafei appear to be opposed to planning in the agricultural sector. Nasser was enamored of this new economic device, of which he had learned from the Indians and Yugoslavs, and he would brook no opposition on the issue, as Marei had learned firsthand when he had expressed some doubts about the value of planning for the agricultural sector. Now he was willing to put that lesson to use against Shafei.

Marei's skill as a political infighter was well displayed in this particular battle. Sensitive to criticisms leveled against individual ownership of agricultural land, most of which turned on the deleterious consequences of fragmentation into small plots, Marei devised a scheme which with one stroke would disarm leftists who were pushing for some form of collectivized ownership and at the same time pry agricultural cooperative societies from Shafei's grasp. The scheme took the form of an experiment in the village of Nawag in the district of Tanta. Marei induced the villagers there to imitate the prevailing practice in agrarian reform areas of dividing the entire land area into three sections in which each owner would have a parcel, thereby enabling large areas to be planted with the same crop and permitting a rational crop-rotation system organized by the local cooperative society. Marei made sure that his experiment was given press coverage, and he also called it to the attention of foreign observers.[21]

Thus prepared, Marei confronted Shafei in a cabinet meeting, claiming that the Nawag experiment resulted in a 30 percent increase in production. Shafei contested the figure, but when challenged he shifted ground and argued that the experiment had entailed oppression of the peasantry by forcing them to submit to Marei's scheme. Perceiving that the minister of social affairs' underlying interest lay in preventing Marei from demonstrating that he, as minister of agriculture, could make better use of cooperative societies than Shafei, Nasser overruled his old officer comrade, declaring that the issue of cooperatives would be taken up at a later date and that Marei should proceed with his experiment, replicating it elsewhere.[22] The writing was on the wall for Shafei. In 1960, agricultural cooperative societies were plucked from the Ministry of Social Affairs and placed temporarily under the presidency, to be transferred a few months later to the Ministry of Agriculture. The circuitous route was designed as a face-saving device for Shafei.

Virtually the only civilian in Nasser's government powerful and brave enough to joust with ranking officer-politicians, Marei also succeeded in besting Abd al Latif Baghdady. As minister of municipal affairs, Baghdady had snatched a choice piece of real estate at Mamura, on the beach east of Alexandria, away from the HCAR, which previously had confiscated it from Prince Touson. Baghdady earmarked this delightful setting for a tourist complex to be developed by the Commercial Bank, the chairman of the board of which was a Jewish Egyptian. Following the Suez Crisis of 1956, the assets of the Commercial Bank were seized and placed under the Ministry of Finance, with Hassan Abbas Zaki, a longtime friend of the Marei family, assigned to supervise the Commercial Bank's holdings. Although Baghdady retained his portfolio of Rural Affairs when he obtained the additional one of Planning, he was not quick enough to rescue this Mamura property from Marei's fast dealings.

At the end of 1956, Minister of Finance Abd al Moneim Qaissouny traveled to the United States to attend a World Bank meeting, and Marei was appointed acting minister in his absence. Taking advantage of his temporary authority, he arranged with Hassan Abbas Zaki to loan the Commercial Bank £E4,000,000 in return for his signature on a document granting the return of the Mamura real estate to the Agrarian Reform Organization, whose director was

Marei's client Saad Hagrass. Shortly thereafter Marei saw to it that Nasser received from this former royal estate a choice beachfront plot on which a presidential villa was eventually built. If Baghdady had notions of appealing his case to the *ra'is,* he forgot them.[23]

By 1958 Marei was able not only to hold his own in interministerial squabbles but also to influence cabinet appointments. As a result of the union with Syria, the government was overhauled in early October, partly for the purpose of achieving better coordination between the two regions, and partly to enable Nasser to kick some of his ambitious underlings upstairs into important-sounding but essentially meaningless portfolios. Marei, who had since March of that year been minister of agriculture in the Executive Council of the Egyptian region, was made minister of agriculture and agrarian reform in the central cabinet. From this post he was in theory to coordinate activities between the two regions, while the ministers in the Executive Councils of Egypt and Syria were to be responsible for day-to-day business in their respective geographical areas. Ahmad Mahruqi, whose name had been put forward by Marei when Nasser began the search for a suitable candidate, was appointed to the Executive Council for Egypt. Some months earlier, Mahruqi had been plucked by Marei out of Kemal Ramzy Stino's Ministry of Supply and promoted to under secretary in the Ministry of Agriculture. He was widely regarded as a Marei client. The new minister of agrarian reform in the Executive Council of the Egyptian region was Hassan Baghdady, who had begun his political career with Gamal Abd al Nasser's brother Leithy in the Alexandria branch of the Liberation Rally, the regime's first attempt at a single party. From there Baghdady had been recruited into the Ministry of Supply, from which he went directly into the cabinet. Regarded by agronomists and even by Leithy Nasser as neither competent nor industrious, Hassan Baghdady was in the cabinet mainly to keep the chair warm for Marei.

DOWNFALL

By consolidating his hold over the HCAR, the Agricultural Credit and Cooperative Bank, and the Ministry of Agriculture, and by adding agricultural cooperative societies to his domain, Marei, following Magdi Hassanein's demise, had become the undisputed overlord of the entire agricultural sector. After the mini-crisis of 1956, when Gamal Salem had been discarded from the elite and Nasser had taken an unhealthy interest in his accounting procedures, Marei had entrenched himself in the elite by cementing his friendship with Muhamed Hassanein Heykal, by loyally serving Nasser, and by continuing to add both personnel and functional responsibilities to his sprawling domains. He was, moreover, becoming a figure of international standing as a result of wide publicity given in the West to his efforts in agrarian reform and because that reform was imitated by several other Middle Eastern countries.[24] In 1957 he published in French, English, and Arabic a widely circulated book on Egyptian agriculture and agrarian reform, a volume which did nothing to downplay his role in both.[25] Within Egypt he received more press coverage than any other civilian cabinet member. His picture, human-interest features, and short biographical sketches of him, and articles written by him, appeared regularly in Cairo's dailies and weeklies. Careful not to trigger Nasser's suspicion by offering unsolicited advice or by making pronouncements in fields other than agriculture, he nevertheless was occasionally consulted by the president on topics unrelated to his specialty, including foreign policy. His career by the late 1950s was at least as impressive as it would have been had the Free Officers never seized power.

But his enviable success and flamboyant manner were grating on officer-politicians in the elite. Some disliked him because he was a civilian, some because they perceived him as a feudalist, and others because they had come out second-best in political struggles with him. All resented the fact that Nasser was less suspicious of him, simply because he was a civilian, than he was of his former colleagues in the military. So they eagerly awaited their opportunity to trip Marei up. It finally came in the summer and fall of 1961, when voracious cotton leafworms ate up a good third of that invaluable crop and when, following Marei's narrow escape from the political fallout of that ecological disaster, they were able to administer the coup de grace as he became increasingly ensnared in a web of corruption charges.

That Marei, as undisputed overlord of the agricultural sector, could preside over the worst loss suffered from worm infestation of the cotton crop in living memory, and then manage to convince the president that he was not to blame and retain his cabinet post, is suggestive of Nasser's faith in Marei and of Marei's shrewdness. The crop had finally been saved from total destruction not by the Ministry of Agriculture, which inexplicably never mobilized itself to take appropriate preventative actions, but by a special committee formed by Kemal al Din Hussein, who was then a vice-president in charge of local administration. Hussein, one of the most ambitious of the inner group of the Free Officers, deeply resented and envied Nasser's preeminence and detested those who had risen into the elite by virtue of patron-client or *shilla* ties to his competitors. Having taken charge of the campaign to combat the infestation, Hussein then turned his attention to exposing the guilty parties, fully expecting to nail Marei and several of his cronies to the wall. Summoned to testify before Hussein's committee, Marei at first demurred, finally agreeing to appear only after being ordered to do so by Nasser himself. Adjudging a good offense as the best defense, Marei, appearing before the committee, launched into an attack on Hussein for allegedly prejudging the case, and then defended himself by arguing that he had at an early date informed the minister of agriculture in the Executive Council for Egypt of the severity of the infestation but that the minister, Ahmad Mahruqi, had not responded.

Marei was too important for the outcome of this battle to be decided in Hussein's committee. Instead it was adjudicated in the highest court in the land—Nasser's office. Hussein got to the president first and convinced him that Marei was the man responsible and had to be punished. Nasser informed Marei through Heykal that he wanted him to assume full responsibility for the disaster, leaving unspecified the consequences for Marei's career. Marei was not to give up so easily. He requested a meeting with the president, which was at first denied and then accepted on the condition that Minister of Agriculture Mahruqi be present. So Marei and Mahruqi argued their cases before Nasser, with Marei making much of the distinction between the two portfolios, which theoretically required of the regional minister implementation rather than formulation of policy. For whatever reasons, Nasser decided the issue in Marei's favor and demanded Mahruqi's immediate resignation.[26]

Kemal al Din Hussein and other of Marei's opponents, outraged that he had managed to "squirm off the hook," as one of them put it, did not want to give up on ousting Marei this close to their goal. Adhering to their basic strategy of causing Nasser to lose confidence in Marei, they switched tactics by focusing on two other issues, namely sabotage of official policy and corruption. The policy in question was land reclamation, which was associated with Nasser's sacred cow, the High Dam, and which was highly attractive to Nasser in its own right. He had come to believe that Egypt's agricultural future lay in reclaiming vast tracts of desert land, a belief fostered in part by Magdi Hassanein and numerous other officers involved in reclamation work, or of leftist proclivities. Ali Sabry, skilled at telling Nasser what he wanted to hear, informed him that 200,000 feddans a year could be reclaimed by water provided by the High Dam. Marei, far more familiar with the virtually intractable problems associated with reclaiming sandy soils, cautioned Nasser that the annual maximum was more likely to be 40,000 feddans or even less.[27] This difference of opinion provided an opening for Marei's opponents, who attributed to him motivations of obstructing revolutionary progress out of ancien régime proclivities.

The more sustained and ultimately more damaging assault on Marei took the form of a campaign to demean his integrity and link him with some of his clients and *shilla* partners, who could more easily be brought before the courts on charges of embezzlement. Since the early days of the agrarian reform, suspicions about Marei's financial dealings had lingered, for the HCAR was a perfect satrapy to plunder if he were so inclined, and he did, after all, display all the obvious signs of wealth. His highly irregular accounting procedures had done nothing to dispel rumors. So what remained for his opponents was to catch his hand in or even somewhere near the till, thereby proving the veracity of the rumors and leaving Nasser little choice but to sack Marei.

In September 1961, as Marei was breathing a sigh of relief at having made it through the cotton worm episode, a rumor campaign sprung up against him, spurred on by a series of reports in Cairo dailies from the Directorate of Supervision (a kind of government accounting organization) that cases were about to be brought against employees in the Ministry of Agriculture and the Liberation Province Organization. Eventually specific charges were made against Ahmad Samni, an under secretary in the ministry who had for several years been the number-two man in Liberation Province. He was accused of taking commissions on purchases of equipment used in reclamation, including overhead sprinkler systems, pumps, and motor vehicles. He was jailed awaiting trial, and rumors began to fly thick and fast that before the event was over Marei would be implicated.[28]

Just at this moment the Syrians seceded from their unequal and unhappy union with Egypt. Convinced that this blow had been dealt him by feudalists and reactionaries who disliked the Socialist Decrees of that July, Nasser became ill-disposed toward those suspected of falling into those categories. Already in trouble as a result of the cotton worms, trouble now exacerbated by the Samni case, Marei was pointed to by several officers in the elite, who were scrambling to obtain top cabinet portfolios for themselves and their clients, as an anomalous reactionary in the new socialist regime. Ali Sabry, who was participating in discussions to form the new cabinet, had decided to cast his lot with the left and hence did not defend Marei. Abd al Hakim Amer, the former proconsul of Syria, now shorn of his domain, was keen to reestablish his position in the Egyptian hierarchy. He urged Nasser to appoint his former security advisor in Syria, Abd al Mohsen Abu al Nour, who had been a classmate of Magdi Hassanein at secondary school, as minister of agrarian reform and land reclamation, thereby restoring military control to Liberation Province. Kemal al Din Hussein, miffed by his failure to pin the blame for the cotton worm disaster on Marei, demanded that his client, Muhamed Neguib Hashad, whose brother had been a second-ranking Free Officer, be appointed minister of agriculture. So Nasser, whose confidence in Marei had in any case been shaken by the cotton worm and corruption issues, and who was beginning to have doubts about Marei's revolutionary credentials, and who in addition, viewed as politically unwise a knock-down, drag-out battle with Amer and Hussein over the formation of the cabinet, conceded. Sabry telephoned Marei on October 2, the day before the new ministry was announced, to inform him that his name was not on the list.

In the following week, Marei's home was filled with mourners from the Ministries of Agriculture and Agrarian Reform, some being reduced to tears by the thought of their boss being axed from the cabinet and its implications for their own careers. No longer in a position to protect his *shilla* partners and clients, and having been ejected from the cabinet at a time that would suggest to the public that he was responsible for the cotton worm disaster and/or was corrupt as rumored, Marei could provide his colleagues little comfort, for he was caught up in his own defense.[29]

Out of the government, and possessing reduced but nevertheless usable resources with which to combat his opponents, Marei found himself confronted by a renewed attack on his integrity. In his speech on November 25 to the opening session of the Preparatory Committee of the National Congress of Popular Forces, which had been called to reform Egypt's political system following the setback in Syria, Nasser launched into a scathing attack on bribery and corruption, blaming capitalists and feudalists as the chief offenders and referring unmistakably to the hapless Samni: "Some people were arrested, others were imprisoned. The under secretary of the Ministry of Agrarian Reform was imprisoned. He is still in prison with the agricultural engineer who collaborated with him. One took 2%, the other 1% [as commissions]."[30]

Marei's first task then was to disassociate himself from Samni's alleged activities. Employing Minister of Public Works Ahmad Abdu Sharabassi as a *wasit* (middleman), Marei approached the minister of justice, Ahmad Husni, to have a *niyaba* (public prosecutor cum court investigator) take Marei's deposition on the affair. Duly called, the *niyaba* became curious as to why Marei, as central minister, who in theory was to coordinate activities of the two regions and to be responsible for planning in the agricultural sector, involved himself directly in the mundane purchase of reclamation equipment. This was especially germane given Marei's previous statement to Nasser that following a dispute with Minister of Agriculture Mahruqi in 1958 he had abandoned day-to-day management of the ministry entirely to him. Marei claimed to the *niyaba* that he personally took charge of the acquisition of equipment, which was purchased locally without tender, because he was "in a hurry to carry out Nasser's orders on reclamation."[31] While this rationale may not have been too convincing in court, Marei was saved the inconvenience of cross-questioning in the witness stand, for Samni was acquitted in the early spring of 1962 and no further related cases were pursued.

But the net continued to close around Marei from a different direction. Another case that had been initiated prior to Marei's departure from the cabinet was brought to trial just after Samni was found not guilty. This one involved Marei's client Aziz Wifai, a top-ranking employee in the Ministry of Agrarian Reform. Wifai and several of his underlings were accused of raking off commissions on purchases of equipment arranged through a middleman by the name of Wadi Tadrous, who also happened to be Marei's insurance agent. To avoid disaster, this time Marei employed his connection with Heykal, whom he requested to have published in *al Ahram* an account of his dealings with Wadi Tadrous. On March 9, 1962, a photograph of Marei appeared on the front page of *al Ahram,* accompanied by a statement written by Marei in response to courtroom proceedings of the previous day, during which Major Muhamed Fahim of the Directorate of Supervision had implied that Marei was involved in the rake-offs through his insurance agent. Marei denied that the payoffs had been effected by the payment of his life insurance premiums, either by Tadrous or by any other third parties. He presented a list of the policies held on his family and himself, which were in the amount of £E16,000, all purchased prior to 1952. But it was not this evidence, which in any case said nothing about who actually was paying the premiums, that was important. What counted was the fact that Marei had access to the front page of *al Ahram* with implied presidential approval, thereby demonstrating that he was still a politician of standing unlikely to be disgraced in court. A month later, Aziz Wifai and his fellow defendants, possibly benefiting from Marei's intervention in the case by way of *al Ahram,* were acquitted on all charges. On April 16, 1962, five days after the story of the acquittal was carried on the front page of *al Ahram,* complete with pictures of the rejoicing defendants and their wives, Marei's picture was once again also on the front page of that paper. A small item accompanying the photograph announced that Nasser had received Marei for one and a half hours at his home in Minshiya al Bakri. With this Nasser signaled that Marei's ordeal with the rumormongers should come to a halt, as it immediately did.

As a result of these events, Marei was destined to take a vacation from politics, but it was clear from the manner of his departure that he still had a political future. For the remainder of 1962 though he was in semiofficial disgrace, dividing his time between his sumptuous flat in Zamalek, his horse stud farm adjacent to the pyramids in Mansouriya, and his estate in Kafr al Arbain. His *shilla* partners and clients still employed in the Ministries of Agriculture and Agrarian Reform wisely kept away from their old boss, for loyalty to him would indicate disloyalty to their new chief, Abd al Mohsen Abu al Nour. Hafiz Awad, who had been relieved of his post in agrarian reform; Ali Talaat, a landowner; and Adil Serafy, who worked for an agricultural company in the private sector, kept Marei company, for none of them could readily be made to suffer for violating Marei's "isolation."[32] Marei himself accepted his period of forced retirement with equanimity, contenting himself with drafting a long letter to Nasser debunking all allegations of corruption, inveighing against those who had plotted against him, and reaffirming his loyalty to the president. By not maintaining too close contact with employees in the agricultural sector, and by refraining from any other political or even semipolitical activity at a time when many who were disgruntled with the regime, including Marei's younger half brother, Omar, were grumbling among themselves, Marei demonstrated to Nasser's satisfaction that his sympathies were still with the government. He had, therefore, only to wait for the dynamics of elite politics once again to change and thereby provide him the opportunity for reentry.

THE LATE NASSER ERA: STRUGGLING FOR POLITICAL SURVIVAL

THE POLITICAL CONTEXT

Egyptian politics under Nasser described large swings to the left with periodic smaller swings back toward the right. During one of these swings to the left, which occurred in the summer of 1961 when Nasser issued the Socialist Decrees and the new agrarian reform, followed then by his search for feudalist and reactionary scapegoats in the wake of the Syrian secession, Marei lost his job. On his resumption of an active role in politics in spring 1963, the momentum of leftward movement was temporarily spent. He was therefore able rapidly to reestablish something of his previous position. By 1964–65 he was sufficiently entrenched in the elite to begin skirmishing once again with powerful opponents. This phase was destined to be short-lived, however, for in 1966 in the wake of the February Baathist coup in Damascus and ensuing radicalization of Middle East politics, Nasser again abruptly redirected Egyptian politics to the left. With the formation of the Committee for the Liquidation of Feudalists in May, the Jacobite phase of this leftward lurch set in. Having by this time already diagnosed the situation as unfavorable, and having terminated his campaign of harassment against his enemies, Marei was nevertheless still politically visible and vulnerable. Long considered one of the principal feudalists to have escaped revolutionary retribution, he was put through the wringer of the Committee for the Liquidation of Feudalists, from which he emerged bruised and battered but with most of his property and political resources still intact. He would have been much less fortunate had the political system not been thrown into disarray by the disaster of the June War. That calamity not only saved him, but it had a profound effect on the remaining years of the Nasser era.

In the first weeks following the military defeat, it seemed that a swing to the right might gain momentum and carry Egyptian politics back to a previous, less radical phase. The argument that Arab Socialism and Nasser's colleagues (but usually not Nasser himself) had led the country to disaster was widely heard and had its repercussions in policy changes and personnel shake-ups. Threatened by this reversal, those on the left were quick to reassert themselves. They contended that the defeat was due not to too much socialism but to not enough. Had the socialist transformation really taken place, according to their viewpoint, disaster could not have struck. So the remedy they offered was more of the same medicine they had been dispensing in the period leading up to the June War.

The stage was thus set for a head-on confrontation between those who wanted to reverse some of Nasser's policies and those who wanted to carry them further. Those in the first group wanted greater democratization, and many also wanted private-sector economic activity to be encouraged at the expense of the public sector. They hoped to achieve these goals by emphasizing growing public dissatisfaction with Nasserism. Meanwhile, their opponents utilized the ever more vital Soviet connection to pressure Nasser to resist demands to forsake socialist gains. Caught in the crossfire, Nasser prevaricated, hoping to prevent either side from gaining a complete victory. But because those on the left enjoyed Soviet patronage and had a decided edge over the right with regard to incumbency in the state apparatus and the single party, their position improved as the salience of the June War receded and the War of Attrition began. By 1969 Nasser had to struggle to keep his political balancing act from toppling over to the left. Those to his right, who had boldly reasserted themselves in the immediate post–June War period, had once again to go on the defensive and rely on Nasser's dwindling political resources for protection. For Marei and others, this weak and eroding position was reversed only when Sadat managed to consolidate power and radically redirect Egyptian domestic and foreign policies.

MAREI'S ROLE UNDER NASSER

Sayed Marei was indisputedly one of the most successful civilian members of the political elite during the Nasser period. Like other civilians, his longevity was due to the fact that as a nonofficer he posed no political threat to Nasser and, like other technocrats, he legitimized his presence in the elite by a claim to technical expertise. But Marei was never truly a technocrat in the same sense as Aziz Sidqy, Abd al Moneim Qaissouny, Mustafa Khalil, and other of his colleagues. Unlike them, he had extensive political experience during the ancien régime, and also unlike them he lacked a Ph.D. His B.Sc. from Cairo University was taken at a time when the syllabus was oriented in a traditional, nontechnical direction, and he never took steps to acquire further scientific expertise. But what he lacked in formal education and technical knowledge he made up for with practical experience and political sense. Familiar with Egyptian agriculture on a firsthand basis, he was impressed by the continuity of agricultural methods and Egyptian rural society through the millennia and was thus not as inclined to tamper with them as were those less familiar with the countryside. He viewed progress as coming through incremental improvements of existing arrangements and saw peasants as being suspicious of and therefore predisposed to be hostile to technical and social changes. This view contrasted markedly to that held by Ali Sabry, Abd al Mohsen Abu al Nour, and many other powerful members of the urban-oriented elite, who saw rural society and agricultural practices as being highly plastic and amenable to rapid change, and who set demanding and possibly unattainable goals for the modernization of rural Egypt. It is hardly surprising that they seemed to fail in contrast to Marei, who was far more cautious in defining goals and who therefore appeared to be much more successful in achieving them.

Winning respect from Nasser and some of his colleagues on account of his successful pragmatism, Marei also demonstrated remarkable competence in managing personnel. Virtually all of his subordinates appreciated his willingness to delegate responsibility and admired his ability to identify organizational goals and to coordinate activities to attain them. More of a politically astute bureaucrat-manager than a technocrat, Marei succeeded with the support of his staff in effectively implementing programs, something which few other members of the political elite, either civilian or military in background, managed to do. Nasser recognized Marei's managerial talents and thus backed him for important posts, despite the occasional political cost in so doing.

Another of Marei's crucial resources was his network of personal connections within the political elite and the bureaucracy, based on contacts established through his family, university graduating class, and/or professional and political activities. Arrayed below him in the agricultural bureaucracy were clients and *shilla* partners, useful to him as loyal employees when he held the relevant portfolios and vital to him when out of office as subverters of opponents' policies and as conduits of information. Within the political elite, Marei had benefited from patronage resulting from his lopsided friendships with Ali Sabry (in the 1950s), Gamal Salem, and Anwar Sadat. His participation in the *shilla* grouped around Heykal legitimized his claim to being a man of expertise; reinforced his ties to Aziz Sidqy, Mustafa Khalil, Abd al Moneim Qaissouny, and Mahmoud Fawzy, and through them to the industrial, financial, and foreign affairs bureaucracies and public and private sector enterprises; and bestowed on him the patronage and protection of Nasser's closest confidant. Without such connections Marei would never have made it into the Nasserite system. Equally, had he been a much less competent bureaucrat-manager, he would have been jettisoned at some point along the way.

Fluctuations in Marei's career and influence were determined by the ebb and flow of the fortunes of his patrons and *shilla* partners in the elite and by the teeter-totter relationship between the *ahl al thiqa* (people of trust, i.e., political loyalists) and the *ahl al khibra* (people of expertise, i.e., technocrats). When the former rose, as, for example, they did in the wake of the Syrian secession from the United Arab Republic and the resultant shift to the left in domestic politics, the technocrats fell. The dynamic for these relations, change in which is not altogether correctly referred to as shifts to the left or right, was provided chiefly by Nasser's personal power considerations. These in turn were determined by his interactions with the great and superpowers and with states and liberation movements in the Middle East, and by economic and political factors wholly domestic in origin. Correctly predicting that Nasser would continue as the real center of power in the system, Marei remained loyal to the *ra'is* from beginning to end.

MAREI'S RETURN TO POLITICS

Nasser's test of Marei's loyalty did not end when he signaled in spring 1962 through the medium of *al Ahram* that attacks on Marei should cease. In July of that year, Nasser's intelligence service arrested Marei's half brother Omar for plotting with Moslem Brothers to overthrow the government. Not even this, however, was to provoke Marei to take injudicious action. While he did work behind the scenes to have his half brother's death sentence converted to a term of imprisonment, he did not raise a hue and cry or grumble publicly about the system, as so many others who had suffered from Nasserism were inclined to do. So by the end of 1962, Marei had just about passed the loyalty test. Nasser decided it was time to question Marei, and he requested Heykal to send him around. In the interview that followed, Nasser stated bluntly that he suspected Marei of being "far from" him, a feeling which Marei denied as having any foundation. But Nasser's suspicion was not so easily allayed. When Marei seemed to qualify his willingness to work for the regime by wanting to do so only in the agricultural sector, Nasser took it to mean that he was demanding to be reinstated as minister of agriculture and/or agrarian reform. This Nasser was unwilling to do, and so he dismissed him, sending word through Heykal that he was displeased with Marei's intransigence. As a result of Nasser's suspicion, reinforced through this misunderstanding, Marei had to sit it out for three more months, until March 1963.[1] On this occasion Nasser delegated Ali Sabry to do the questioning. Sabry came right to the point: "Do you cooperate with the system or not?" When Marei assured Sabry that he did, he was given the good news that his reentry into public life was to be through Bank Misr, of whose board of directors he was to become a member.[2]

Marei immediately set about rekindling his political career. At Bank Misr for less than a month when elections in the newly created Arab Socialist Union (ASU) basic cells were held, he offered his candidacy. He won more votes than his two fellow board members who were also running: Muhamed Rushdi, son of Marei's old Abbasiya neighbor Rushdi Bey, and Ahmad Fuad, who had eleven years earlier helped draft the agrarian reform law. All three went on to represent the bank's employees at the higher levels of the ASU. In the summer of the following year, Marei ran unopposed for parliament from the family seat in Sharqiya and won with some 41,000 votes, the highest number received by any candidate throughout the country.[3] Marei achieved these successes without significant external support, but his next upward step was facilitated by his lopsided friendship with Anwar Sadat.

Sadat had been chosen by Nasser to head the new parliament, and he in turn backed Marei to become deputy speaker. His reasons for doing so were both personal, in that they were mutual friends and participants in the Heykal *shilla*, and political, for Sadat knew that as speaker he would be locked into a struggle with Prime Minister Ali Sabry, a struggle in which there could be no better ally than Marei, who had his own reasons for disliking and opposing Sabry.[4] Sabry, hoping to derail Marei's candidacy, endorsed for the deputy speakership Muhamed Abu Nosseir, the orphan who had been raised in the Marei family but who had turned on his benefactors. Nasser did not want Sabry to dominate both the cabinet and parliament, so to ensure that Sadat as speaker would be an effective counterfoil, he facilitated Marei's election as his deputy.

Nasser's plan to balance off Sabry and his government with the counterweight of Sadat, Marei, and the Assembly worked well at the outset. The first round in what was to be a bitter contest was won by Sadat and Marei, who to implement their plans developed a network of supporters in the Assembly. Marei's standing was further enhanced when Sadat assigned to him two chairmanships, that of the Committee on Agricultural Development and of the important Committee of Reply. The chief task of the latter body is to respond to the government's program for the coming year, having in this capacity the power to summon ministers to testify. Thus prepared, Marei and Sadat began to harass Sabry and his ministers over various aspects of the government's performance and program, including its failure to maintain adequate food supplies, as well as the "crisis" of higher education, and in June 1965 they forced Sabry to submit a new draft budget.[5] Sabry complained to Nasser of Sadat's and Marei's oppositional activities, arguing that they were intent upon toppling his government, but Nasser refused to rein them in. So Sabry turned to the newly created ASU as a tool with which to counteract Sadat's and Marei's influence.

In the early 1960s, Nasser became determined to organize the ASU along the lines of the Yugoslavian Communist Party, adding to that model a secret vanguard organization which was to direct the "mother organization," hence public life in Egypt from behind the scene. In discussions held in late 1964 among members of the Executive Committee and General Secretariat of the ASU, in which Marei as a member of the latter participated, Nasser's new determination to make the political organization the preeminent authority became evident.[6] During these discussions, Marei suggested that ASU units in the villages take a back seat to agricultural cooperative societies. His reasoning was that since cooperatives served peasants' utilitarian needs, they would remain the real focal points for their activities. Nasser did not agree. Not to be deflected from his goal of blanketing the country with ASU units, he lashed out: "It is presumed that the ASU is the basic organization. He who fights it will be dismissed. He who stands against it will be dismissed."[7] He then questioned Marei: "Are the members of the cooperatives members in the ASU and are they also members of the village councils?" Marei responded that members of the ASU and the board of the cooperatives were both elected, hence equal.[8] But Nasser did not want cooperatives on an equal footing with his new organization. He dismissed Marei's suggestion with the threat that if cooperatives "counter the work of the ASU we will dissolve them."[9]

Ali Sabry played his cards much more astutely. Instead of suggesting probable complications in future relations between the new ASU and preexisting organizations, as Marei had done, he extolled the virtues of the political organization and its secret vanguard organization. He was rewarded for his perspicacity with a leading role in the ASU and its semisecret nucleus, which in turn provided him with the means to overcome Sadat's and Marei's opposition to him in the Assembly. He set about organizing a branch of the vanguard organization within parliament, with which he was soon able to short-circuit the connection between Speaker Sadat and Deputy Speaker Marei, on the one hand, and the Assembly's membership, on the other. Unable effectively to combat the vanguard organization within the Assembly, Sadat and Marei had little choice but to sit by and watch their power in the Assembly ebb away.[10] Given that Nasser was then intent on establishing the ASU, in part to counterbalance Field Marshal Amer and the military, it would have been political suicide to attempt to use parliament to frustrate the growth of the political organization in either its overt or covert forms. Anwar Sadat was not a member of the Higher Executive Committee of the ASU, nor was he in the General Secretariat, so he could not affect that organization's policy from within. In December 1964 Marei had been appointed to the newly created secretariat as subsecretary for national capitalism, and he did participate in the discussions leading to the organization of the ASU, but he had little power in the organization, as his subsequent defeat in the 1968 Higher Executive Committee elections demonstrated. Essentially powerless in the now all-powerful ASU, Sadat and Marei lost their temporary advantage back to Sabry.

THE AGRICULTURAL SECTOR

From the spring of 1963, Marei's return to politics proceeded simultaneously on different levels. At the most visible level, he rose to deputy speaker of the Assembly, in the meantime scrambling, like most other ambitious politicians, to obtain a position of influence in the ASU. Regenerating his political career within these bodies, Marei also worked to reestablish influence in the agricultural sector, or at a minimum to curtail the power of his enemies, by whom he had been displaced in 1961.

This venture into his old fiefdom was risky. Agricultural issues had become highly politicized, and despite the presence of Marei's innumerable supporters in governmental bodies responsible for executing agricultural policy, those now in charge of these institutions were his sworn enemies. Abd al Mohsen Abu al Nour, who in the mid-1960s began to shift his allegiance from Abd al Hakim Amer to Ali Sabry and his ideology from right to left, remained in his post as minister of agrarian reform and land reclamation until June 1967. In the Ali Sabry cabinet of March 1964, he had been promoted to deputy prime minister. At that time, Sabry jettisoned Minister of Agriculture Muhamed Neguib Hashad, who was a client of Kemal al Din Hussein, and replaced him with Shafiq Kishin, an agronomist who had cast his lot with Sabry and the ASU. Neither Abu al Nour, Kishin, nor Sabry wanted to cool Nasser's ardor for land reclamation, tied as it was to the High Dam and implemented for the most part by former officers who had shifted into state reclamation companies. Nor did they advise caution in other problematical areas of agricultural development. Thus Marei confronted Nasser's commitment to reclamation and other technically dubious agricultural policies, a commitment reinforced by misleading information provided by self-serving former officers now active in the agricultural sector. But regardless of the high risk involved, Marei reentered the arena of agricultural policy-making. This decision reflected his profound interest in agriculture, its abiding importance to his political career, and the fact that he possessed the resource of technical knowledge reinforced by still-loyal personnel within the bureaucracy. Last and most important, he could afford to adopt a forward strategy because he enjoyed the protection of Muhamed Hassanein Heykal.

The erstwhile editor of *al Ahram* had need of Marei for his own purposes. In the never-ending struggle between the *ahl al thiqa* (political loyalists) and the *ahl al khibra* (technocrats) which developed under Nasser and which intensified in the months leading up to the

June War, Heykal cast himself as a defender of the latter. To legitimate his claim to being a purveyor of scientific rationality, Heykal had to have on side those publicly identified with it. Marei of course had built a career through fostering his reputation as a technical expert. Aware of Nasser's personal power requirement of balancing off contending individuals and of his desire to prevent anyone or any group from gaining absolute control over a specific structure, hence its functional area, Heykal knew it was to his benefit to thrust Marei and his views on agriculture into the limelight. As such, Marei's suggestions for policy would be seen by Nasser as possible alternatives to policies pushed by Sabry and Abu al Nour. Marei himself might also be considered by Nasser as a possible replacement for Abu al Nour.

The sparring between Marei and Abu al Nour that was made possible through Heykal's sponsorship began even before Marei had won reelection to parliament. In mid-July 1964 the editor of *al Ahram* made available the pages of his newspaper to Marei to cast doubts on the wisdom of Abu al Nour's policies. In a series of long articles, Marei adopted the role of defender of producers, referring to himself in the collective, "We the farmers. . . ." Implied was incumbent Minister Abu al Nour's unfamiliarity with agricultural problems on a firsthand basis, which was one of the standard arguments used against officers now operating in many technical fields. Further implied was that Abu al Nour represented the interests of an urban-oriented government. In that this attack came when food supply was an increasingly chronic and politically sensitive problem, it was all the more bold.[11] In March and April of the following year, *al Ahram* carried another series of Marei's articles. This time they were addressed to an even more sensitive issue, namely tenure policy for the reclaimed lands. As the area reclaimed with water from the High Dam began to approach 500,000 feddans, the question of who was to own it became salient. Sabry, Abu al Nour, and the left argued that it should remain with the state and be exploited as state farms. Others were of the opinion that it should be farmed by companies, either private or public, or by small holders. Marei contended that the agrarian reform model of small private holdings coupled with compulsory membership in agricultural cooperative societies was most desirable. Nasser kept his own counsel on the issue but was generally thought to favor companies or the agrarian reform model. What was clear was that he did not want to expend political capital in a struggle over the tenure issue, which was in any case not of crucial importance to him. With the president thus remaining aloof, those contesting the issue had more scope to argue their cases. Lacking any direct means to influence policy, for Abu al Nour was the incumbent minister and as such was doing everything in his power actually to create state farms, Marei once again could but chide him from the pages of *al Ahram*.

Given repeated access to the editorial page in March, April, and May 1965, Marei made an excellent case against state farms and for the agrarian reform model. He launched his critique on March 7 by juxtaposing private capitalist agriculture, which under the control of large landowners he deemed to be exploitative and inefficient, to collective agriculture of the Soviet variety, which he described as a nightmare of inefficiency that served no one's interests adequately. Egypt, according to him, could afford to import neither model, for both were inappropriate for her own social, economic, and political conditions. Instead, the indigenous agrarian reform cooperative model, ideally suited to the Nile Valley and having been proven to be more efficient than any of the alternatives (some data in support of this proposition being provided), was proposed by him as the natural and ideal solution to the problem. To counter the charge that the state, having paid to reclaim the land, should then benefit from it, he proposed that it should be sold to peasants on an installment basis, as was the case with the original agrarian reform.[12]

Through his clients, Marei had other means to challenge Minister Nour's competence and the advisability of creating state farms in the new lands. Saad Hagrass, recently transferred to the Ministry of Planning, contributed a highly unfavorable assessment of those farms in the *Follow Up and Appraisal of the First Five Year Plan,* which was issued by the Ministry of Planning in 1966. Hagrass, having already been chased from the Ministry of Agrarian Reform, could not further be harmed.

But disaster was to strike the indefatigable Muhamed Sobieh. In 1957, after becoming minister of agriculture, Marei had made Sobieh editor of *al Ta'awun* (Cooperation) and *al Magalla al Zira'iya* (The Agricultural Magazine), professional journals for Egyptian agronomists published by the public relations department of the Ministry of Agriculture. Sobieh had used his editorships to good effect, presenting occasional articles which cast doubts on developments in the agricultural sector under Abu al Nour's tutelage. But Sobieh finally went too far. In April 1965 in the pages of *al Magalla al Zira'iya,* he lambasted state farms in the desert as extravagant failures. This was the last straw for Sabry, Abu al Nour, and those grouped around them. Kemal Rifaat, a leftist-inclined former Free Officer, and at that time ASU secretary for the propagation of socialist thought, under-took the task of ridding the agricultural press of Marei's influence. He brought the two professional journals under the direct jurisdiction of the ASU and replaced Muhamed Sobieh with Suleiman Mazhar, who had been a colleague of Free Officer Khaled Muhi al Din's at the leftist *al Masa'*. Henceforth Mazhar devoted the pages of his journals to theoretical discussions of the transformation of class relations in the countryside.

Lacking the vital resource of incumbency, Marei was unable to defend his client. Moreover, his position was now to be further threatened by developments in the Syndicate of Agricultural Engineers, which had been established in 1949 as a result of Marei's successful legislative effort. In the early 1950s he had run for the presidency of the syndicate, but he had been outmaneuvered by Omar Tarraf, whose brother, Dr. Nur al Din Tarraf, was a former member of Misr al Fatat and as such was close to several members of the RCC and was thus in a position to further his brother's candidacy. The syndicate, in any case, disposed of too few resources to be of much interest to Marei as he rose higher in the elite, so he took little interest in its affairs.[13] But he did not want it to fall into the hands of his enemies to be used against him, nor did he relish the syndicate being used to intimidate his supporters in the agricultural sector. Yet by late 1965, Sabry had so increased his power within the elite that he no longer had to tolerate the semiautonomous status of the syndicate, so he took steps to bring it under his control.

The incumbent president of the syndicate was at that time Ibrahim Shukry, the Misr al Fatat deputy who had called for a 50-feddan limit on landholdings in the 1950 parliament. Marei and Shukry had become allies in 1964 when the former served as chairman of the parliament's Agricultural Development Committee and the latter as deputy chairman.[14] Seeking to avoid domination by Abu al Nour, who was now deputy prime minister with responsibilities for agriculture, Marei absented himself from the committee chairmanship, turning it over to Shukry, who likewise had little time for Sabry or Abu al Nour. But Shukry was to pay for lending Marei a hand. In November 1965, Sabry client Ahmad Talaat Aziz announced his intention of challenging Ibrahim Shukry for the presidency of the syndicate. In the succeeding weeks word went out that agronomists in the employ of the government who voted for Shukry would risk such retributions as posting to Upper Egypt and delayed promotion. Adjudging the situation hopeless, Shukry withdrew his candidacy, and Aziz was declared president.

With the loss of Sobieh in the agricultural press and Shukry in the syndicate, Marei was in an exposed and vulnerable position. It had been made clear that his influence was insufficient to protect those of his supporters who made it through the first purge following his dismissal from the cabinet in 1961. More threatening, from Marei's own viewpoint, was that Heykal's power was also declining as the left, consisting most importantly of Sabry and the former officers working with him, began to clear the decks of any and all suspected of being opposed to them. Not wanting to be upstaged in the Arab arena by the radical Baathists who had come to power in Syria in February 1966, and at home having to balance off the ambitious Field Marshal Amer with the ASU, Nasser had little choice but to continue to support Sabry and his associates, who were using the political organization to build their own personal clientage networks. That what appeared to be Marei's final denouement was at hand became evident in spring 1966, when the alleged murder by a wealthy landowner of an ASU official in the village of Kamshish sparked off a witch-hunt that was only to be terminated by the intrusion into domestic politics of the aftereffects of the June War.

NEAR-LIQUIDATION AS A FEUDALIST

In May 1966, as lurid descriptions in Cairo's dailies of the murder of Muhamed Abd al Fattah Abu al Fadl—Moslem Brother turned ASU official—by a member of the al Faqi family began to give way to more general descriptions of class relations prevailing in the countryside and the means by which large landowners had evaded provisions of the agrarian reform laws, Nasser was forced to act. He established a Committee for the Liquidation of Feudalists (CLF), but instead of placing it under Ali Sabry and the ASU, which would have made the committee correspondingly radical, he appointed the more conservative Abd al Hakim Amer as the committee's chairman. Not to be left out of the action, ASU supporters in parliament successfully demanded on May 23 that the issue be debated in the Assembly, with M.P. Abd al Hamid Ghazi initiating proceedings with a call for the seizure of all illegally held land and its immediate distribution "to the people."[15] The demand was reiterated by M.P. Fikri Gazzar, but in a way much more threatening to Marei. Gazzar wanted all agrarian reform files reopened so as to determine whether errors of omission or commission were committed by the authorities. This was a veritable Pandora's box, the opening of which would itself discredit Marei, and were any damaging evidence to be found, Marei's political future would be very bleak indeed. As it turned out, Marei was saved from the most unlikely quarter. Abd al Mohsen Abu al Nour, deputy prime minister for agriculture and irrigation, minister of agrarian reform, and member of both parliament and the CLF, was not keen on having his fiefdom of agrarian reform invaded by deputies in the National Assembly or by anyone else. He argued that reopening the files was unnecessary, because more than 1,000,000 feddans had in any case been seized from feudalists and because he had already taken care of the al Faqi family himself.[16]

Although temporarily saved by Abu al Nour's shared interest in preventing the agrarian reform bureaucracy from being invaded by M.P.'s and others, Marei was not yet out of the woods. As the discussion progressed to a general indictment of the system as one which permitted landowners to continue to exercise arbitrary and unjust power, Marei could hardly defend landowners' interests openly, nor, given his prominent role in the agrarian reform and his status as an alleged feudalist, was it advisable to remain silent. Marei's answer to the dilemma was to take the floor and argue that the Kamshish incident and its aftermath was a foreign plot inspired by Israel and her supporters in order to divide and fatally weaken the Egyptian home front. This being the case, to wage a divisive campaign against so-called feudalists was to fall into the trap set by Zionists and imperialists.[17] The parliamentary debate, which had threatened to crystallize in one or two demands that would be extremely discomforting to Marei, was partly as a result of his clever analysis diverted into bickering over interpretations of the cause, significance, and possible resolutions of the crisis.

A similar lack of unanimity prevailed in the CLF itself. Chairman Amer, supported by Kemal Rifaat and air force chief Shams Badran, opposed suggestions by Sabry, supported by Abu al Nour and security specialists Sami Sharaf, Sharawi Gomaa, Salah Nasr, and others, that the maximum limit on landownership be lowered to 25 feddans and that violent means be used if necessary to ensure compliance with the law.[18] But Amer and Sabry, unable to agree on how radical the purge of feudalists should be, did find common cause in their dislike of Marei. They agreed to instruct the regional branch of the CLF for Sharqiya, Menoufiya, and Qalyubiya provinces to investigate the Mareis and to strip them of any land held in excess of the legal maximum. Fearing the worst, the Mareis had already begun to sell land at bargain-basement prices to peasant tenants, hoping thereby both to obtain something in return for their holdings and, at least as important, to avoid embarrassment or worse at the hands of the CLF.

At the outset of the investigation, Marei had relatively little to fear. The provincial branch of the CLF demanded to see all titles to land belonging to the Mareis, and Sayed Marei provided them. Whatever the case with regard to the legality or illegality of the size of his and his family's holdings, he was certainly astute enough to ensure that he would not be given away by formal evidence of ownership. When the third inspection of this evidence by members of the provincial branch of the CLF failed to turn up anything incriminating, the members tried a new and more threatening method. They went to Azizeha and began to question peasants about the land-holdings and general affairs of the Mareis. When those peasants, many if not most of whom were Nasrs and all of whom were loyal to the Mareis, refused to divulge any damaging evidence, the committee members repaired to the town's main coffeehouse, where they interrogated village women. This strategy grew out of their assumption that while Marei may have coached his peasant retainers and relatives, it was highly unlikely that he would have done so with their womenfolk.

With this development Marei was thrown into panic. He went immediately to Anwar Sadat asking for his intervention. Sadat responded by telephoning Sabry, demanding that he order the CLF provincial committee to desist from such tactics and in the future to investigate Marei strictly through formal legal channels. Not wanting to test the strength of his relations with Nasser against those of Sadat, and at any rate having his troubles with Amer in the CLF, Sabry ordered the investigation terminated.[19]

Whether Marei was saved from disaster just in the nick of time is unclear, although his response suggests he had cause to worry. In any case, his fortunes were at a low ebb. He had been shorn of influence in his post as deputy speaker in the Assembly. His clients and supporters in the agricultural sector had been sacked from their positions or were too intimidated to be of use. In the wake of the investigation by the CLF, his national reputation had once again been sullied, and this time even his standing in Sharqiya was damaged by the CLF's activities. By spring 1967 he was contemplating the final break with Nasserite politics and began sending out feelers to international organizations in the hopes of beginning a new career.

THE SECOND COMEBACK

The disastrous June War rocked the foundations of Nasser's political system. The defeat was interpreted by many as the consequence of Nasser erring in aligning Egypt with the Soviet Union against the United States and in pushing too far, too fast, in transforming the domestic political economy. Nasser's resignation on June 9 and nomination of Zakariya Muhi al Din as successor was tacit recognition of this criticism. By juxtaposing Muhi al Din, who stood for the pro-Western, conservative option, to himself, Nasser was saying that if you reject Nasser and Nasserism, this is what you will have. It was made clear by the huge demonstrations in support of the *ra'is* that the majority of Egyptians preferred him to Muhi al Din and to anyone else. It was much less clear that Nasserism, at least as it had been practiced in the period leading up to the war, was so popular. So after June 1967, Nasser labored to reestablish his authority by deradicalizing domestic politics, so that those alienated from the system might be brought back into it or at least be neutralized. This option was open to him because Marshal Amer had been discredited by his military's performance and was by the end of summer to be eased completely out of power. This in turn meant that Nasser no longer had to rely so heavily on Sabry and his ASU to counterbalance Amer and the military, and hence he had more room to maneuver than at any time since the early 1960s.

Marei was thus not only spared liquidation by the CLF as a result of the war, but the new political equilibrium which emerged following the war facilitated his return to a prominent position in the elite. Marei further benefited from Nasser's need to demote or remove Amer's clients. Abd al Mohsen Abu al Nour was kicked downstairs from deputy minister for agriculture and irrigation to minister of land reclamation in the cabinet formed on June 19, 1967. As the Nasser-Amer relationship continued to deteriorate during the summer, Nasser struck at Abu al Nour once again. When in a cabinet meeting Abu al Nour called for the formation of a citizen's militia to combat the Israeli threat, Nasser congratulated him on his excellent idea and asked him if he would care to take charge. Abu al Nour leapt at the chance and in so doing moved into checkmate. Nasser dryly remarked that in order to do the new job properly Abu al Nour would have to devote all his attention to it, so he should resign from the cabinet. When Abu al Nour protested, arguing his ability to manage both the militia and the ministry, Nasser changed the suggestion into an order. The militia, due to Nasser's opposition, was never to be formed.[20]

In early August, Nasser added Abu al Nour's old portfolio of Land Reclamation to those of Agriculture and Agrarian Reform, which he had given to Marei in the June 19 cabinet. Marei's return to the cabinet in this grand style resulted from Nasser's need to prune Amer's clientage network, but it also presaged the redirection of the political system in a rightist direction. Nasser wanted to conclusively demonstrate his good faith to the bourgeoisie who had become isolated in the previous period, so on July 26, 1967, he quietly ordered Marei, now in his post as minister of agrarian reform, to begin handing back the property of eighty-eight individuals who had undergone sequestration at the hands of the CLF.[21]

In the meantime, Marei had begun to rebuild his dominant position in the agricultural ministries. On his triumphal return as minister to the Ministry of Agriculture on the morning of June 20, he was greeted by a tumultuous reception from the several thousand employees of the ministry. Packing the ornate if dilapidated reception hall of the lovely old building, they chanted, "Marei, Marei, Marei."[22] Basking in this adulation, Marei immediately set about regrouping his old team, bringing Saad Hagrass back from the Ministry of Planning, shuffling Abu al Nour's people out of the way, and promoting his old *shilla* partners and clients, who had been languishing under Abu al Nour for the past six years. Having thus brought these sprawling bureaucracies under his personal control once again, as Nasser of course knew he would, Marei was ready and waiting when the order came on July 26 to begin to undo some of the damage caused in his absence. Losing no time, Marei ordered Hagrass, newly reinstated at his old post of director of the General Organization for Agrarian Reform, to place his organization on an emergency footing, to permit no news of its activity to leak out to the press, and to implement Nasser's desequestration order as rapidly as possible. Realizing this was a golden opportunity to strike a blow at his enemies, to win legitimacy for his organization and for himself, and to ingratiate himself with Nasser, Marei also appreciated that Nasser could no longer operate with a free hand, since opposition to desequestration would inevitably be mobilized.

Marei further understood that in the highly fluid political situation that had emerged after the war he could take some initiatives without fear of serious reprisal. He nursed a grudge over his defeat on the issue of land tenure in Liberation Province, which had reverted to state farms following his dismissal from the cabinet in 1961. Within a week of returning to the ministry, he took steps to begin to distribute land in South Liberation Province to peasants employed there. On June 25 it was announced that discussions to that effect were taking place, and shortly thereafter the Ministry of Agriculture began to distribute small plots of land.[23] Long an opponent of expensive reclamation schemes in the desert, Marei took the initiative in calling a halt to all such work. In the future, Marei announced in his ministerial statement to parliament on November 27, 1967, "priority will be given to areas where large drainage and irrigation projects have been completed [and] to muddy land before sandy land."[24] He also announced that no new areas would be brought under sprinkler irrigation, an expensive and frequently ineffective technical innovation much favored by officers active in reclamation work since the early days of Liberation Province. In an attempt to pave the way for a partial dismantling of the state-controlled "cooperative" marketing system that Abu al Nour had spread throughout the country, Marei initiated a pilot project in one province in which private agricultural companies would be permitted to buy cotton directly from producers.[25]

Yet another issue in the agricultural sector on which Marei and his predecessor differed, and which was salient in the general political arena, was that of agricultural cooperative societies. As Marei's creations, they were closely identified with him and his reputation, and in 1965 he had attempted unsuccessfully to convince Nasser that they, rather than the basic units of the ASU, should be the preeminent village organization.[26] Marei's opponents were ambivalent toward cooperatives. On the one hand they sought to use them as vehicles for mobilizing the peasantry against landowners, while on the other they preferred that the ASU become the most important political organization at the village level. As a result of this ambivalence, policy toward cooperatives was erratic and ultimately ineffective during Abu al Nour's protracted tenure as minister, and the cooperatives themselves deteriorated. Corrupt practices by members of the boards of cooperatives, 80 percent of whom according to the cooperative law of 1956 had to be peasants whose landholdings did not exceed 5 feddans, were endemic. By the summer of 1967 and Marei's return to the cabinet, it was clear that something had to be done to improve the situation. Cooperatives had been assigned a vital role in distributing virtually all agricultural inputs, including credit, and were responsible as well for purchasing crops, but were performing neither task adequately.[27]

It remained to be determined just what steps should be taken to rectify the situation. The left argued that the problem of cooperatives was not too much democracy but rather was not enough, alleging that supervisors rather than board members typically dominated cooperatives. Those holding this view feared that Marei would reform the cooperatives, either by abolishing the provision requiring four-fifths of the members to be small peasants, or by canceling altogether elections to the board, converting them into appointive bodies and thereby enhancing the influence of Marei's clients in the supervisory central cooperative organizations and, by implication, Marei himself. Hilmy Yassin, a contributor to the leftist monthly *al Tali'a*, writing in the editorial section in September 1968, observed that Marei had stated in a speech in Assiut in August that, "studies are to be carried out in order to come to a decision about the formation of the boards of directors of agricultural cooperatives; whether they should be appointed from the 'good' elements or elected from each [geographical] sector so that family influence would not interfere." Yassin, concerned that Marei favored appointment and had the power to act on his preference, argued that "to use the method of appointment means that only influential persons will be appointed [and] appointment contradicts the Charter."

Yassin and those who shared his views did not need to be so concerned about Marei taking unilateral action, for by 1968 Marei's honeymoon in the Ministries of Agriculture, Agrarian Reform, and Land Reclamation had come to an end. Able to operate almost independently in the near political chaos that prevailed in the wake of the June War and supported from behind the scene by Nasser, Marei had taken several provocative steps, such as handing back some desequestrated property and decollectivizing parts of South Liberation Province. But as the left began to reassert itself once the immediate crisis of the military defeat had passed, and as Marei's measures antagonized powerful opponents, he became more cautious lest he overreach himself.

POLITICAL VOLATILITY IN THE LAST YEARS OF THE NASSER ERA

The first indication that the left was not in total disarray, and that Marei therefore would not have it all his own way, came shortly after the desequestration order arrived from Nasser in July. Despite Marei's order to Hagrass to proceed quickly and with utmost caution to prevent information leaks, news of the partial desequestration mysteriously appeared in the press in August.[28] The battle over this issue, which was nominally an agricultural one but which had wide-ranging implications, had begun. Sami Sharaf, head of Nasser's personal intelligence network and in tactical alliance with Ali Sabry and the left, called Hagrass and ordered him to stop restoring land to its original owners, except in those few cases in which procedures had been initiated but not yet completed. Marei contacted Nasser to see where the matter stood and was informed by the president that he could proceed on some cases but that there was no longer a general order for desequestration.[29] With the tide rapidly turning, Nasser had been forced to compromise. Marei, however, was not to abandon this cause so quickly, for he appreciated the strength of his position as minister of agriculture and agrarian reform in the relatively freewheeling political situation that now prevailed. He instructed Hagrass to form a technical committee in the Ministry of Agrarian Reform to gather information on all cases of sequestration, which numbered 334, in order to place that information before the ASU's Political Committee, chaired by Kemal Rifaat and charged officially with determining the future of sequestration. The data Hagrass presented was highly supportive of Marei's position. It demonstrated that of the 334 cases, only 25 came about as a result of violation of the 1952 or 1961 agrarian reform laws, while the remainder were sequestrations by the CLF on political grounds.[30] But the ASU committee prevaricated, refusing to give Marei a green light on desequestration. Nevertheless, Marei, aware of the strength of his position, quietly ordered the resumption of desequestration, which proceeded in fits and starts throughout the remainder of the Nasser era.

Realizing that the weight of public opinion was behind desequestration and that Marei controlled the responsible ministry, Sabry and others who originally had ordered the property seizures, and who did not want to be overruled, adopted suitable tactics to counteract Marei's moves. Instead of opposing his desequestration policy head-on, they began to find fault with the manner in which he was handling specific cases. In the February 12, 1969, session of the Central Committee of the ASU, they charged Marei with favoritism toward feudalists. Specifically, they alleged that when Marei restored properties to wealthy landowners he first canceled all rental contracts, thus denying peasant tenants usufruct rights, which as a consequence of provisions of the 1952 agrarian reform law had become more important and remunerative than ownership itself. Another charge was that Marei's Ministry of Agrarian Reform was selling its orchards to wealthy landowners. A further attempt was made to embarrass Marei by forcing him to disclose the fact that one of the families whose sequestrated property had been restored was none other than the al Faqis—those charged with the murder of the ASU official and thus responsible for having given rise to the CLF and the wave of sequestrations in the first place.[31]

Marei defended his position before the Central Committee by arguing that the landowners had obtained court orders to have peasants removed from their land and that his ministry had nothing to do with this. He also argued that the Ministry of Agrarian Reform sold off scattered orchards only to reduce administrative overheads, and that the total acreage involved was small. But despite Marei's command of the facts and figures in specific sequestration cases and his presentation of technically plausible rationales for other of his ministry's actions, his position in the ASU Central Committee and in the political elite, which had already begun to slip, was further damaged.

This diminution of Marei's influence had been presaged by an indirect attack on him which had appeared in June 1968 in the Sabry-dominated daily newspaper, *al Gumhuriya*. A team from that paper had investigated the sociopolitical conditions in ten villages, with Marei's village of Azizeha being conspicuous among the ten. Their report, published in two parts on June 13 and June 20, stated that in Azizeha the position of *umdah* had remained in the hands of the richest family in the village for more than one hundred years. It was of course no mystery to the readers of *al Gumhuriya* that the unnamed family was the Marei-Nasrs. It was also reported that the agricultural cooperative society was dominated by two well-off peasants, one owning 18 feddans and the other owning in excess of 50. Since the law at the time required that cooperative society board members own no more than 5 feddans, the article intimated that Marei had overlooked flagrant violations of this law even in his own village. In short, Marei and his family were portrayed as being an integral part of the feudalist landowning class that dominated rural life and deprived peasants of their rights.

Another indication of Marei's political decline was that in the cabinet announced in March 1968, he was striped of the Land Reclamation portfolio, which was given to Muhamed Bakr Ahmad, who was independent of Marei's influence and who had ties to former minister Abu al Nour and agronomists associated with him. A heavier blow was to come later in the year. Encouraged by his cabinet colleagues Aziz Sidqy and Hassan Abbas Zaki, Marei nominated himself as a candidate for membership on the Higher Executive Committee of the ASU, which was to be the new eight-man ruling body for the political organization. Sabry and Abu al Nour, having control of the elections, engineered a crushing defeat of Marei, who received a meager 33 votes in comparison to Sabry's 134 and Abu al Nour's 104, with political lightweights Labib Shuqair and Dia al Din Dawud, other Sabry clients, also outpolling Marei and winning seats on the committee.

Shorn of influence in the ASU, Marei was then subjected to further humiliation by being placed on political probation for being "soft on feudalists." This step prevented Marei from offering his candidacy for the parliamentary elections held in January 1969, for the ASU was officially charged with supervising those elections. For the first time since reaching the minimum age required of deputies, Marei did not contest a parliamentary election.

To add insult to injury, Marei's relative Muhamed Abu Nosseir, who had caused Sayed Marei's brother Hassan's fall from the Ministry of Commerce and Industry in 1954, was, as a result of Sabry's urgings, made minister of justice in the cabinet formed in March 1968. From that post Abu Nosseir began to harass the judiciary, alleging to Nasser that judges of ancien régime backgrounds who frequented the Judges' Club were conspiring against the regime, as evidenced by their verdicts in favor of wealthy malcontents. Marei suspected that the autocrat Abu Nosseir was simply seeking justification to purge anyone unfortunate enough to be under his authority and less than enthusiastic about it. He went to Nasser to explain his viewpoint, but the purge continued, suggesting to Marei that his influence with Nasser did not match Sabry's.[32]

Within a few months, however, the dictates of Nasser's political balancing act demanded once again that he trim the growing power of the left, and specifically that of Ali Sabry. The first indication that a change was coming was Nasser's announcement at the General National Congress of the ASU on July 23, 1969, of new policies on land tenure and on agricultural cooperatives. He declared a new agrarian reform, lowering the maximum limit of legal landownership from 100 to 50 feddans, but because a more drastic reform had been anticipated and was demanded vociferously by the left, and because Marei as minister of agrarian reform was to implement the new measure, it could not be considered especially radical, or a harbinger of drastic new steps to follow. In any case, a mere 28,500 feddans were confiscated.[33] Moreover, Nasser signaled that the principle of private ownership was not under attack by declaring a new and moderate tenure policy for reclaimed lands. He argued that technical considerations required much of the land to be distributed to private owners, either as individuals or in the form of companies, so that maximum production could be obtained. Some land would be retained and farmed by the state. Finally, a new cooperative law was announced. It raised the maximum landownership permitted a member of the board from five to ten feddans and further required that board members be literate and not in debt. These measures virtually terminated the possibility of small peasants being elected to cooperative boards. One observer of the new law commented: "The individual who owns ten feddans in the Egyptian village is really a wealthy peasant. He must be related to the old wealthy and exploitative families. We are, therefore, depriving the needy elements of services and control of the cooperatives."[34] Lest there be any doubt that a shift back to the right was in progress, in the following month Ali Sabry's client Minister of Justice Muhamed Abu Nosseir was forced by Nasser to resign in the backwash of the purge of the judiciary and several well-publicized incidents of unlawful detention.[35] Then in early September, Nasser struck at Sabry himself. On his return to Cairo from an extended visit to the Soviet Union, Sabry was arrested on a charge of smuggling and dismissed from his post in the ASU.

But as Nasser's health deteriorated, as the front with Israel began to collapse, and as Soviet influence increased as a result of arms transfers and then direct military intervention in the War of Attrition, the center of political gravity was being forced to the left. Sabry, a key contact with the Soviets, simply could not be left on the shelf, so on April 26, 1970, Nasser announced that he was to be the secretary of the new Foreign Affairs Committee in the ASU; on May 17 that he would represent Egypt at Soviet celebrations of Lenin's one-hundredth birthday; and on June 29 that he was to be the new assistant for defense affairs with the honorary rank of general, a promotion not published in the Egyptian press.[36]

In the meantime, a serious threat to Marei was developing. Always resented by members of the elite because of his unique relationship with Nasser, Muhamed Hassanein Heykal, who insinuated in his Friday columns that the Soviet connection was not paying sufficient dividends and who offered acerbic comments on the excesses of "centers of power" and "dawn visitors," became after the 1967 war the bête noir of the left. The battle between Heykal and the left was fought out partly in the press, with al Gumhuriya, under ASU control, lashing out at Heykal and al Ahram. A more important manifestation of the personal struggle, at least from Marei's viewpoint, was treatment meted out to the clients and associates of the contending parties—such treatment usually being a signal from Nasser that Heykal or his enemies had gone too far. Gamal Oteify, for example, a leading member of Heykal's *al Ahram* brain trust, was jailed during this ceaseless struggle. He was freed a week later after Sadat, acting as *wasit,* patched up the quarrel between Nasser and Heykal.[37] Then in April 1970, Heykal's fortunes took a sudden and dramatic turn for the worse. *Al Ahram* in-house leftist and editor of *al Tali'a* Lutfi al Kholi, along with Heykal's personal secretary, Mrs. Nawal al Mahallawi, were arrested.[38] Almost simultaneously it was announced that Heykal had been appointed minister of information. The cabinet appointment was an especially serious blow. As president of *al Ahram,* Heykal could snipe away at his enemies, and they could snipe back from their newspaper strongholds, and both could damage one another's clients, but Heykal could not be called to account in cabinet meetings, in parliament or any other such setting. He alone had enjoyed this privilege. Now that he was being brought into the cabinet it could only mean that his influence, hence that of his *shilla* partners, would inevitably recede.

Thus, by summer 1970, Marei was again in a difficult position. Sabry had bounced back from temporary disgrace and Heykal, not able to protect even his private secretary, had been transformed from omnipotent press baron at *al Ahram* to humble cabinet minister. Marei's ally Anwar Sadat had been promoted to vice-president, but that was assumed to have resulted from Sadat's weakness rather than his strength, and in any case the position was not a powerful one so long as Nasser was alive. Then, as the summer progressed, a rumor began to circulate in Cairo that a drastic new agrarian reform was in the works in which the limit would be lowered to 25 or possibly even fewer feddans. It was further rumored that land confiscated would be converted into state farms.[39] Whether true or not, such rumors reflected the prevailing belief that the leftward trend was rapidly gaining momentum. Yet fate once again was to intervene and change the situation dramatically and to Marei's benefit. This time it took the form of Nasser's death and Anwar Sadat's succession to the presidency.

9 | FROM TECHNOCRAT TO PARTY BOSS AND DIPLOMAT UNDER SADAT

MAREI AS *WASIT* (MIDDLEMAN) UNDER SADAT

Primarily an agronomist bureaucrat-manager responsible for implementing agrarian reform and agricultural policy under Nasser, Marei under Sadat became a political manager charged with implementing the new president's political liberalization. This transformation came about as a result of his intimate relationship with Sadat and because of systemic change. In Sadat's Egypt there are no men of expertise equivalent to those who under Nasser presided over Egypt's development efforts and who became personally identified with those efforts. Marei, for example, had become known as "the father of agrarian reform," while Aziz Sidqy had been identified as "the man of one thousand factories." Under Sadat there have been too few large-scale development projects and too much cabinet instability for technocrats to establish power bases or reputations similar to those of Marei, Sidqy, and others in Nasser's Egypt.[1] The civilizing of the regime, and Sadat's lesser stature as compared to his predecessor, has contributed to this situation. Ambitious challengers such as Aziz Sidqy and Muhamed Hassanein Heykal, who might pose a threat to the president now that the keys to the political kingdom are not held exclusively by the military, are not permitted the latitude they or other technocrats enjoyed under Nasser. In addition, the growth of the private sector and atrophying of the public sector has rendered governmental satrapies relatively unattractive to the politically ambitious, who are now inclined to pursue their political interests in one of the parties and/or in parliament, and their economic interests in private enterprise. Thus politics, which was a dirty word in Nasser's Egypt and which was in theory replaced by administration, has returned under Sadat and has placed him in need of political managers rather than technocrat-administrators. In that policy formation remains the prerogative of the president, however, his political managers are more akin to political technocrats than political decision-makers. They may influence policy through its administration, but not in its formulation.

Marei is one of Sadat's key political managers or political technocrats, but his role differs somewhat from that of other such implementors of policy as Mamdouh Salem, Fikry Makram Obeid, Mustafa Kamel Murad, and Mahmoud Abu Wafia. Among this galaxy of political stars, only Marei stands out as playing what can be discerned as a slightly independent political role. That he is able to do so results paradoxically from his close relationship with Sadat. Their long association since first meeting in the home of journalist Ihsan Abd al Quddous in 1952, rendered more intimate by their close cooperation in parliament in the mid-1960s and then cemented in the summer of 1975 by the marriage of Marei's son Hassan to Sadat's daughter Noha, is for Sadat probably unrivaled by any other politically relevant personal friendship. This intimacy and Marei's record of loyalty to the previous president has led Sadat to permit Marei greater political latitude than that granted any other member of his entourage, latitude in which Marei has maneuvered skillfully. Able occasionally to distance himself from official policy, Marei has cast himself as a *wasit* (middleman), or bridge between Sadat and various individuals and constituencies inclined to opposition.

As a political middleman, Marei has become a vital asset to Sadat in his erratic campaign to liberalize Egyptian politics. Thus his political career has risen and fallen in direct relationship to liberalization. When Sadat has encouraged political activity, Marei has been assigned to supervise it. When such activity reaches and then exceeds the limits with which Sadat feels comfortable, Marei is replaced by an uncompromising political manager, such as Mamdouh

Salem, whose job is not to mediate but to intimidate. Marei's political prominence and power, associated with swings to the right in the Nasser era, have under Sadat reached their peak on those occasions when politics, especially of a leftist nature, are in full bloom.

FOLLOWING NASSER'S DEATH: FOR SABRY OR SADAT?

Until May 1971, when Sadat purged Ali Sabry, Minister of Interior Sharawi Gomaa, Head of Presidential Intelligence Sami Sharaf, and their supporters, it was not clear who would win the succession struggle. The fragility of Egypt's untested constitutional succession system and the presence of powerful challengers suggested that Sadat, known until then as "colonel yes yes" for his obsequiousness to Nasser, might be brushed aside. As the struggle intensified in early 1971, rumors began to circulate as to who was conspiring with whom to oust the president. One rumor had it that Sayed Marei, then the deputy prime minister for agriculture, agrarian reform, and land reclamation, had decided to cast his lot with Ali Sabry, who at the time appeared to control directly or indirectly the ASU, broadcasting, presidential intelligence, and the Ministry of Interior and to have the upper hand in the military through Minister of War Muhamed Fawzy. When the crunch finally came in mid-May, however, Marei turned up in the Sadat camp, although rumors persisted that he did so only after Sabry's demise was evident.

In his memoirs, Marei devotes considerable attention to his activities at this time, presumably in an attempt to prove his unswerving loyalty to Sadat and to scotch rumors of disloyalty.[2] His account may be accurate, but it does seem contrived, and in any case it leaves open the possibility that he was sitting on the fence waiting to see who would come out on top before committing himself. Because this episode is crucial, it is worth reviewing in detail.

On April 29, 1971, in the presence of Labib Shuqair, (then speaker of the Assembly and later to be arrested as a conspirator), Sharawi Gomaa, and Sami Sharaf, Marei telephoned Sadat and informed him that the assembled group thought it advisable for him to reverse his decision to appear before parliament to argue his case for a merger with Libya. Marei assured Sadat that his presence was not required to secure the desired outcome. Whether Shuqair, Gomaa, Sharaf, and Marei had identical reasons for keeping Sadat away from the Assembly is not clear, but it does seem strange that Marei should act in concert with these supporters of Ali Sabry at a time when Sadat was desperately casting around for allies. More unusual behavior followed. Marei, invoking the memory of the events of spring 1954, advised the president to address a crowd of peasant beneficiaries of agrarian reform in order to demonstrate his popularity. Sadat agreed, so Marei left for Beheira Province to make the necessary arrangements. After some delay, he decided that the preparations were inadequate and postponed the event, whereupon he drove to his flat in Alexandria, took his phone off the hook, and fell asleep. Late that evening, May 13, he awoke, replaced the receiver, and the phone immediately rang. It was Sadat, who had in the meantime ordered the roundup of his opponents and who requested Marei to return to Cairo posthaste. Three hours later the crisis had passed and Marei was at Sadat's side.

This account raises some questions. The very suggestion of visiting an obscure agrarian reform area to demonstrate mass support is itself suspicious. The year 1971 was not 1954, and agrarian reform was no longer such a salient issue. The battle was to be won or lost within the confines of the elite—not on the basis of popularity in Beheira. Might it have been an attempt to lure Sadat away from Cairo? Possibly. That Marei should find the arrangements to be unsatisfactory, cancel the event without informing Sadat, and repair to Alexandria and cut communication at a crucial time suggests that he was getting out of the way because he knew the struggle was coming to a climax and preferred not to take sides prematurely. In short, the episode remains shrouded in ambiguity. Marei's explanation notwithstanding, it remains plausible that he was taking steps to ensure his political future under a new president.

Whatever the case, Marei made it through the "corrective revolution" of May 1971 with his position and reputation intact and with an almost clear path before him leading to the post of prime minister. The one remaining obstruction was his old *shilla* partner Aziz Sidqy, who as minister of industry had been actively and successfully courting support in the cabinet. His position had, in fact, begun to rival that of Prime Minister Mahmoud Fawzy himself, whom Marei supported out of tactical considerations.[3] Forced to recognize Sidqy's influence, Prime Minister Fawzy, during one of Marei's junkets abroad, promoted the ambitious minister of industry to first deputy prime minister and placed him in charge of the

Cabinet Committee on the Economy, which implied Sidqy's superiority over Marei. This infuriated Marei, who offered his resignation immediately upon his return to Cairo. But Prime Minister Fawzy outmaneuvered Marei by saying that he too would resign, thereby threatening to reveal that Marei's jealousy of Sidqy had been the cause of the government's collapse. Marei backtracked, but not before securing a compromise. Fawzy agreed to divide his ministers into two groups, one under Sidqy in the Committee on the Economy and one under Marei in the Committee on Agriculture, Irrigation, Supply, Agrarian Reform, and Barren Lands. But this was no more than a temporary palliative, and the government was soon immobilized by the Herculean struggle between Fawzy's two deputy prime ministers. The timing could hardly have been worse, for as the cabinet polarized into rival blocs, the streets began to fill with workers and students protesting the uneventful passing of 1971, which Sadat had unwisely declared the Year of Decision. Unable to take military action on the Israeli front, Sadat moved to shore up his domestic political position by separating the combatants in the government. He pulled Marei out of the cabinet, and on January 16, 1972, had him elected first secretary of the ASU as Sidqy, newly appointed prime minister, was naming his cabinet.

Sidqy's victory over Marei—and victory it was, for the ASU had been in cold storage since May 1971—resulted from Sadat's personal power requirements. Regarded with suspicion by the Soviets after having purged their man Sabry, and yet desperately in need of Soviet military assistance, Sadat could not risk promoting the reputedly pro-Western Marei to the prime ministry. Sidqy was the ideal choice, for as minister of industry he had had extensive dealings with the Soviets, and despite his connections with Heykal, whom the Soviets distrusted, he was viewed as a leftist technocrat. Moreover, it suited Sadat's plans for domestic politics to have Marei direct the ASU. He did not want an effective leftist in that position, breathing life into the organization and converting it into what could be a threat to the presidency. On the other hand, he did need a shock absorber to protect his authority from increasingly hostile students and workers, to say nothing of disaffected professionals, so he could scarcely afford handing the ASU over to a nonentity. Given these requirements, Marei was the ideal choice. His ambition and talent would ensure that the ASU would not lie dormant, for as Sadat knew, Marei would work to convert it into an institution which he could then use to undermine Prime Minister Sidqy.

REBUILDING THE ASU

In his meeting with the ASU Central Committee's Subcommittee of Intellectuals on March 29, 1972, Marei candidly described the stimulus for the campaign to overhaul the political organization:

> I did not really propose the ASU reform. I had no intention of doing that. The students' movement pushed and demanded this reform. I held 45 meetings with the professional syndicates and they all asked for this reform. The government was always the authority that suggested reform. This time the masses are the ones to call for it.[4]

In other words, Marei's task was first to defuse the tense situation prevailing on campuses, and second to appease workers and professionals in their unions and syndicates. These were especially significant challenges, considering the reception given by students to news of Marei's appointment. They protested the handing over of the ASU to a "feudalist and capitalist" and chanted slogans against him.[5] The regime tried to calm the situation by drawing attention to Marei's instrumental role in the agrarian reform and by arguing that he was "continuously in contact with the daily life and the problems of the great majority of the people, the peasants."[6] It was clear, though, that students, having waited through the anticlimactic Year of Decision, distrusted Marei at least as much as they distrusted Sadat, and that the former had to take quick action lest antigovernment sentiments and actions not abate.

Appreciating the perilousness of the situation, Marei was all ready to go. Two days after his appointment as first secretary, and following a meeting of the General Secretariat of the ASU, he announced that "the clear attitude now is to have the political organization as the real *minbar* (pulpit) for expressing the different opinions and attitudes of all parts of the alliance of popular forces."[7] There was thus to be no fundamental change—the ASU was to remain the sole political organization. Formal opposition outside the ASU would not be permitted, so what remained was to work out arrangements between the working forces in the alliance (e.g., workers, peasants, national capitalists, intellectuals, and soldiers) within the framework of the ASU. This clarification was necessary to prevent the reform from going too far and, at least as important, to mollify ASU stalwarts who were apprehensive for their futures and for the fate of their organization. In that first meeting, Marei also announced how the reform was to be accomplished. The General Secretariat was to hold meetings with students, faculty, and members of unions, syndicates, and other organizations, to discuss "the role of every citizen and his responsibility to the battle."[8]

The first order of business was to pacify the students, and on the following day, January 19, Marei leapt into the veritable lion's den of student activism, the faculty of engineering at Cairo University. There he met with students and faculty for three hours, leaving with a promise to address the entire student body and to respond to questions. He also used the occasion to fire a shot in his personal battle with Prime Minister Sidqy, remarking pointedly to students that "other responsible people should attend meetings to answer any questions."[9] In the following weeks, he continued to devote much of his attention to students, always following the conciliatory line he had first taken in the engineering faculty. On February 22 he declared that "the organization assures youth that they have the right to find an audience when they speak and to have an answer when they question." He added that the political leadership was being careful not to become too suspicious of students, "even when it has been proven that there is deviation from the correct way in expression and practice." To implement his pledges, Marei announced that it had been decided to reorganize the ASU's youth organization, which until that time had been used to police student activities.[10]

Marei's quick, conciliatory gestures to students were not in vain. Flattered by the attention given them by the first secretary, pleased that he had declared their grievances as justified, and relieved that he was willing to restrict the surveillance function of the youth organization, student activists abandoned the streets for their classrooms.

When it became clear that the immediate crisis had passed, an emergency meeting of the General National Congress of the ASU was called so that the precise direction the proposed reforms were to take could be spelled out. In his opening speech to the Congress, Marei enunciated the basic principles upon which the reform was to be based:

First, the ASU is the only political organization in Egypt;
Second, the Alliance is controlled by four main documents, the Charter, the 30th March Declaration, the Constitution, and the Program of National Action (which Sadat had declared some months earlier);
Third, the ASU embraces the thoughts of the allied forces, and supervises communication between them.[11]

Even with the crisis of student demonstrations now over, it was obvious that the ASU reform was to remain a cosmetic one. Sadat was not prepared to embark on a thoroughgoing and possibly risky overhaul of the political system while his personal reputation as president had as yet to be established and while he had to be preoccupied with foreign affairs. So Marei still confronted the tasks of winning the confidence of politically articulate Egyptians and their allegiance to the ASU, but without being able to grant any fundamental or significant concessions. It soon became clear, however, that he had worked out a successful strategy for doing so. It included openhearted sympathy for those who complained of suffering from abuses of power in the past, some amelioration of their situation, and skillful cooptation of key persons, the most significant and helpful of whom were prominent leftists.

On February 22 Marei announced that the first stage of the reform had been completed. Having listened to suggestions and arguments for more than a month and in over forty meetings, the time had now come to decide on the new plan of work of the ASU. To supervise the overhaul of ASU machinery, Marei announced that a twenty-man Work Committee would be formed, composed of five members of the ASU Central Committee, five members from the National Congress of the ASU and, most important, ten "important personalities."[12] He thus signaled his intention to admit those other than ASU activists into the reform process, thereby ensuring that ASU stalwarts did not dominate the proceedings and in so doing overprotect their institution and their own stake in it.

To ensure that the left felt adequately represented, Marei nominated Khaled Muhi al Din and Lutfi al Kholi for membership on the committee. The choice of al Kholi was particularly astute, for in addition to being influential in intellectual circles, al Kholi was editor of the leading leftist journal, *al Tali'a,* support from which would contribute to the success of the reform effort. Al Kholi accepted the formula of the Alliance and through the spring and early summer worked closely with Marei to hammer out the details of that formula and convince skeptics of its viability. Large portions of the May, June, and July issues of *al Tali'a* were devoted to the proceedings of the Work Committee and to analyses of those proceedings by the journal's staff members. Although Michel Kamel followed Khaled Muhi al Din's line and demanded political clubs "as a means of guaranteeing the people's freedom of expression within the ASU,"[13] and Muhamed Aglan urged the ASU Work Committee to abandon its urban locale and go out into the countryside to meet with the masses,[14] the general reception given by *al Tali'a* editorialists to the reform was favorable.[15] But even more significant than the line taken by individual *al Tali'a* editorialists was the fact that they lavished such attention on the reform, thereby implying that it was a serious effort worthy of consideration by intellectuals and political activists. In that Marei's primary task had been to rivet attention on the ASU and thereby prevent political participation from seeking other channels, *al Tali'a*'s coverage was a significant victory for him.

Throughout the reform, Marei played a game of cat and mouse with ASU officials, who were unanimous in their distrust of him, a feeling which was further exacerbated when Marei brought in outsiders to assist in the reform process. In his first joint meeting with ASU officials and members of the Work Committee, Marei sought to placate them:

> We are here to reorganize the ASU. This does not mean that we are going to repeat the ASU elections. It just means that we are going to change the style of ASU activity. . . . Our discussion of the ASU's failure to satisfy the people's needs and demands does not really constitute an accusation against all those who had previously worked in the ASU. I am sure that they all tried to make something of the ASU.[16]

But in his meetings with professionals, workers, youths, and so on, Marei was not nearly so charitable to these officials. He was, in fact, ready to concede virtually any hostile point made against them, and even added some of his own. In an interview conducted by Fahmy Huweidy of *al Ahram,* Marei listed such a long bill of indictment against the ASU in "the previous stage" that Huweidy replied that "one quarter of these negatives is enough to render any political organization completely immobile."[17] In March, Marei released a draft report to guide the reform, which he prefaced with an eleven-count indictment against the ASU. He accused it of failing in its mission because it was bureaucratic, undemocratic, subjective (i.e., rife with favoritism and nepotism), staffed with opportunistic reactionaries, lacked a program, had no links to other organizations such as syndicates, had an ambiguous relation with parliament and the government, kept the facts from the people, deluged the people with unrealistically high hopes, and paralyzed them through overintellectualization, and finally, and to Marei of greatest importance, the ASU "considered itself as an organization that should interpret and justify the actions of the executive authority" [i.e., the cabinet]. According to Marei, "This made the ASU take responsibility for actions and decisions which it had never considered. This was the ASU's way of pretending to participate in decision-making."[18] The contemporary relevance of this final point was Marei's ongoing struggle with Prime Minister Sidqy, a struggle which almost exactly a year later was to cause the fall of the government and Marei's ejection from the ASU.

While heaping abuse on his predecessor's actions in the ASU, Marei was careful to ensure that the corollary of his position was not the destruction of the political organization and its replacement by a formal or semiformal opposition, be it in the form of syndicates acting outside the framework of the ASU, political clubs, or parties. He repeatedly took pains to spell out the limits of the reform. When in the joint meeting of the Work Committee with the Political Affairs Subcommittee of the ASU Central Committee it was proposed that the charter be amended, Marei replied, "We cannot open this complex intellectual discussion at this stage."[19] In a subsequent meeting Marei was asked: "Are we going to just try to reform the ASU? I thought the committee was to build a new structure and a new system." Marei responded: "No, the committee will do no such thing."[20] In his meeting with intellectuals on March 29, Marei rejected leftist historian Dr. Muhamed Anis's suggestion that individuals be permitted to draft their own papers elucidating their preferences as to how the ASU should be reorganized.[21] Following a particularly difficult session with the Committee of Intellectuals, Marei took steps to circumscribe the limits of debate in his next meeting, which was with the Artists and Writers Subcommittee of the Work Committee:

> I must point out that our attempt to reform the ASU must be done within the framework set by our different political documents—the Charter, the March 30th Declaration, and the Constitution. I failed to make this point clear in our meeting with the Intellectuals Committee, and as a result the discussion got out of hand. Members of the Intellectuals Committee asked that we change the Charter and the March 30th Declaration. They also asked that we make new definitions of the people's working forces. I do not think that there is anything wrong with these documents. They were just never correctly applied.[22]

As the meeting with artists and writers progressed, several prominent writers, and especially Neguib Mahfouz, questioned the possibility of resolving political contradictions within the ASU. Marei once again staked out the limits of the reform:

Do you really think that the present contradictions are so basic that the working forces cannot possibly coexist in the present alliance? I see no reason why we cannot have different views within the ASU. I do not think, however, that we need call these views and organizations partylike organizations or miniparties. Some members of the ASU's Intellectuals Committee have called for the establishment of different political parties, but I do not think that this can really be the solution.[23]

In a sharp exchange with Abd al Khaleq al Shennawi during the meeting with the Professional Syndicate's committee on April 22, Marei made his attitude clear once again on political activity outside the ASU. Shennawi complained that during the ancien régime, engineers opposed to projects had been allowed to participate in debates in parliament. Marei retorted, "It was the presence of a recognized opposition and political parties that delayed the implementation of the Aswan Dam project in the past."[24]

Throughout these long discussions with the various committees and subcommittees of the ASU, Marei patiently went over the same ground time and again, refusing to lose his temper in the face of provocation and generally displaying mastery of the situation. The overriding message he conveyed was that the ASU under its benign and sympathetic new leader would in the future be more responsive to demands for freedom of expression, but that political activity outside the organization would continue to be unacceptable. With regard to intraorganizational reforms to facilitate this freedom of expression, Marei presented on June 2 his report for "evolving the style of work in the ASU." It called for some bureaucratic proliferation and reshuffling, such as creating new Secretariats of National Capitalists, Handicrafts, and Economic and Service Affairs; adding a Higher Council for Youth under a new minister of state for youth; and reorganizing relations between syndicates and the Central Committee. Of greater importance was the recommendation that *minabar* (pulpits) be created inside the ASU "to enable every social force of the Alliance to express its attitudes and opinions."[25] Thus the promise was held out that something resembling the political clubs called for by Khaled Muhi al Din and others would emerge within the ASU and that in future these clubs might lead to a formal legal opposition.

But hopes raised by Marei's June report were dashed the following month as his carefully prepared groundwork for a slight but possibly significant opening up of the political system was laid to waste by Sadat. In announcing to the ASU Central Committee on

July 18 the eviction of Soviet military advisors from Egypt, the president declared his intention to clear the decks for military action and his related decision to cut short the brief experiment in semidemocracy and to consolidate the home front for the coming battle.[26] The General National Congress of the ASU, which met the following week and which was to have been the culmination of Marei's painstaking efforts to reorganize and invigorate the ASU, was instead devoted to a call to national unity. The resolutions of the Congress almost completely ignored the painstakingly prepared arrangements of the previous long months of debate.[27]

That the Congress and its final report had presaged a backtracking from the modest liberalization of the first half of 1971 became absolutely clear on August 15, when Sadat issued as Law 34 a Presidential Decree for Patriotic Unity. It defined the ASU as the sole political organization expressing the Alliance of Popular Forces and forbade the establishment of political or other public organizations outside the ASU.[28] Thus ended meaningful discussion of modifying the ASU to facilitate greater political participation.

Although Marei could look back upon his first half year as first secretary of the ASU with some sense of accomplishment, for he had helped temporarily to reduce political tension, he must have been disappointed that his efforts to overhaul the ASU had only bought time for the regime but had not borne any more substantial fruit. Sadat had unmistakably shifted the focus of attention from the home front to the front with Israel; the task of the ASU now was to prepare the ranks for battle and not to encourage clamorings for political freedom.

Ever a realist, Marei shifted gears in unison with his boss. After July almost all his public statements were concerned with foreign affairs and the role of the ASU in shoring up the home front. From that time he began to dispatch members of the youth organization, the syndicates, and the ASU itself overseas to drum up support for Egypt's cause. Even in the periodic conferences the ASU held in the provinces, Marei devoted most of his speeches to foreign rather than domestic affairs.[29] Questioned in an interview with *al Gumhuriya* published on January 10, 1973, as to why the ASU was disregarding "patriotic and national problems" such as birth control and illiteracy, Marei responded:

> If you attend any village or any place—a conference of young men, workers or intellectuals—and you ask about the first and most important subject in such a conference, will you find that

the subject is fighting illiteracy? If so, then the ASU is mistaken. The people will be distant from it because they have worried very much about the occupied land for six years. When shall we liberate our land? We must liberate it whether the people are literate or not, whether the people have birth control or not. ... This does not mean that we will neglect combating illiteracy or birth control, but we regard these as secondary issues for the time being.

With his responsibilities as first secretary diminished substantially by the turn of events, Marei departed Cairo on January 8, 1973, for a two-week pilgrimage to Mecca. On his return to Egypt he said little more publicly about foreign affairs or the role of the ASU, for by this time his struggle with Prime Minister Sidqy had become an all-consuming passion. It had, in fact, despite its almost subterranean nature, become the focal point of Egyptian politics.

MAREI VERSUS SIDQY

Marei and Sidqy had become acquainted as students at the University of Cairo, but they had only come into close and sustained contact following their promotions into the cabinet in 1956, at which time they moved into the Heykal orbit. They continued to socialize with one another until Nasser's death, sharing as they did mutual antipathy to the officers who blocked their path to the highest offices in the land. But there had always been an element of tension in the relationship. Their personal styles were very different, with Sidqy being a hard-driving, uncompromising, rather dogmatic modernist-technocrat, and Marei being a more tactful, flexible type who extolled the virtues of traditions and peasant earthiness even more than those of modernism and scientific excellence. Their institutional positions also led them to conflict. As minister of industry, Sidqy strove relentlessly to expand the domain of agro-industrial projects, such as canning plants and sugar refineries, so as to include the production of agricultural inputs under his own ministry, while Marei fought just as hard to prevent that from occurring. Sidqy repeatedly insinuated that agriculture in Egypt remained desperately old-fashioned and nonscientific, while Marei put forward the argument that the industrial sector rode the back of agriculture, draining it of reinvestment capital in the process. Bitter as these conflicts were, they could be contained so long as the necessity of unity in the face of a more threatening enemy remained. When Nasser died and Sadat cleared the decks of the "centers of power," that necessity vanished, so Marei and Sidqy turned on one another with a vengeance typically reserved for old friends and members of the family.

Sidqy had emerged from the first round of the fight in a better position, for the post of prime minister was a more impressive prize that that of first secretary of the ASU. While Marei was engaged in quelling student disturbances and trying to reestablish the ASU as a funnel into which political activity could be poured and then bottled up, Sidqy was busy popularizing himself and his government. He inaugurated a television program in which he explained government initiatives to the viewers and informed them how their prime minister and his cabinet were resolving the problems the nation faced. He also arranged for his ministers to appear regularly on television to explain their contribution to the government's program. The new minister of agriculture and agrarian reform, Mustafa Gabaly, who had been handpicked by Sidqy because of his known antipathy to Marei, used these occasions to lambast his predecessor. On national television Gabaly informed the Egyptian people that the Ministry of Agriculture was technically primitive as a result of the shortcomings of the previous minister and that Egyptian agriculture could only be saved from its perilous and unproductive state by the application of modern science and technology, which had in previous years, according to Gabaly, been woefully neglected. This was too much for Marei to tolerate. He went immediately to Sadat, demanding equal time to defend his reputation and that of the ministry which he had built. This he was refused, so he redoubled his efforts in other areas to bring Sidqy and his minister of agriculture to heel.[30]

During the summer of 1972, the minister of agriculture's office released ever more ominous warnings about the magnitude of cotton worm infestation. Then, in a bold move, Gabaly sacked Lewis Mahmoudi, a high-ranking Marei appointee, for failing to take adequate countermeasures. Marei mobilized his resources immediately. A rumor campaign was begun to the effect that the impending cotton worm disaster was a figment of Minister Gabaly's imagination, manufactured by him as part of a plan to demonstrate his competence and to pave the way for a purge of the ministry. Marei also went to Sadat and demanded that his people in the ministry be protected. Sadat responded by ordering Gabaly to reinstate Mahmoudi and desist from further such actions.[31]

While this skirmishing was in progress, Sidqy and Marei became involved in a parallel conflict, each using intermediaries to strike blows against their main adversary. Gabaly, acting on Sidqy's behalf, resuscitated a proposal which had been put forward and rejected during the Nasser era. It was for a tax on profits derived from fruit orchards. In the highly charged atmosphere of 1972, at which time students were protesting loudly and persistently against the in-egalitarian distribution of the wealth, Gabaly's move appeared parti-cularly astute. Orchards are owned primarily by wealthy landowners. More important, Marei, the bête noir of many of the students and the butt of many of their chants and slogans, was widely known as an owner of large fruit orchards. For Gabaly, hence Sidqy, to succeed in establishing a tax on orchards would win for both popularity and suggest that Marei was unable to defend the agricultural sector and even his personal stake in it from Sidqy's depridations.

But Sidqy overplayed his hand. In public and in parliament, Marei said nothing about the tax, lest Sidqy be able to capitalize on it by depicting Marei as a defender of wealth and privilege. As the summer of 1972 wore on and the attentive public watched carefully as this drama unfolded, it appeared as if the government was going to be able to steer the bill through parliament. In the meantime, however, one of Marei's appointees in the Ministry of Agriculture, the head of the Department of Horticulture, was amassing statistics which demonstrated that the tax would lead to a decrease in fruit production, and hence exports, thereby further eroding Egypt's pre-carious balance-of-payments position. These statistics the employee leaked to the old Liberal Constitutionalist minister of agriculture, Abd al Ghaffar, still a wealthy and politically influential Menoufiya landowner and soon to be related to Sadat through the husband of the president's eldest daughter. Although not in parliament, Abd al Ghaffar had numerous supporters who were. When they went on the offensive against the tax, armed with statistics provided surrepti-tiously from Gabaly's own ministry, it suggested that Abd al Ghaffar was urging them on. Parliamentarians were quick to draw the conclu-sion that this in turn implied Sadat's approval of Abd al Ghaffar's activity, and by implication the president's support of Marei rather than Sidqy. Cognizant of these developments and their implications, a majority of deputies voted against the proposed tax. Gabaly then retired to the sidelines as it became clear that Marei's fortunes were on the rise and Sidqy's on the decline.

Sidqy had made a serious tactical error in attempting to embar-rass Marei by one-upping him in his personal domain. Gabaly could sound off in the press and on television about Marei's incompetence and possibly get away with it, but the Ministries of Agriculture and Agrarian Reform, over which Gabaly was the nominal boss, were de facto Marei satrapies. Marei could and did arrange to have his clients and *shilla* partners undermine Gabaly's authority.

Extremely sensitive to any encroachments on his authority and reputation in the agricultural sector, Marei further defended himself by reinstating his old client Muhamed Sobieh, who had been sitting it out in semi-house arrest since 1965, when Kemal Rifaat and the ASU had kidnapped his journal and dismissed him as editor. Fortuitously, *The Agricultural Magazine* and *Cooperation* were in 1972 still under the jurisdiction of the ASU, so Marei, now its first secretary, reappointed Sobieh as editor and gave him the green light to go after Gabaly and Sidqy. Soon the pages of the journals were filled with articles condemning the profligate excesses of the land reclamation program "in the previous stage."[32] Sidqy had begun his career in Liberation Province under Magdi Hassanein, and Gabaly had from 1966 to 1969 been chairman of the General Organization for Development and Utilization of Reclaimed Land. To the articulate public, Sidqy and Gabaly were identified with reclamation of the desert, while Marei was known to oppose it. This and other countermeasures suggest that Sidqy had overestimated Marei's vulnerability in the agricultural sector and underestimated his determination not to be embarrassed within it.

The energy Sidqy and Marei had to pour into their mutual campaign of recrimination appeared to be limitless. As Sidqy was using his post as head of the government to hammer away at his enemy, Marei was utilizing the ASU to restrict Sidqy's authority. His strategy was to focus discussions on reforming the ASU on relations between it and "the executive authority" (i.e., the cabinet). In the meeting with the ASU Work Committee and the General Secretariat of the ASU Central Committee on March 19, in which Marei initially laid out the specifics of the reform, virtually the first topic he addressed was relations between the ASU and the government. After introducing the subject, he let his client Saad Hagrass carry the ball. Hagrass explained that the constitution and the charter required that "the ASU should be the mind of the country. It has the power to direct and supervise government authority." Marei picked up on this line of argument:

The ASU has failed because it has always tried to serve the government by putting the masses in the framework that the government specifies. The ASU has also established itself as the defender of government policies even if it knows nothing about these policies. This political hypocrisy crippled the ASU and prevented it from realizing the goals of the masses.

Following a point of information in support of Marei's argument by Dr. Gaber Gad Abd al Rahman, an ASU careerist who had an institutional interest in building up the ASU and thus was a convenient bedfellow, Marei resumed the attack, although in more pointed terms:

> Let us talk frankly now about this point. The present government has recently issued a series of laws and resolutions without informing or consulting the ASU. We feel that the laws that concern large sectors of the people must come to the ASU. This demand is supported by the Charter, the Constitution, and the March 30th Declaration. But how am I to translate this into reality?

After some discussion Marei went on to answer his own question:

> The ASU's Central Committee is to set the framework of our national policy. The government must never take a decision that contradicts the ASU's general policy decisions. . . .
>
> We must have a role in planning. We have no idea about the budget and we have no control over the appropriation of various funds. The Program of National Action states that the ASU must study the national plan. We want the various popular councils to participate in the discussion of their various governorate's budgets with the executive authority. This way we would be developing the system of local government.

Following more discussion along these lines, Marei brought the issue to a head:

> I want to finish the discussion of one important point now. Does anyone think that the ASU must, by virtue of its structure, become a government organization? In other words, do you want us to establish government power over the ASU? (The majority answers: No!) Then you all agree that the ASU must not become a government organization. In the past decade the ASU was really only justifying the government's decisions. The government is still asking us, "Why don't you explain the government's decisions to the masses?" I say that we are not prepared to defend the different government decisions because we were not consulted before these decisions were taken. The masses support

some of these decisions and condemn some of them. The ASU is not going to compromise itself by defending all government decisions. It is our duty to represent the masses. Because the ASU can not attack the decisions it does not approve we are just going to keep quiet. . . .[33]

On May 15 the Work Committee issued its report, in which it demanded that the government submit to the Central Committee the national plan and its general proposals for foreign and domestic policy. The report also called for the creation of Committees of National Work in all villages, composed of ten members of the ASU basic unit and another ten or so local functionaries.[34] The stated purpose of these committees was to facilitate decentralization and the ASU's access to decision-making at the lowest levels.

But events were to overtake Marei and render impotent his strategy to use the ASU to contain Sidqy and his government at the national and local levels. The expulsion of Soviet advisors and Sadat's decision against liberalization wrecked Marei's carefully laid plans. With the president falling back on executive authority, Marei and his ASU were the odd men out.

This setback caused Marei to grumble more openly about Sidqy. By the year's end his public references to the prime minister had become clearly derogatory. In an interview with *al Gumhuriya* he explained the difference between his political outlook and that of Sidqy's who, although not mentioned by name, was clearly identified:

> To be a successful politician you must talk with the people about the subjects with which they are concerned. . . . The political leader adapts himself to the surrounding people and to their feelings. He should live with the people and with their problems. . . . As a politician you have two jobs. First, to lead the people and second, to have the people influence your opinion. *If you think that you should be broadminded and intelligent in order to be distant from the people, then you will never succeed. There are many examples of this. If there is an expert in economics with great opinions, he will never be able to apply any of his opinions if he is distant from the people. There may be a politician who buys his popularity. This is also wrong.* [Emphasis added.][35]

The final point is a reference to Sidqy's handouts while on tour in the provinces, drumming up support for himself and his government in 1972.

Sidqy's retaliation took the form of a rumor campaign. Not averse to displaying his wealth in public, and widely suspected of

acquiring that wealth illegally, Marei was highly vulnerable to innu-
endo. A rumor began to circulate to the effect that Marei's avarice as
a cattle owner was the cause of the high price of meat. While speaking at Assiut University, where the rumor had clearly reached, Marei
was asked if he owned six hundred Friesian calves. To combat the
rumor, Marei released information from the Ministry of Agriculture
to the effect that there were but two hundred Friesian calves in the
whole country.[36] But in its place a new rumor sprang up, this one
alleging that he as a large producer had manipulated the price of
grapes and watermelons to his advantage. From that point the campaign began to get out of hand. The high price of poultry was rumored to be the result of Marei supplying his fox farm with suitable
food, while another story had it that he was operating a snake farm
for which he imported special hormones.[37]

As the slander campaigns were sinking into the gutter, Deputy
Prime Minister for Information Abd al Qader Hatem, a friend of both
Sidqy and Marei, attempted to mediate the feud. The compromise
arranged by him, whereby two ministers would act as liaisons between the ASU and the government, was, however, never successfully implemented.[38] Shortly thereafter Sadat called an emergency
meeting of Sidqy, Marei, and Hafiz Badawy, speaker of the Assembly. Sadat wanted to cool down the dispute, and he obtained an
agreement from Marei and Sidqy to meet weekly on the more or less
neutral turf of Badawy's office to "coordinate activities." That too
failed, for Sidqy, apparently confident in the strength of his position,
failed to appear for the second scheduled meeting. Marei stormed
home from Badawy's office and the battle resumed.[39]

In the end it was the president's need to balance off Sidqy and
his government with a competitive institution that enabled Marei to
overcome the prime minister. With the ASU having been defanged
in the summer, Sadat had no choice but to turn to the Assembly,
where in late November and December Sidqy and his government
were destroyed as the president stood by watching. On November
17, Sidqy delivered the government's policy speech to the Assembly.
It met an uncharacteristically harsh reaction. Mustafa Kamel Murad,
a former Free Officer close to Sadat, criticized the government's
inadequate preparations for war. Other deputies found fault with
different parts of the government's program. As the tenor of the
debate in succeeding sessions grew increasingly critical, the question
arose as to how far the deputies would be permitted to go in their
criticism of Sidqy and his cabinet. The answer was eventually provided indirectly by the only person who could—the president him-

self. He authorized his brother-in-law, M.P. Mahmoud Abu Wafia, to lash out at Sidqy's budget. With Abu Wafia thus signaling a green light, Marei's good friend at *al Ahram,* Gamal Oteify, who had also been chosen by Marei to serve on the Work Committee to reorganize the ASU, delivered the coup de grace to Sidqy. A skilled parliamentarian, Oteify proceeded to discredit the proposed budget, demonstrating convincingly that it had been improperly and incompletely drawn up, and that the reason for this might be that the government was attempting to disguise its fiscal and budgetary intentions.[40] Severely discredited, Sidqy had become almost overnight a lame duck whom Sadat could dismiss at will.

In the end, the timing of Sidqy's dismissal was determined by yet another round of demonstrations and strikes. November and December had witnessed at least one attempted coup, a purge of the military and dismissal of Minister of War Sadeq, pro- and anti-Sadat students fighting on campus, and outbreaks of Coptic-Moslem hostility. Then in January a new wave of violence swept the campuses with students at the faculty of engineering again in the forefront. Classes were suspended for a month, and on February 4, the day universities were reopened, Sadat employed the ASU to purge the media. The Disciplinary Committee expelled sixty-four journalists from the political organization, thereby depriving them of the right to practice their professions.[41] While the president defended this step in a hard-line speech to the Assembly, the first secretary of the ASU, Marei, kept his own counsel and quietly slipped out of the country a short time later, staying abroad for almost a month. Sadat had crossed his Rubicon and in so doing rendered Marei's role in the ASU completely superfluous. Sidqy's turn could not be far off. On March 26 Sadat struck, taking over himself as prime minister while simultaneously replacing Marei with Muhamed Ghanem. Sadat defended his action, declaring:

> The people see how people abroad are talking about the struggle between the government and the ASU, between the ASU and the government, between the People's Assembly and the ASU, and between the People's Assembly and the government. In a state of institutions this is not possible, otherwise it would be a state of contradiction, not of institutions.[42]

Several days later, Ihsan Abd al Quddous, editor of *Akhbar al Yom,* struck a similar note while explaining the cause of the latest reshuffles. He stated that the differences between the government and the ASU had reached the point at which there were two governments in Egypt: the official government and the government of the Socialist Union, each ignoring the other in its actions. . . . There came a time when the principal forces destroying the government and its decisions came from within the Socialist Union and the principal forces weakening the Socialist Union and hampering its popular capabilities were from within the government. . . . No doubt all this was the responsibility of the persons in leadership and was commensurate with their motivation of personal ambitions.[43]

On March 31 it was announced that Sidqy and Marei would become advisors to the president. For Sidqy this meant political obscurity. Realizing his fate, he quietly set up a consulting agency, with his primary client being Fiat, the automobile manufacturer he had invited into Egypt when minister of industry. Marei, on the other hand, did not miss a beat in his busy round of political activities. Having already embarked on a campaign of mobilizing world support for Egypt's cause while first secretary, he simply carried on in his new capacity as presidential advisor. But neither Sidqy nor Marei was about to forget this epic struggle or forgive his adversary. To this day they refuse to see one another.

DIPLOMAT EXTRAORDINAIRE

Marei's dismissal as first secretary and appointment as advisor to the president simply formalized his extrication from a role in managing domestic politics, a task which Sadat assumed himself. Having in the previous months gradually shifted his attention from domestic to foreign affairs, Marei was now charged specifically with preparing the Arab World for the coming war with Israel. This he did by traveling throughout the region and by receiving visiting delegations, a function he performed in his eleventh-floor office in the ASU building, which he formerly had occupied as first secretary. Lest there be any doubt as to who was the more powerful, the new first secretary, Muhamed Hafiz Ghanem, was installed in a less desirable office on a lower floor.

The climax of Marei's nascent diplomatic career was to come only some six months after it was launched. On the evening of October 7, 1973, the day after Egypt initiated its attack across the

Suez Canal, Sadat summoned Marei to his headquarters and charged him with heading a mission to the Arab oil-exporting countries in order to "coordinate strategy." Sadat wisely refrained from placing specific demands on the Arabs, leaving it to the Saudis, Kuwaitis, Bahreinis, and so on, to calculate moral obligations and political considerations in barrels per day and dollars. Marei, who had previously called for pressure to be applied to the West in the form of economic boycotts and sanctions, but who had little familiarity with the world of oil, went immediately to Heykal for advice. With the cooperation of Mustafa Khalil, who under the auspices of *al Ahram's* Center for Strategic Studies had been analyzing options for the use of the oil weapon, and with the assistance of former Prime Minister Mahmoud Fawzy and Heykal himself, Marei determined that total cessation of exports to the West would be self-defeating. The group concurred that the optimal strategy was one which would punish individual Western nations but would not push them to the brink. With this strategy in mind, and occupying a powerful bargaining position by virtue of Egypt's military success and Sadat's instructions, Marei departed Cairo on the morning of October 10 for Riyadh,[44] accompanied by his personal physician Ali Aissa, by Mustafa Khalil, Nasser's son-in-law Ashraf Marawan, and General Saad Qadi.

Marei executed the strategy brilliantly. The linchpin was King Feysal and Saudi Arabia, for the response by Riyadh would determine those of the other oil-exporting countries on the Peninsula. With his enthusiasm stimulated by General Qadi's optimistic appraisal of the course of the war, Feysal offered an oil-production cutback of 10 percent, arms supplies, and $100 million to Egypt. Marei accepted the offer, suggesting that a 5 percent cutback might be sufficient at the outset. But Marei, mindful of the disastrous state of the Egyptian economy, was disappointed with the amount of financial assistance offered, although he did not violate the protocol of Feysal's *maglis* by appearing ungrateful or by bargaining. Following the interview, Rashed Pharaon, an advisor to King Feysal, accompanied the Egyptian delegation to the doorsteps of Feysal's palace, where he asked Marei if he was satisfied with the $100 million. Marei responded in the negative, commenting that the war in the Sinai was costing Egypt $10 million an hour. Pharaon reported back to Feysal, who immediately telephoned Marei at his guest palace to inform him that the amount would be increased to $400 million. With the bargain thus struck, the delegation left for Kuwait and the Lower Gulf, where the ruling sheikhs, apprised by Feysal of Saudi Arabia's contribution, had little choice but to match the ante in terms relative to their own oil production and revenues. Marei thus returned to Cairo triumphantly, having secured immediate financial assistance well in excess of half a billion dollars and a commitment from Feysal et al. to use the oil weapon.[45]

Having established himself as a statesman of the first rank in the Arab World, and known as one of Sadat's intimates, Marei's visibility as a prominent Egyptian diplomat came at a time when the attention of the Middle East and of the world was focused on Egypt. In December 1973, he accompanied Sadat to the Arab summit meeting in Algiers, and in the following month he was at Sadat's side during the Aswan round of disengagement negotiations.

But it was not in Sadat's interest for Marei to become too prominent. He wanted to utilize Marei's skills in such a way that Marei's accomplishments as a diplomat and political leader would not distract attention from his own. For his part, Marei, having tasted success as a diplomat on the world stage, was keen to operate in a capacity in which he could formulate policy rather than just implement it. The opportunity for both to realize their goals came in January 1974, when Marei, riding the wave of Arab diplomatic success caused by Egypt's and Syria's performance in the October War, won endorsement from the Third World for the position of secretary general of the World Food Conference.

HEAD OF THE WORLD FOOD CONFERENCE AND WORLD FOOD COUNCIL

The World Food Conference, and the World Food Council that emerged from it, were the United Nations' answers to the food crisis of 1972–74, when adverse weather conditions caused crop failures in Asia and drought ravaged the Sahel. World grain reserves were reduced to less than one-month's supply. Grain prices tripled, and food aid to the poorest countries dwindled as malnutrition and starvation threatened their populations. The nonaligned countries in their September 1973 meeting in Algiers adopted a resolution calling for an international conference on food. A month later the U.N. General Assembly voted to convene in Rome a World Food Conference for November 5 to 16, 1974.

The Third World's demand for a review of the world food system and for a modification of it was gathering momentum just as the Arabs successfully demonstrated that they could stand up to the West economically and to its surrogate in their region militarily. Having dramatically improved their terms of trade at the expense of the West, the Arabs were viewed as the ideal choice to spearhead the drive to achieve a better and more egalitarian system for the distribution of the world's most vital commodity—food. It was altogether natural then for the U.N. General Assembly in January 1974 to nominate Sayed Marei, the Arab World's most prominent agronomist, to be secretary general of the forthcoming conference.

Marei, who in 1969 had been offered a U.N. post but who had been forced by Nasser to turn it down, was this time encouraged by his president to accept the offer. Sadat was to continue as prime minister for almost a year following the war and to rule more or less dictatorially, so he had little need of Marei's skills in the domestic arena. Moreover, it was advantageous for Sadat to have Marei serving as head of the highly visible World Food Conference. His presence there would demonstrate Egypt's leading position in the Middle East and the Third World, which in turn would help establish Sadat's credentials in the nonaligned movement. Also, by enhancing Egypt's status, Marei would in turn strengthen Sadat's hand in the negotiations with Israel, upon which he had just embarked. As if to symbolize the fact that Marei had been promoted and that their friendship was thus on a new and higher level, Sadat and Marei announced on January 24, 1974, the engagement of Noha, the president's daughter by his second wife, Jihan, to Marei's youngest son, Hassan.

If Sadat's calculations of the personal and national benefits to be derived from Marei's occupancy of the role of secretary general of the World Food Conference were more or less as outlined here, then he had every reason to be pleased with the outcome. Marei performed his task brilliantly, causing the spotlight to focus on him and the demands of the Third World. Choosing to interpret his role in a political rather than bureaucratic context, he succeeded in putting First World food exporting countries on the defensive and in preventing the FAO bureaucracy, threatened by the creation of the World Food Conference outside its jurisdiction, from subverting his or the conference's aims.[46] While he did not succeed in creating a World Food Authority, which would have deprived food-exporting countries of their unilateral control over the distribution of foodstuffs, that was an extremely ambitious goal, impossible of achievement given Third World food importers' relative lack of mobilizable political resources. He did, however, skillfully utilize this goal as a bargaining counter to trade off against the attainment of politically more practicable solutions, such as the creation of the International Fund for Agricultural Development (IFAD), for which a contribution of $200 million from the United States was obtained, and the World Food Council.[47]

From the outset, Marei defined his role as being an active proponent of a specific program rather than a neutral chairman. At his speech to the inaugural meeting of the committee established to prepare the conference which was held in Rome on February 11, 1974, Marei proposed an agenda focused on his major concerns. These were stimulating food production in less-developed countries (LDCs) through the provision of capital and technology; increasing food aid to the LDCs; and creating a world system for grain storage over which both producers and consumers would share authority, thereby depriving the leading exporting countries of their unilateral control over world grain supplies.[48] Better to achieve these goals, Marei converted the conference's secretariat from an apolitical, neutral administrative organ into a politicized body endorsing his line. This was considered a presumptuous violation of accepted rules governing international organizations by those most opposed to Marei's proposals, chief of whom were the representatives of food-exporting countries and the FAO.[49] In the face of this combined opposition Marei had to give ground, but he nevertheless secured the essence if not the form of some of his ideas. Forced to drop the proposal for a World Food Authority to supervise an international grain stockpile, Marei readily agreed to a World Food Council to perform other follow-up tasks and to publicize the need for strengthening the world food system.[50]

Widely recognized as having performed effectively as secretary general of the conference, Marei was chosen to be president of the newly created Council. From this position he tried to incorporate his original proposals for a World Food Authority, which would have had a high degree of control over world food supplies, into the Council, thereby winning back what had been lost at the November Conference. This effort was ultimately to fail, however, for the First World, and especially the United States, refused to surrender control over food supplies. The first meeting of the Council, held in June 1975, ended in deadlock, and no official report was released. Marei then embarked on a series of trips to world capitals in an attempt to work out a compromise, but the issue was too contentious and the second meeting ended similarly deadlocked.

Cutting his losses, Marei began to devote his energies to raising funds and otherwise facilitating the establishment of IFAD,[51] and to popularizing his ideas for stimulating agricultural production in the Third World through the application of Western technology financed by petrodollars. He argued that the principal stumbling block was not capital or the lack of technical resources or capabilities, but the absence of political will. In 1975 he published in Arabic with Saad Hagrass *If the Arabs Want,* a book in which they argue that the Arab World could be converted into a food-surplus region if only political leaders would take the necessary steps to do so.[52] A similar message was conveyed in his *The World Food Crisis,* published the same year in English.[53] Marei reiterated this theme in numerous speeches and interviews during and after his term as president of the World Food Council, but by 1977 his emphasis began to change from a collaborative effort to solve the world food problem to greater self-reliance on the part of Third World and especially Arab countries.[54] In an interview given shortly after being replaced as president of the Council, Marei stated:

> I see that the solution to the food problem in the future is in the hands of the Third World. It is about time that they do not depend in every step they take upon outside help. . . . So I stress the importance of holding a conference of the countries of the Third World where they can meet, discuss their problems, and exchange their skills. . . . We should apply the motto of the Chinese: To work by ourselves for ourselves.[55]

He began also to shift his emphasis on international financing for Third World development to Arab financing for Arab agricultural development, lauding the efforts of the Arab Authority for Agricultural Investment and Development, an agency of the Arab Fund for Economic and Social Development which began an ambitious development program in the Sudan in 1977.[56] These modifications of his original position, which had tended to focus on international efforts to deal with the world food crisis but which now emphasized the role of the Third World and Arab World more specifically, may reflect his mounting frustration with collaborative efforts in the form of the World Food Council and IFAD.

It would hardly be surprising if by 1977 Marei was exasperated with the intransigence of OECD countries within IFAD and the World Food Council and had become embittered as a result of their attitude toward him. Despite his frequent appeals to prevent the bureaucratization of the World Food Council and its transformation into yet another lethargic satrapy of international bureaucrats,[57] this was precisely what was happening, and it, he may have reasoned, was entirely the fault of OECD countries. For their part, they had tired of Marei's constant prodding, and word was sent out through the foreign services of numerous OECD countries that Marei should not receive support for reelection in the third meeting of the council, which was to be held in Manila in June 1977. One reason given was that he had refused to devote himself full-time to his job as president, having resumed an active role in Egyptian politics even before serving as secretary general in the November 1974 World Food Conference.[58] Despite the growing momentum to oust him, Marei announced his intention on March 11 to nominate himself for reelection.[59] During the next two months the Egyptian Foreign Ministry lobbied actively on his behalf, but by mid-May it was clear that the OECD countries remained opposed to him and that sufficient votes therefore could not be obtained. On May 12 he announced his decision to withdraw his candidacy for the post.[60] At the June meeting he was succeeded by Arturo Tanco, the Filipino minister of agriculture.

The curious paradox was that Marei, considered by many in Egypt to be "a feudalist and a capitalist," had become a leading spokesman for the grievances of the Third World against the First. His political outlook and personal style were such that he saw his role as stimulating negotiations so that the world food crisis could be resolved in a way beneficial both to food importers and to exporters. He assumed that the developed countries could be made to perceive the situation in similar terms—that they would realize that the gains from the export of technology would offset any losses due to a decrease in food exports. It must have come as a shock, therefore, for him to discover that he could not transcend the structural context and induce the participants to view the solution to the conflict in the non-zero-sum way that he did. Unaccustomed to being forced into political dead ends and failing in important missions, he must have come away from the presidency of the council with at least partially changed attitudes. The fact that his subsequent comments made reference to the Chinese model suggests that he had lost considerable faith in the possibility of adopting workable cooperative solutions to world problems.

Whatever Marei's thoughts were on the fundamental nature of the world political system, he did not have the luxury of time to contemplate this or other semimetaphysical issues. During almost the entirety of his career as an international politician-bureaucrat, he had simultaneously been supervising the most ambitious political change undertaken in Egypt since Nasser had consolidated his rule in the early 1950s. As the speaker of the People's Assembly, Marei was overseeing the political liberalization that Sadat had embarked upon in 1974. By the early summer of 1977, that liberalization had reached a critical phase. How that had come to be, and what happened subsequently, are the subjects of Chapter 10.

10 | SPEAKER OF THE PEOPLE'S ASSEMBLY

POLITICAL LIBERALIZATION

In the wake of the October War, Sadat resumed the campaign of liberalization which he had begun in early 1972 but had completely terminated by the spring of 1973 in order to stifle rising discontent and to prepare the country for war. His decision to pick up where he had left off resulted from a variety of motives. He seemed personally to prefer a system more open than that which had been established by Nasser, although his commitment to democracy did not take precedence over his desire to keep a firm grip on the reins of power. Presumably his calculations were that liberalization would make ruling easier, especially in that as "the hero of the crossing" he had won considerable legitimacy. By elevating himself to the position of supreme arbiter, he could observe the political battles played out beneath him, intervening occasionally to ensure desired outcomes.

Foreign policy considerations must also have played a role in his decision to liberalize. His approach to the West, and to the United States in particular, required that at least a facade of democracy be erected. This need was further enhanced by his strategy of attempting to win U.S. support for Egypt in her negotiations with Israel and, more generally, to make Egypt the United States' most favored Arab nation. Another contributing factor was that as his war of words with the Arab states escalated as Egypt moved gradually but unmistakably in the direction of a separate peace with Israel, Sadat could embarrass opposing Arab heads of state whose domestic positions were far too precarious to permit political liberalization, a fact to which he gleefully drew attention.

In that Sadat's commitment to liberalization was based more on tactical than normative considerations, there were limits on how far he would go in support of it. These limits were eventually reached in the late spring of 1978, when the New Wafd, having reemerged from the dustbins of history, in combination with the Nasserite left and Islamic fundamentalists, threatened to encroach upon Sadat's domain as exclusive policy formulator. By that time the liberalization campaign had roller-coastered through several ups and downs. In the first phase, which lasted from the spring of 1974, when Sadat issued his October Paper devoted to a restrictive definition of liberalization, until July 1975, when at the ASU General National Congress he announced that *minabar* (literally pulpits, but meaning "proto-parties"; singular = *minbar*) would be allowed to form within the ASU, the thrust of liberalization was much as it had been in the first half of 1972. The institution earmarked to implement the reform remained the ASU, this choice implying careful control of the pace and sequence of events—a liberalization from the top down. But by 1974–75, the articulate public could not be mollified by such half-hearted measures, so Sadat was forced to press the liberalization forward. Following his announcement in July 1975 that *minabar* could be created, the liberalization process temporarily faltered, as if no one knew how to respond to the offer or whether it was to be taken seriously or not. Then, in late October, the pace suddenly and dramatically accelerated, as one group after another declared the formation of their *minabar*. By January 1976 the total of registered *minabar* exceeded forty, a far too large and unwieldy collection on which to base the newly liberalized polity. A Committee of *Minabar* under Marei's chairmanship was then formed to rationalize the situation, and in the spring of 1976 the forty-plus *minabar* that had been fed into the committee were ground out as left, right, and center *minabar,* with the government clearly identified with the center *minbar* and the prime minister acting as its leader. The stage was thus set for the October 1976 parliamentary elections, which were hotly contested by the three *minabar* and by independents. The government desisted from open manipulation of voting but used all administrative leverage possible to ensure a resounding victory for the center *minbar.* [1] Emerging from these elections confident of his ability to stage-manage a more open political system, Sadat declared immediately after the elections that the *minabar* would be converted into political parties and that other parties could be formed once parliament passed the necessary legislation.

The president's faith in liberalization was to be tested almost immediately thereafter. On January 18 and 19, 1977, the worst riots since the final months of King Farouk wracked Cairo and other parts of the country, leading Sadat to crack down on the formal and informal oppositions, expel a leading deputy from the Assembly, and ram through a referendum demanding drastic penalties for political agitators. But Sadat was still willing to give liberalization a chance, albeit within a carefully circumscribed framework. This framework took the form of the new law for political parties, approved by parliament in mid-June 1977. Sadat had, however, seriously underestimated the degree of hostility to his rule and the desire of opposition politicians to organize. Despite heavy-handed government intimidation, the New Wafd, the Islamic right, and the Unionist Progressives—the leftist party headed by former Free Officer Khaled Muhi al Din—began to challenge not only domestic policy but also, and more important, Sadat's handling of foreign affairs and his decision to go to Jerusalem and embark on a separate peace with Israel. In the spring of 1978, Sadat cast about for a way to contain his critics, and when the kid-gloves approach failed to achieve the desired results, he resorted to the mailed fist. As the New Wafd receded into history once again and the left and the right were muzzled, Sadat announced the creation of what was in effect the president's own party, rife with implications for those who failed to join.

During this dramatic four-year period, Sayed Marei, despite his commitment to the World Food Conference and then the World Food Council, played a decisive role. Sadat laid out general guidelines for the liberalization, and Marei, acting in various capacities but chiefly as speaker of the Assembly, provided the operational definitions. As the implementor of the liberalization policy, Marei defined for himself a role as a middleman, or bridge, between the president and the various constituencies vying for power and influence in the now rapidly changing system. This role had at least two different facets, or subroles. First, as a recognized spokesman for the president, Marei set the limits of debate and action acceptable with regard to specific issues. In this capacity he acted as a surrogate president in the hurly-burly of day-to-day politics, enabling Sadat thereby to project an image of Olympian grandeur and removal from the dirty business of political maneuvering. Marei thus had the tough job of rejecting specific demands and forcing recalcitrant and ambitious politicians to accept restraints on their activities. In that this subrole was performed in a formal manner in public settings, it required Marei to toe the Sadat line to the last inch. Thus Marei's speeches, his press interviews, and his pronouncements from the speaker's chair or other platforms all demanded complete support for Sadat and identified Marei with presidential preferences and positions. In the public record, Marei followed Sadat's line through all its twists and turns, backtrackings, and contradictions.

But the public record, reflecting as it does but one facet of Marei's role as a middleman, is a misleading and incomplete guide to his thoughts and less-public political behavior. If Marei had only echoed Sadat's opinions he would have been ineffective, for it is not enough just to announce policies—they have to be sold to reluctant politicians. In private, therefore, Marei had to have room to maneuver, to admit frankly that he did not agree with thus and so, to give a different interpretation of events than that formally endorsed by the president, and so on. In short, Marei had to win politicians' confidence if he was to convince them to accept Sadat's policies. To do that he had to concede in private at least some points against Sadat and his policies, and occasionally to indicate his strong support for oppositional criticism.

This bargaining should not be seen as mere political salesmanship. Marei, in fact, was not in 100 percent agreement with the president and did not want to think of himself as simply the implementor of someone else's policies. But he could not affect policy by opposing it openly or he would quickly lose his job, so he did not. What he did do was signal his opposition to strategically placed members of the political elite, who thus informed of potential support could then go on to mobilize further opposition to policies which Sadat had endorsed. In that this method of influence-wielding was subtle and semisecretive, it was only active members of the political elite who were even aware that it was taking place. The general public saw the first subrole—that of Marei defining the limits of debate and opposition—but not the second. For most of those on the periphery of the political system, therefore, Marei was nothing more than an apologist for the regime, totally aligned with the president and willing to sublimate his own preferences in deference to those of Sadat. Within the elite, however, Marei's image was different, for active politicians perceived the nuances of his behavior and many adjusted theirs accordingly. Within this context he was, and still is, considered a liberal or progressive and one frequently at odds with the president. His intraelite alliances, which during and after the 1974–78 period have included such odd bedfellows as Marxists who were imprisoned by Nasser, and which are based on the ties discussed in Part One and on sheer tactical considerations, defy analysis based exclusively on the public record and conceptualized in single analytical categories.

MAREI AS SURROGATE PRESIDENT

In this facet of his middleman role, Marei reiterated Sadat's position and frequently elaborated on it. In some cases this led him to argue publicly against policies which he was known in private to support. With regard to foreign policy, for example, he followed the president's zigs and zags faithfully, constantly arguing that Egypt had not and would not abandon the Arabs and stood fast with them against the Israeli threat. As coordinator of the oil embargo, as one of Egypt's main contacts with Arab states, and as a former close associate of Muhamed Hassanein Heykal, widely known for his pro-Arab opinions, Marei was committed personally and ideologically to close relations with those states. But this did not prevent him from giving a ringing endorsement to the Sinai II negotiations in his speech to the Assembly on his reelection as speaker in October 1975.[2] Even when Sadat announced his intention of going to Jerusalem in November 1977, Marei immediately endorsed that decision.[3] He also secured the Assembly's support for Sadat's initiative, while preventing disgruntled M.P.s from using that arena to air their grievances. Instead of convening the Assembly to discuss the trip, Marei held a meeting in his office of "the Assembly Bureau and the bureaus of the parliamentary committees," or, in other words, the leaders of the Center Party in parliament, none of whom would dare speak out against the president's action. This intimate group issued a statement on November 19 in the name of the Assembly stating that it "stood behind President Anwar al Sadat and blessed his peace initiative."[4] It was not until well after Sadat had returned from Jerusalem that the Assembly as a whole was permitted to debate the trip and then the press refrained from publishing the most scathing indictments offered by M.P.'s.[5]

Marei's public utterances on formal political opposition are like a barometer of Sadat's feelings on the issue, moving gradually between 1974 and 1977 in the direction of favoring parties. On November 1, 1974, just one week after his election as speaker of the Assembly, Marei stated to students of Alexandria University:

> There has been talk about the formation of one or two parties or an opposition. Opposition is necessary in the People's Assembly so as to listen freely to all points of view. However, I can't imagine that we will endeavor to create an opposition or sit down and say "let's have parties."[6]

Six months later, after he had served as chairman of the Quartet Committee, which had been formed by Sadat for the purpose of working out some formula for political opposition within the ASU, Marei was asked by an *al Ahram* reporter about opposition within the assembly. He replied that "shifting opposition," by which he meant opposition by different deputies to different issues, existed and was permissible, but he took pains to ridicule "fixed opposition," linking it to the negative experience with parties in the ancien régime.[7]

At the end of 1975 and a week after he had been nominated by Sadat to preside over the Committee of 100,* Marei began to set the limits for the upcoming discussions by cautioning against excessive optimism about the future of independent political organizations. In the opening session on February 2, 1976, when asked whether the decisions of the committee would be resolutions with the effect of law or would simply be proposals, Marei responded that they would be the latter and would be forwarded to Sadat for his consideration.[8] In an interview three days later, Marei reaffirmed that "the decisions of the Committee on the Future of Political Work are not obligatory because they are proposals which will be presented to the president."[9] When asked by the editor of the Kuwaiti newspaper *al Qabas,* just before the committee issued its report, whether he agreed to the establishment of parties, Marei responded, "No. The general trend is against establishing parties for the time being."[10]

Once the framework for the fall parliamentary elections had been established by the report of the Committee on the Future of Political Work, political discussion began to focus on various procedural issues. The opposition, which depending on the issue included a heterogeneous grouping of independents and members of

---

*Later referred to as the Committee of *Minabar* and finally renamed by Marei, who was anxious to imply as broad a mandate as possible, the Committee on the Future of Political Work.

the left and right *minabar,* demanded that the country be redistricted prior to the election in order to correct the underrepresentation of urban areas. Marei, in a question-and-answer session following a speech to graduating seniors of the Alexandria University faculty of medicine, responded to a question about redistricting by saying that he preferred no change in districts at that time, "so that it won't be said that they are being prepared for someone in particular."[11] Proportional representation was put forward by the left as another means to ensure a more accurate reflection of the popular and especially the urban vote in the composition of the Assembly. Marei similarly opposed this and defended single-member districts favorable to high status rural notables such as himself, "for all the people find that direct elections are the way by which an individual practices his freedom in the election of his representative."[12] When it was then demanded that the government of Prime Minister Mamdouh Salem, since it was now also the core of the Center Organization, be replaced by a neutral caretaker government to supervise the elections, Marei responded:

> There is no reason to fear that the government is manipulating the elections, despite the presence of candidates from it. What happens in the whole world is that the existing government runs the elections. In England the Labour Government ran the elections and the Labour Party lost.[13]

Having won all the struggles over electoral laws and procedures, the government then issued a military order on September 14, two days before the official beginning of the election campaign, in order to deal with the politically sensitive issue of key money charged tenants by owners of apartments.[14] The most significant provisions of the order called for stiff fines for violations of the existing law against charging key money and imposed a tax on income from apartments. Its purpose was to defuse the volatile housing issue just prior to the election, but given the government's stated intention of liberalizing and establishing a state of institutions under the rule of law, issuing a military order was a provocative act that seemed to make a mockery of government promises. Furthermore, in that the constitution called for the Assembly to pass on all tax matters, it appeared to be unconstitutional. As speaker of the Assembly, Marei might have been expected to defend his institution's constitutional prerogative, but he did not. While he was not conspicuous in his support of the military order, he did defend it when asked his opinion by a journalist, saying,

"The Constitution allows this because we are in a state of war. This [military order] will be exhibited to the next People's Assembly at the beginning of its session in the form of a draft law together with the new proposed tax law."[15] As it turned out, the tax bill passed in that session included the provisions of the military order, but the legislation was vetoed by Sadat.

Marei's indefatigable defense of the Sadat line on foreign policy and on the policy of liberalization was not unique. Whatever the issue, if Marei chose to speak publicly on it, he supported the president and his regime. With regard to the general issue of corruption, for example, Marei steadfastly defended the record of the parliament in investigating numerous allegations, although that body, crippled by various restrictions of its investigatory powers, failed to turn up incriminating evidence in a single case. When *al Akhbar's* Gamal al Hamamsy pointed out the Assembly's failings in this regard and suggested that the parliament enhance its investigatory powers by seeking the assistance of appropriate executive and judicial agencies, Marei responded in an open letter to the press that the implementation of this proposal would violate the independence of the legislative branch and that the record of the Assembly was in any case above reproach.[16] Similarly, when the New Wafdists, Independents, and the Unionist Progressives (the left party) criticized the government's ill-fated commando raid on Cyprus in February 1978, which had been intended to kill or capture the guerrillas responsible for the death of Yusuf al Sibai, chairman of the board of *al Ahram,* but which had ended in disaster, Marei defended the mission.[17]

As interpreter of the president's will to the public, Marei clearly acted as a brake on criticism and as a bulwark against attempts to democratize the system faster and further than Sadat desired. In this regard he was indistinguishable from other hardline men of the regime, such as Mamdouh Salem. But his comparatively higher visibility and his known intimacy with Sadat, cemented by the marriage tie, made Marei in the public mind Sadat's number-one associate and apologist. Yet Marei was not content with the role of spokesman for and defender of the president, as several other politically less adroit individuals quite obviously were. Marei's progressive inclinations, his confidence in his own powers of reasoning and debate, and his ambition to rise ever higher, indeed to the top of the Egyptian political pyramid, led him to court public opinion while simultaneously taking the hard line against any challenges to presidential authority.

CONSTITUENCY POLITICS

Despite the liability of close association with the president and his frequently unpopular policies, Marei attempts constantly to cultivate ties to powerful constituencies, regardless of their attitude toward him. The Islamic right, for example, has long been distrustful of Marei, whom they accurately look upon as a secularist. As speaker of the Assembly, he and the even more ardent secularist, Deputy Speaker Gamal Oteify, frequently teamed up to head off attempts to provide official legal sanction for various provisions of Islamic law, such as that prohibiting the consumption of alcohol.[18] In the late summer of 1977, when the Egyptian and Sudanese parliaments held a series of joint meetings in Cairo, Marei was particularly hard put to withstand the challenge of Islamic fundamentalists, reinforced as they were by a large delegation from the Sudan. Preferring to avoid head-on confrontation, he professed sympathy for their demands for implementation of the *sharia* (Islamic law), but he cautioned that this was not the time for such action. In that Egypt was passing through a delicate stage in negotiations with Israel and desperately needed the support of Western countries to pressure the Jewish state, Marei counseled deputies that it would not be wise to veer in a fundamentalist direction, for this would inevitably be given the wrong interpretation in the Christian West and would provide ammunition for Egypt's enemies.[19] Several years earlier, while first secretary of the ASU, Marei had made a point of going on the pilgrimage lest he be accused of being an atheist socialist. He had at that time also laced his speeches with religious imagery.[20]

As the Islamic resurgence continued to gain ground through the 1970s, Marei intensified his contacts with the religious establishment, meeting frequently with the Sheikh al Azhar and throwing his support behind a project to open a branch of al Azhar University in Sharqiya's capital of Zagazig. He also endorsed the call for courses in Islamic studies to be required for graduation from universities, and at the end of January 1977 Marei volunteered to meet with al Azhar students who were threatening to strike over various issues.[21] Throughout the period, Marei continued to attend Friday mosque services in the company of the president and/or other dignitaries and to be widely seen and photographed for the front pages of Cairo's dailies while doing so.

Despite these activities, Marei did not succeed in alleviating the suspicion felt toward him by many on the Islamic right. Among his most formidable opponents in the Assembly, for example, were

Moslem fundamentalist deputies from Upper Egypt. That Marei felt threatened by Islamic fundamentalists is suggested by his lamentation to a Kuwaiti reporter that he and Sadat were frequently exposed to the attacks of *imams* (Islamic clergymen) in their Friday speeches.[22] But despite lingering bad relations between himself and fundamentalists, Marei never abandoned his efforts to keep lines of communication open to this constituency of increasing political importance.

He applied the same principle to another significant constituency which was predisposed to distrust him. From early 1972, when he had assumed the post of first secretary of the ASU, until his departure from the speaker's chair of the Assembly in October 1978, Marei was a frequent target of students' hostility toward the regime. As head of the ASU he was ridiculed by student leaders as "a feudalist and a capitalist."[23] During student and worker demonstrations in 1975, and again in 1977, demonstrators protesting the high price of commodities chanted, "Sayed Bey, Sayed Bey, kilo lahmah bi etnein gineh" (Sayed Bey, Sayed Bey, a kilo of meat for £E2). In the riots of January 18–19, 1977, as student protestors converged on the Assembly building, Marei appeared briefly on a balcony. Observing him there, the students shouted, "There's the thief." Always sensitive about his image, Marei tried to dissuade the correspondent for the American news magazine *Time* from filing the story. When that failed, Marei's chief assistant contacted the magazine's foreign editor, demanding the story be retracted, a demand which was rejected.[24]

Unlike other members of the presidential entourage, Marei refused to let taunts by students prevent him from maintaining as close contact as possible with this amorphous but potentially powerful constituency. In the tense winter months of 1974–75, when students took to the streets to protest deteriorating economic conditions and the failure of the government to deliver on its promise of liberalization, Marei embarked on a series of meetings with students. In his public statements on demonstrations, he was careful to point out that students had real grievances. He implied that the situation which had given rise to violence was the fault of the government (i.e., Prime Minister Hegazy) for mishandling the economic open-door policy and the fault of the ASU (i.e., First Secretary Muhamed Hafiz Ghanem) for failing to provide channels through which complaints could be expressed.[25] While this conciliatory tone resulted to some degree from Marei's intention to unseat Prime Minister Hegazy and undermine First Secretary Ghanem, it was typical in any case for him to placate students. In the wake of the 1977 riots, for example, he accompanied his professions of sympathy for demonstrators' complaints with numerous formal and informal meetings with students and faculty members.

The favorable impression of Marei held by many who are self-declared enemies of the president is especially common among those on the left. In the Heykal camp in the Nasser era, Marei established numerous contacts with leftist intellectuals, and especially those associated with al Ahram publishing house. In subsequent years, Marei has been careful not to let those contacts wither. Over the years he and Lutfi al Kholi, former editor of the leftist monthly *al Tali'a,* have socialized regularly. In the wake of the January 18–19, 1977, riots, Sadat sacked al Kholi and vilified him in a televised speech, saying that no atheist (i.e., al Kholi) could be editor of a mass media journal. Al Kholi, not wishing to embarrass Marei, ceased visiting him at his home or office, but they maintained contact over the telephone.[26] Marei also keeps lines of communication open to the younger generation of leftist intellectuals entrenched in the media. He intervened with Sadat to have released from jail Muhamed Salmawi, a journalist at *al Ahram* and son of one of Marei's *shilla* partners from the 1937 class of the faculty of agriculture. Salmawi, long a friend of Marei's, had been arrested following the January 1977 riots, allegedly for inciting them, a charge that was later dropped.[27] Self-professed Marxist at *al Tali'a* and former M.P. Abu Seif Yussef reflects the opinion held by many such individuals toward Marei. Abu Seif thinks of Marei as a progressive liberal in the Keynesian tradition and as such a person with whom a Marxist such as himself can easily strike up a working relationship.[28]

Many of those on the left also perceive Marei's policy preferences to be very close to their own. He is, for example, considered to be the most committed supporter of political liberalization within the presidential entourage. He is seen as having bravely withstood attacks from the conservative right during the 1972 ASU reforms, when Upper Egyptian M.P. Muhamed Mahmoud, later to become an important figure in the Center Party, accused him of opening the door to leftist Nasserites and Communists. The left did not hold it against Marei when he had to accept Sadat's strict limitations on ASU reform. Understanding Marei's middleman position, they appreciated his attempt, futile though it was, to pry the system open even slightly.

Another issue on which many on the left see themselves in agreement with Marei is that of the economic open-door policy. In his public utterances on the open door, Marei has taken an ambivalent position, arguing that in theory it is a good idea but that in practice it has not been correctly implemented. He has railed against those who have profited unduly from it; condemned the "boutiquification" of the economy; and criticized the government for making too many promises to the people and then failing to provide even the basics, such as inexpensive clothing and housing. And in parliament Marei has spoken against granting too many exemptions and privileges to companies operating in the free zone at Port Said. He has also pointed out that the purpose of the open door should be to stimulate investment in large productive enterprises, a line similar to that pushed by former Prime Minister Aziz Sidqy.[29]

Marei's ambivalence toward economic liberalization led by the private sector has not been lost on the left, which sees Marei as a supporter of the public sector against attacks from the extreme right. When Marei's younger brother Marei Ahmad Marei lost his post as head of the Chemical Mouassassat (Organization) when the *mouassassat* system of public holding companies was abolished in 1975, he assembled Mouassassat employees and delivered a speech in which he lashed out at the destruction of the system and its replacement by private sector "parasitical" firms importing rather than manufacturing their products in Egypt. This incident became widely known and further burnished Sayed Marei's credentials as a defender of the public sector.[30]

Yet another issue area in which Marei is seen as being in sympathy with those on the left is that of Palestine and Arab identification generally. He is known to have excellent contacts with the Palestine Liberation Organization (PLO) and to argue within the elite for Egyptian support for the Palestinian cause. Following Sadat's trip to Jerusalem and then the Camp David Accords, Marei made it known to the left that he was not in favor of a policy of abandoning the Palestinians and the Arab cause. Many interpreted Marei's retirement from the post of speaker of the Assembly in October 1978 as the direct consequence of his disagreement with Sadat over the course of Egyptian policy toward Israel. Whether correct or not, the existence of this interpretation points to general perceptions of Marei's stand on this issue.

MANEUVERING BETWEEN SADAT AND THE OPPOSITION

Another constituency with which Marei as speaker had sustained dealings were the Independents. They consisted of a mixed bag of former Wafdists, members of Misr al Fatat and the Moslem Brotherhood, and even a former member of the Revolutionary Command Council, but they nevertheless shared a desire for greater political liberty. Nineteen Independents had won election to the 1976 parliament, and in what seemed to be the springtime of freedom they were intent upon using their newly won positions to secure more concessions from the regime. To many of these Independents, Marei, with whom they had little previous experience, was initially perceived as simply a spokesman for the president and hence a brake on their efforts to liberalize. Independent Hilmy Murad, minister of education in 1968–69 and a supporter of Misr al Fatat in the ancien régime, and the husband of the sister of Ahmad Hussein, the founder of that organization, decided in 1976, just after the elections, to launch an immediate attack on Marei in the hopes of forcing further open the doors of democracy. He sent a circular to the three parties, outlining the reasons for his stated intention of voting against Marei as speaker of parliament, simultaneously forwarding a copy to *al Ahram*. Publication of the circular was delayed by the paper until Marei had completed a rebuttal, which was printed alongside Murad's indictment.[31] Murad's argument against Marei consisted of three points: (1) that there should be "renewal in leading positions," (2) that it was unconstitutional for the speaker of the Assembly to be related to the president, and (3) that to implement the rules and regulations fairly the speaker must truly be independent, whereas Marei was "from the core of the Center Organization," hence only nominally independent.

Marei's response, rather more lengthy than Murad's indictment, consisted of a mélange of red herrings, straw men, bits of misinformation, and a veiled threat against Murad. In sum, it was a masterful if crude self-defense, warning Murad that he had picked a fight with a tough and seasoned campaigner. It no doubt was intended to dissuade further such attacks. Among Marei's arguments was the following:

> If we take this principle [renewal in positions] as absolute, Dr. Murad himself would not have won in his election district, because he cannot assume that he is a new face in public life. He held presidential or professorial posts at the university, then in the ministry, and so has become, according to his definition, an old face.

The threat against Murad took this form:

> I don't want to discuss with him today what he recalls from his disagreement with Nasser, although I was one of its witnesses, because I do not want to divert this discussion from its course.

The day may come on which I will testify about this session to satisfy the truth.*

Marei went on to argue that his marriage connection to Sadat was irrelevant because his political career had not benefited from presidential support, because he had in the previous two parliamentary sessions proved his commitment to defending the Assembly's integrity, and because Egyptian law did not recognize relationships by marriage. He concluded by avoiding the sensitive issue of his connection with the Center Organization, stating evasively,

> I will not nominate myself for any position in the People's Assembly except if it is so decided by the political organizations, especially the Arab Socialist Organization [Center], which is the majority of the People's Assembly and so has the right to choose the president of the Assembly.

With that Marei had the last word, for *al Ahram* refused to publish Murad's response.

But the matter did not end there. As Marei was nominating himself for speaker in the inaugural meeting of the new parliament, Independent M.P. Ahmad Hussein Nasser was distributing inside the chamber a circular written by Hilmy Murad critical of Marei and endorsing the candidacy of Independent Mahmoud al Qadi. Called upon by Marei immediately after the elections to defend his actions, Ahmad Hussein Nasser argued that assembly rules which prohibited soliciting votes within the chamber were no longer appropriate because they had been formulated prior to the liberalization.[32] Marei responded that the circular should have been placed in M.P.s' pigeonholes in the chamber's anteroom after the beginning of the session, a suggestion to which Nasser objected on the grounds that this would have precluded M.P.s from receiving it prior to the election. Although Marei clearly had the upper hand in this contest, as was indicated by his 311 votes as opposed to Mahmoud al Qadi's 35, it was also evident that he had begun the 1976–77 parliamentary session on the wrong foot as far as the Independents were concerned.

But having revealed the tough side of his political character to Hilmy Murad, Ahmad Hussein Nasser, and the Independents more generally, Marei then proceeded in the coming months to woo them.

---

*This day did come. In his autobiography, published not quite three years later, Marei presented an account of Murad's dismissal from Nasser's cabinet which was highly unflattering of Murad and which contradicted a widely held belief that Murad had bravely and selflessly resisted Nasser's authoritarian tendencies. See *MM* (see Preface, note 3), pp. 595–600.

As Minister of Finance Abd al Moneim Qaissouny was announcing in his budget speech on January 18, 1977, that subsidies would be lifted on several basic commodities, Marei abandoned the speaker's platform for a seat next to Hilmy Murad, in so doing signaling his discontent with the measures and the fact that he had not been consulted about them. Later, when referring to the riots that broke out following Qaissouny's announcement, Marei commented that Murad had demonstrated greater political foresight and acumen than the government by immediately predicting that there would be mass demonstrations.[33]

Marei and Murad were to be forced together again by events less than a month later when Sadat, angered by a telegram sent him by Kemal al Din Hussein, protesting in intemperate language the proposed referendum designed to demonstrate support for the regime and to head off further disorders, responded by demanding that Hussein be expelled from the Assembly. Acting as a spokesman for the Independents, of which Hussein was one, Murad approached Marei to work out a compromise so that the principle of parliamentary immunity and Hussein's membership could be preserved. Not wishing to make his long-standing enemy Hussein a martyr, Marei agreed to present Sadat with Murad's compromise formula of a resolution sponsored by the Independents condemning Hussein's telegram. But the president could not be budged from his stand. So on February 14, Hussein was expelled from the Assembly, although twenty-eight deputies voted against the expulsion and a further forty-eight abstained.[34] Having attempted to assist Murad in protecting his fellow Independents, and having then distanced himself from the expulsion proceedings, leaving it to Prime Minister Mamdouh Salem to prepare and read the bill of indictment, Marei came out of the affair with an enhanced reputation among Independents.

The working arrangement bordering on a tactical if subterranean alliance between Marei, on the one hand, and Murad and Independents, on the other, was further cemented in May and June as the Assembly struggled over the law to regulate parties. The draft bill called for any new party to be approved by the Central Committee of the ASU and further required that it have the support of twenty deputies in the Assembly, not to mention several other, less contentious clauses. On May 29, following the rapid approval of the first four clauses of the bill by the automatic majority of the Center Party, the Independents, Unionist Progressives, and Socialist Liberals (rightists) walked out of the Assembly. Marei immediately repaired to the speaker's office, where he invited protesting deputies to express their opinions on the remaining clauses so that he could present their case to the leaders of the Center Party in hopes of inducing them to permit amendment of the more contentious clauses scheduled for debate. This mollified the opposition, and the Center Party was persuaded to accept some amendments, but it stood fast on the more restrictive clauses, the key one being the requirement of twenty deputies to form a new party. This in turn stimulated a second walkout on June 12, which prompted Marei to lash out at the opposition:

> There is something which must be said—that is, if the first withdrawal of the opposition from the previous session had parliamentary significance and was based on parliamentary reasons, the withdrawal that happened today in this session had no democratic meaning and is not supported by any democratic principle (applause) because a planned withdrawal is an unsound parliamentary tactic in the history of parliaments, and this is advice for all of them. If any of them thinks himself an old parliamentarian, I am older than they are in parliamentary practice by many years. . . .[35]

There were, in other words, clear limits on Marei's support for the opposition. As long as deputies remained within the guidelines of an agreement negotiated between them and the speaker, they could expect support from the chair. If, however, they transgressed and asked for more, Marei would attack them. For Hilmy Murad and others in the opposition, therefore, Marei was not a permanent ally, but he was a reasonable man with whom arrangements could be made. Political coalitions, after all, do not demand identity of views. Even though Marei was seen as being fundamentally a man of the regime and one who had as a result a tactical but not a normative commitment to democracy, he was credited by the opposition with having "political vision" and "political horizons," traits which few others at the top of the elite were assumed to possess.[36] After many months of parliamentary infighting, Hilmy Murad and most of his colleagues had come to the conclusion that Marei was by far the best they could hope for as speaker of the Assembly. When Marei ran for reelection in the fall of 1977, he was unopposed.

PATRONAGE AND POWER IN THE AGRICULTURAL SECTOR

The patronage Marei dispensed in the 1970s to his clients and *shilla* partners was, in comparison to the Nasser era, of reduced quantity and political significance. After January 1972, Marei did not occupy any formal role in the agricultural sector, hence his power of appointment was limited. Moreover, the bureaucracy itself had declined in status and power and no longer paid salaries competitive with the private sector. Another new factor was that Marei's old associates were by the mid-1970s reaching retirement age and hence were looking for nice quiet positions that paid well but did not require arduous activity on behalf of their patron. Finally, Marei was now a politician in his own right, with his presence in the elite legitimized by virtue of his activities as an ancien régime parliamentarian as much or more than by his fame as an agronomist, so his tie to the agricultural sector was not as crucial as it had been when he posed as a technocrat in the Nasser era. In that he no longer had to justify his presence in the elite by claims to technical proficiency, he had less of a need to maintain a fiefdom in the agricultural sector.

His new strategy was based on the limited goal of preventing the agricultural sector and its key positions from being used against him, as Sidqy had attempted to do in 1972. Having helped topple the Sidqy government and thus Minister of Agriculture Mustafa Gabaly, Marei proceeded to ensure that Gabaly's influence would be eradicated from the agricultural sector. When in 1975 the government of Mamdouh Salem, motivated by Salem's animosity toward Marei, threw its weight behind Gabaly's candidacy for the position of director general of the FAO, Marei demanded of Sadat that this support be withdrawn. Marei prevailed, and Gabaly, on whose behalf the Foreign Ministry had been lobbying foreign governments, was left hanging just a few votes short of victory. The Lebanese Edward Saouma went on to win the post, and Gabaly, positively enraged with Marei, sought solace in a consulting position with the Iraqi government.

With one prominent exception, Marei prevented anyone similar to Gabaly from obtaining a portfolio in the agricultural sector after 1973. Ministers of agriculture, agrarian reform, land reclamation, agricultural and industrial complexes, and Sudanese affairs, the latter having a large agricultural component, were generally either political lightweights (such as Muhamed Zaki, who served in the 1973–74 Sadat government, or Mahmoud Abd al Akhar, who was Prime Minister Hegazy's minister of agriculture) or were individuals of some political standing who were acceptable to Marei. In this second category were Osman Badran, Ibrahim Shukry, and Abd al Aziz Hussein.[37]

The one exception was Abd al Azim Abu al Atta, the only nonagronomist (he is an irrigation engineer) to hold the portfolio of

Agriculture since the ancien régime. This was sufficient in and of itself to cause Marei to oppose him, for the struggle between the Ministry of Public Works, staffed by irrigation engineers, and the Ministry of Agriculture, which employs agronomists, is a constant of Egyptian cabinet politics. In what appeared to be a clear case of the former colonizing the latter, Abu al Atta, who had been awarded the portfolio of Irrigation in Mamdouh Salem's first cabinet, was then, in violation of long-standing tradition, also given the portfolio of Agriculture in Salem's next government, formed on March 19, 1976. While Marei had in the past worked with Abu al Atta, they had never been close, in part because Abu al Atta's brother was married to the sister of Marei's long-standing enemy, Kemal al Din Hussein, and in part because Abu al Atta, former head of the High Dam Purchasing Office in Moscow, was a keen advocate of land reclamation. Aware of Abu al Atta's positive and Marei's negative position on this issue, and cognizant of Sadat's increasing interest in reclamation, Salem saw the ambitious Abu al Atta as an ideal minister of agriculture. Salem was further aware that Marei and other agronomists' complaints against Abu al Atta as an irrigation engineer could be offset by the fact that he hailed from Sadat's home province of Menoufiya. The president had a reputation for assisting fellow Menoufiyans.

Abu al Atta did not disappoint his prime minister. He immediately launched an aggressive publicity campaign in favor of reclaiming vast tracts of desert while simultaneously developing ties with top-ranking employees in his new fiefdom. The most crucial relationship was with Salah al Abd, whom Abu al Atta promoted from first under secretary in the Ministry of Land Reclamation (which is a ministry in name only) to be first under secretary in the far more prestigious Ministry of Agriculture. Al Abd's central importance to ministers in the agricultural sector results from the fact that he is the Egyptian director of the World Food Program, which in recent years has been donating annually some $12 million to Egypt. Marei had first appointed him to this key position and had also appointed his cousin and his brother to other top posts in the agricultural bureaucracy, all being relatives of his old *shilla* partner, Abd al Qader al Abd. Salah al Abd's switch to a new patron was thus disturbing to Marei, and all the more so because Abu al Atta, with seemingly limitless financing, assumed by informed observers to be coming via al Abd from the World Food Program, mounted a successful campaign for parliament in the 1976 elections.[38] Running as a member of the Center Organization from the Doqqi constituency, in which the Ministry of Agriculture is located, Abu al Atta challenged the well-known former leftist Free Officer Kemal Rifaat, whom he could not possibly have defeated in the absence of government support and ample financing. Abu al Atta, assisted by al Abd, thus entered parliament as one of Mamdouh Salem's close allies and Speaker Marei's most bitter enemies.

But as Abu al Atta was winning the election, his hold over the Ministry of Agriculture was weakening. Numerous top-ranking employees, most of whom remained loyal to Marei, were complaining ever more loudly about their new boss' lack of appropriate credentials and his use of the ministry's resources, including cars and employees' time, to say nothing of cash, to further his political career. In order to appease Abu al Atta's critics, Prime Minister Salem, in the cabinet reshuffle of early November 1976, added agronomist Abd al Aziz Hussein as minister of state for agriculture and Sudanese affairs, leaving Abu al Atta in the top spot. But this failed to mollify Marei and his loyalists in the ministry. As their protests continued, Salem had to give in. In his new cabinet, formed on February 1, 1977, Salem stripped Abu al Atta of the portfolio of agriculture, although he kept him in the cabinet as minister of irrigation.

This political minuet involving Marei, Salem, Abu al Atta, and al Abd reveals the limitations of Marei's influence in the agricultural sector after 1972. His former clients, aware that his career had propelled him beyond the level of being a mere minister, were now scrambling to make contacts with new incumbents or were retiring. Decay of Marei's influence was further hastened as a result of intra-elite conflict, for Prime Minister Mamdouh Salem was intent on reducing Marei's power across the board. The fact that Salem could impose Abu al Atta on the agricultural bureaucracy was suggestive of Sadat's support for his prime minister against Marei, and the very perception within the political elite of the president's preference was itself a valuable political resource for Salem. Marei thus had to suffer the indignity of being almost at the pinnacle of the political elite, yet being unable to defend his old satrapy.

MAREI VERSUS THE ASU

By virtue of his position as speaker of the Assembly, Marei was locked into the triangular struggle of power between himself, the first secretary of the ASU, and the prime minister. This conflict had become a basic feature of Egyptian politics after Sadat had up-graded the Assembly in 1971–72, and it remained so until the ASU was, to all intents and purposes, dissolved in the wake of the 1976 elections. After that time institutionalized conflict in the government became even more intense, since there were but two main competitors in what had become a zero-sum contest. This conflict, moreover, was not an incidental feature of the system, but was the direct result of Sadat's patrimonial necessity of dividing in order to rule.

The battle between Marei and the ASU commenced almost immediately after he assumed the post of speaker of the Assembly in October 1974, and it steadily gathered momentum through the next year and a half. Anxious to defuse the increasingly tense political situation, Sadat, in December 1974, created the so-called Quartet Committee, consisting of Marei as chairman, First Secretary of the ASU Muhamed Hafiz Ghanem, Prime Minister Hegazy, and Deputy Prime Minister and Minister of the Interior Mamdouh Salem. The job of the committee was to decide upon a means of invigorating the ASU in order to contain political activism. The composition of the committee suggested a reform of the ASU almost completely from the outside, this in itself being a violation of precedent. The added fact of Marei's chairmanship was a further insult to the organization and its first secretary, Ghanem. It was also an indication that Marei and the Assembly were gaining the upper hand.

In mid-January 1975, following another round of demonstrations by students, this time accompanied by workers, Marei submitted the committee's report. It simply echoed the suggestions of the 1972 ASU reform and Sadat's October Paper, calling for syndicates and unions to have better representation in the General Secretariat of the ASU. The facts that the report was given such little prominence at a time of serious political disorder, that Marei in his speech presenting the committee's recommendations dealt with them only after having first outlined steps being taken in the Assembly to deal with "internal conditions,"[39] and that political events had so obviously passed this lukewarm reform by—all were evidence that the ASU, at least in its historical form, was doomed and that Marei was going to attempt to place the Assembly, rather than the ASU, in charge of the liberalization.

With the players' cards now on the table the struggle intensified. In discussions to reorganize the means of control over the press, Marei pressed for reducing the role of the ASU in the about-to-be-formed Higher Council for the Press.[40] In retaliation the ASU seized all copies of *Hurriya,* a weekly which had just begun publication and which was edited by Marei's old client Muhamed Sobieh. Marei also began sniping away at the ASU's leaders, referring to their threats against various journalists and suggesting that such bellicosity resulted from an undue sensitivity on the part of ASU. He obviously took delight in contrasting the ASU's heavy-handed approach to the Assembly's tolerance of the criticism directed at it by the press.[41]

In April, Marei's strategy of undermining the ASU bore fruit. Muhamed Hafiz Ghanem was relieved of his post as first secretary and was replaced by Rifaat Mahgoub. Marei was then to succeed in isolating the ASU from its traditional leftist constituency. As 1975 wore on and it became increasingly evident that the ASU, out of motivations of institutional preservation, was dragging its heels on liberalization with regard to the formation of parties and censorship of the press, the left turned on it. In an ill-fated attempt to muzzle criticism of his organization, Rifaat Mahgoub decided to intimidate the increasingly popular *Ruz al Yussef* by imposing on it a new editor loyal to himself. The weekly fought back tenaciously, ridiculing Mahgoub and his unseemly tactics.[42] The other prominent leftist journal, *al Tali'a,* also began attacking the ASU,[43] thereby signaling its support for greater political freedoms and hence for the Assembly to assume a yet more prominent role.

With the ASU having thus contributed to its own isolation from any support base, Marei moved in for the kill. This he was to accomplish from his post as chairman of the Committee on Minabar, which had been formed at the end of 1975 outside the jurisdiction of the ASU. For First Secretary Mahgoub it was bad enough that Marei was once again in charge of an overhaul of his organization, but that Marei was also given authority to recruit non-ASU members into his committee was altogether too much. Mahgoub decided to try to subvert the committee's work. He called a series of semisecret meetings of ASU stalwarts in Cairo and Alexandria to mobilize their support in opposition to Marei and his reforms.[44]

Marei's tactics for dealing with this threat and with the larger issue of the future role of the ASU were twofold. On the one hand, he ensured that the ASU would not be able to set the agenda of his committee, declaring in the opening session on February 2 that the committee was not bound by the Report on the Development of the ASU, which his Quartet Committee had issued and which assigned to the ASU a prominent role. He also rejected an attempt to have the General Secretariat of the ASU present its views in the form of a report on "the Constitution and the parties" to the Committee.[45] Marei's other tactic was to disarm mounting opposition among ASU members to himself, his committee, and to its recommendations by assuring them that the ASU would be strengthened rather than weakened by the decision to create three principal *minabar.* On March 19 he affirmed in a speech that the establishment of *minabar* did not imply destroying the ASU, "but will strengthen it and organize opposition within it."[46] Four days later he declared that "the formation of the *minabar* will not destroy the ASU but will activate it politically and socially."[47] He went on further to assure ASU activists:

> Some of the leaders of the Socialist Union falsely believed that the *minabar* were formed at the expense of the political organization. However the *minabar* did not signal an abandonment of the Socialist Union, but were created so as to express different opinions present in the political organization. They will not deviate from the socialist line and they will not attack the Socialist Union.

Marei then intimated that the ASU would be better off with his reform than with that being demanded by others: "The *minabar* will be formed so that the Socialist Union remains, which is contrary to the goal of those who are calling for parties—and that is to get a hold on the Socialist Union."

Marei needed to allay the fears of many ASU activists in order to thwart Mahgoub's subversion of the reform. This deception, implemented successfully, made it possible to shoulder aside the ASU for the last time. The key role promised the ASU Central Committee, which was to be reinvigorated through elections to then carefully supervise the three *minabar,* never materialized. Elections were not held, and Mahgoub was dismissed from his post and replaced by Marei's old friend Mustafa Khalil. As Sadat relied increasingly on the Center Party to implement his will, the ASU became ever more anachronistic until finally, in 1978, it was completely dissolved. But it was Marei who had paved the way for that eventuality by defanging the ASU between 1974 and 1976. It was more than incidental that in so doing he gathered many of its former powers into his hands as speaker of the Assembly, thereby causing the Assembly and his position in it to become the principal foci for political activity in Egypt.

MAREI VERSUS PRIME MINISTERS HEGAZY AND SALEM

The conflict between Marei and Prime Minister Hegazy was short and sharp. Marei was just settling into his new job as speaker when he launched an attack on Hegazy as being responsible for the riots and demonstrations that rocked Egypt in January 1975. He lectured the prime minister for being insensitive to the needs of the people; for having injudiciously elevated economic principles over political realities; for having falsely inflated the hopes of the public by over-estimating the immediate benefits of the open door policy; and for failing to take even remedial steps to alleviate the most chronic problems, such as shortages of housing, food, and inexpensive clothing.[48] A much more flexible individual than former Prime Minister Sidqy, Hegazy was already beginning to doubt the wisdom of the open-door policy and may have seen some truth in Marei's criticisms. But Marei was not interested in a compromise on specific issues, for he wanted to replace Hegazy, so he threw his lot in with Salem and others who shared that goal. With Marei, Salem, and others arrayed against him, and with his obvious reluctance to adhere to Sadat's prescriptions for the economy, Hegazy had become expendable. On April 16, 1975, he was removed after having served less than six months as Egypt's prime minister.

Marei received scant reward for his labor to overthrow Hegazy. The coveted post of prime minister went to Mamdouh Salem, while the vice-presidency, which had been rumored to be going to Marei, was on April 16, the day Hegazy was sacked, awarded to Air Force General Hosni Mubarak. Sadat explained his reason for overlooking Marei as being a constitutional one:

> Those who say that [I have actually been preparing Sayyid Mar'i, the speaker of the People's Council, as my successor] simply did not read our Constitution. The only person who cannot become president of the Republic is Sayyid Mar'i. The Constitution provides that in the event of the death or resignation of the president of the Republic, the speaker of the People's Council is to supervise, within 60 days, the election of a new president. The speaker of the People's Council is banned from advancing his candidacy to the post, according to the Constitution.[49]

Denied the possibility of rising higher than prime minister, it became logical for Marei to concentrate his efforts on unseating Salem. But

Marei was locked into his struggle with the ASU at this time and did not want a two-front war. He maintained good relations with the new prime minister for almost a year, as is suggested by his lack of criticism of Salem and by his frequent comments on the good relations between the Assembly and the government. In summarizing the accomplishments of the parliamentary session which ended in late July 1975, for example, Marei observed that "there was complete cooperation between the Assembly and the government during this session."[50] In his speech to the Assembly following his reelection as speaker on October 18, 1975, Marei reaffirmed the theme of cooperation with the government:

> . . . Our Assembly is not working in a vacuum but in the heart of a living society. Thus we comprehend our role as a constitutional organization whose task is legislation and observation of the work of the cabinet on the basis of common responsibility of all the organizations and cooperation between them, and not on the basis of a struggle over authority and specializations.[51]

This was in marked contrast to his acceptance speech of the previous year, when he had lectured Prime Minister Hegazy on his responsibilities toward the Assembly and warned him that the fruits of economic development had to be distributed equally.[52] But in the fall of 1975, Marei scrupulously maintained his truce with Salem, commenting in early November after a heated discussion in the Assembly about public transportation: "We will face the problems of the people through complete cooperation between the Assembly and the government. The Assembly will help the government in solving these problems, even if it takes place in stages."[53]

This uncharacteristic cordiality between the speaker of the Assembly and the prime minister was, however, destined eventually to degenerate into the acrimony more typical of the relationship. The change, which became noticeable in the spring of 1976, was precipitated by Marei's final victory over the ASU, which freed his hands to deal with the government, and by the emergence of the three *minabar* which were to contest the fall parliamentary elections. Prime Minister Salem had been designated by Sadat as the leader of the Center Organization, which implied that were Marei to join the organization he would be in a subordinate position. It was unthinkable that Marei should join the rightist or leftist opposition, and it was generally assumed that as a man of the president, Marei had no choice but to cast his lot with the Center and thus submit to Salem's preeminence within it. But Marei wanted to avoid that outcome at all costs, so he devised a plausible justification for remaining independent. In his first clarification of the results of the deliberations of the Committee on the Future of Political Work, Marei stated that the president, the speaker of the Assembly and the first secretary of the ASU would not belong to any of the *minabar*. [54] On May 7, he issued a formal announcement that he would not join any of the organizations and that he would offer his candidacy in the coming parliamentary elections as an independent.[55] Realizing that Marei had thrown down the gauntlet, Salem assigned Abd al Azim Abu al Atta the portfolio of Agriculture in the cabinet formed following the issuing of the report by the Committee on the Future of Political Work. It was obviously to be all-out war.

Salem enjoyed much the stronger position, for he was both leader of Sadat's *minbar,* which was to become the Center Party immediately after the elections, and the prime minister. Moreover, Marei's strategy of remaining independent was too clever by half, for if parliamentary tradition demanded that the speaker be independent, so too did it require that he not play a leading political role. Marei had also to suffer the indignity of being attacked by various members of the Center Organization, who demanded that the speaker be chosen from among their ranks. He was rescued by Salem himself in what was portrayed by the prime minister as a magnanimous gesture but which probably was an act forced on Salem by Sadat. To add insult to injury, Salem recruited Saad Hagrass, one of Marei's most enduring and loyal clients, to his cause. Hagrass was awarded for his defection from his former patron with a top position in the Center Organization. The final straw for Marei was that Salem also forged an alliance with Fuad Muhi al Din, a cousin of Marei intimate Abd al Aziz Muhi al Din. As minister of state for parliamentary affairs, Fuad Muhi al Din was in direct competition with Marei for the role of liaison man between the president and the Assembly, as no doubt Sadat intended. An aggressive, politically ambitious doctor with excellent ties to the military, Fuad Muhi al Din simultaneously worked as a parliamentary whip for Salem, mobilizing Center Party members to vote as Sadat desired and in so doing greatly reducing Marei's ability to influence the course of events on the floor.

Cut off from an organizational base as a result of the creation of *minabar,* attacked in his old fiefdom of the agricultural bureaucracy by Salem's nominee Abu al Atta, and clearly losing his influence with Sadat, for how otherwise could Salem take such liberties, Marei resorted to the opposition, with whom he cultivated relations, in order to bolster his position. This strategy began to emerge more clearly in the wake of the January riots, for this massive civil disobedience provided Marei the opportunity to cast doubts on the wisdom of Salem and his minister of finance, Abd al Moneim Qaissouny. Marei's connection to the opposition was further reinforced as a result of the expulsion of Kemal al Din Hussein from the Assembly, and it was cemented by the government's crude efforts to intimidate supporters and potential supporters of opposition parties.

This last governmental tactic was adopted for the purpose of preventing any twenty deputies from banning together and forming a new party under the provisions of the 1977 parties law. In order to dissuade defectors from the Center Party, the government threatened to investigate cases of alleged electoral fraud or financial improprieties. Given the automatic majority of the Center Party in the Assembly, where such cases were to be tried, this was no idle threat. It was, moreover, directed at some of Marei's supporters. Ahmad Younis, for example, had played a role in the defeat of Prime Minister Sidqy's orchard tax in 1972 and had cooperated with Marei over the years. He intimated his intention to leave the Center for the Wafd. Without delay, the government stripped Younis of his parliamentary immunity and announced that it was reopening its dormant case against him, which was based on allegations of fraud in his capacity as head of the Federation of Cooperatives. Not in a position to protect him or others, Marei had to sit by as Salem continued to broaden his powers at the speaker's expense. Paradoxically, the public continued to think of Marei as one of the two or three most influential men in Egypt and to blame him for disliked policies.[56]

EARLY RETIREMENT

By this time, Marei's role as middleman was being seriously threatened as a result of the changing context of elite politics. Frightened by the riots of January 18–19, Sadat had forced Marei to side with him against Kemal al Din Hussein and those demanding more lenient conditions for the formation of new parties. Worse followed. The parties law, despite its various requirements and despite governmental intimidation, could not prevent the New Wafd from coming into legal existence, which it did on February 4, 1978.[57] Instead of providing a counterweight to the left, as Sadat had hoped it would, the New Wafd moved into alliance with other oppositional elements on the basis of the mutual desire for greater democracy. The domestic political scene was immediately electrified. Fuad Serag al Din, president of the New Wafd, was acclaimed at a mass rally on May 12 as "leader of the nation," an accolade formerly applied only to Saad Zaghloul and one with threatening implications for Sadat. Meanwhile the organ of the Unionist Progressives, al Ahali, tore into government policy. Sadat's adventuresome foreign policy, almost but not quite beyond the realm of open public debate, contributed greatly to the rising level of tension.

By the spring of 1978, Sadat's liberalization had reached the point of no return. Either the newly created and relatively open system could be permitted to operate as it had been designed, in which case there was a chance that the New Wafd or some other party or coalition of parties might someday have to be allowed to form a government, or Sadat could crack down and revert to authoritarian rule. In late March he signaled his intentions. The Center Party, acting on the president's behalf, demanded that Wafdist deputy Sheikh Ashour Muhamed Nasr be expelled from parliament. Sheikh Ashour had lost his temper in the Assembly and shouted that parliament was a sham and "Down with President Sadat."[58] In this case there was to be no prevarication or mediation. Prime Minister and Center Party Chief Mamdouh Salem presented the bill of indictment against Sheikh Ashour to the Assembly. When Hilmy Murad rose to speak against it, Speaker Marei denied him the floor, at which point all twenty-four Wafdist deputies walked out in protest.[59] Marei's days as a mediator had almost come to an end.

In the spring and early summer of 1978, Sadat reeled in the democratic freedoms which he had played out since 1974. Before the New Wafd could test its claim to massive latent electoral support in the by-election to fill Sheikh Ashour's empty seat, Sadat initiated the changes that were shortly to transform the system back into an authoritarian one. He announced a plebiscite for May 21, the purpose of which was to tighten control over the press and to deprive key groups, and especially the leaders of the New Wafd, former members of the Revolutionary Command Council (RCC) and leftists, of their right to participate in politics. In this frigid climate, support for the New Wafd evaporated. The Center Party's candidate overwhelmed the New Wafdist trying to regain Sheikh Ashour's seat, and on the following day 98.29 percent of the ballots cast in the referendum affirmed its proposals. On June 2 the New Wafd, preferring political oblivion to a leadership purge similar to that conducted against it by the RCC in 1952, adjourned sine die.

With that troublesome contender out of the way, Sadat directed his attention to outspoken journalists. Seven of them, including Muhamed Hassanein Heykal, were ordered not to leave the country and were targeted for investigation "for publishing articles detrimental to Egypt's interests."[60] Then came the turn of the left, with Khaled Muhi al Din being called to account for articles published in al Ahali, and the paper itself being seized. The final blow came on June 26, when with Marei absent from the speaker's chair the Assembly, in accordance with the May referendum, voted to expel from parliament Abd al Fattah Hassan, Serag al Din's protégé and deputy leader of the New Wafd, and leftist Abd al Ezz al Hairiry, for "taking part in corrupt political life before the 23 July Revolution."[61]

By this time there was no safe room left between the president and the opposition in which middleman Marei could maneuver. With the expulsions of four deputies in a little more than a year, parliamentary immunity had been made a mockery. The government itself had trammeled over the parties law, which Marei had skillfully sold to the opposition. Accompanying the crackdown was a change in power relationships within the elite. In choosing to revert to authoritarian rule, Sadat turned to former policeman Mamdouh Salem and other hard-liners in the Center Party and away from Marei, whose skills were appropriate and useful in a liberalization, but irrelevant and useless for rule by decree.

Marei's middleman strategy had thus foundered on Sadat's intransigence. Preferring semiretirement to occupying a formal role that had little prestige and even less influence, Marei gave no signs of disappointment at being kicked upstairs to the post of presidential advisor in October 1978. That is not to say, however, that he forswore political ambition or his informal political role. As presidential advisor, he has continued to act as middleman, presumably staying active in anticipation of another liberalization or a more fundamental change. On the one hand, he has remained a prominent member of the presidential entourage, performing a variety of ceremonial functions and publicly restating and reinforcing Sadat's line. On the other hand, in private and to the opposition, Marei has continued to signal his displeasure with Sadat's policies, not the least being that of negotiating a settlement with Israel. Less willing than Sadat to isolate himself from domestic and regional constituencies, Marei has communicated his sentiments widely, as the following interview with Yasser Arafat suggests:

Q: Are you threatening Sadat?
A: Sadat will pay the price sooner or later. I know Egypt better

than you. I know the Egyptian people. Looking at the resignation of Said Marei in Egypt. He sent me a message: "I want to clear my conscience. I had nothing to do with it [Sadat's trip to Jerusalem and ensuing negotiations]." The Egyptians will not keep silent. Everyone is against it.[62]

Lest Marei's message to the chairman of the Palestine Liberation Organization be interpreted as a final break with Sadat, it should be pointed out that Marei had met secretly with Menachem Begin in Bucharest on August 25, 1977, to discuss a possible meeting between Sadat and the Israeli prime minister.[63] Marei's strategy, in short, is still that of a middleman—keeping his lines of communication open to the president's enemies while simultaneously cultivating good relations with the president himself. It has been the structural context of Egyptian politics since the summer of 1978, and not a fundamental change in Marei's strategy, that accounts for his reduced prominence.

11 | CONCLUSION

Some brief remarks on micro-macro linkages may help relate the particularities of this case to the Egyptian political system and possibly to other Middle Eastern or even Third World political systems. Above all else, it must be emphasized that the seemingly infinite resourcefulness and flexibility of Sayed Marei reflects not only his own astuteness but, at least as important, the dynamic political context of which he was a part. The relative significance of the social collectivities in which he has pursued his political interests has changed in response to both the expansion and contraction of governmental power and to socioeconomic development.

Taking the factor of governmental power initially, the Egyptian political system can be seen to have traced an inverted U-shaped curve, with the ancien régime and the Sadat era being characterized by relatively dispersed power and limited governmental capabilities, while Nasser's regime was typified by concentrated power and a rise in governing capability. In short, Nasser may be thought of as a classical defensive modernizer in the tradition of Muhamed Ali or Ataturk, for fired by nationalism he gathered the reins of power into his hands and greatly increased the scope of governmental activities. In so doing, Nasser devalued the political resources of family connections, provincial class loyalties, and rural clientelism, while simultaneously revaluing the resources of those social collectivities placed closer to the center of power. For Marei those collectivities were his organic and political *shillal* and the clientage network he was able to establish within his bureaucratic fiefdoms. Conversely, as power under Sadat has ebbed down into the system, and as the private sector has turned the tide against the public sector, Marei has rekindled his provincial connections while permitting his *shillal* and patron-client relationships almost to extinguish. Simultaneously his family has reemerged as a more vital politically and economically relevant resource.

Stylistic changes have also accompanied the expansion and contraction of state power and consequent fluctuation in the political importance of social collectivities. In the weak, comparatively decentralized ancien régime, Marei was overtly a party politician, gaining and justifying his presence in the political elite on the grounds of family background, party loyalty and political commitment. Under Nasser, Marei had to change tack, basing his claim to participation on technical competence and personal loyalty to the president. For Sadat, Marei has performed vital services as a political technocrat, managing the more decentralized political system by juxtaposing himself between the president and the opposition. He has, in short, survived by juggling the political resources at his disposal and by tailoring his political personae to suit prevailing conditions.

The cyclical changes in governmental capabilities and concentration and dispersion of power occurred against the backdrop of linear socioeconomic change. The modernization of agriculture is, presumably, a once-and-for-all occurrence. Hence latifundia-style labor-intensive cultivation, the socioeconomic context for extended rural clientelism, is giving way irrevocably and forever to capital intensive agriculture. Rural sociopolitical patterns must therefore evolve into new forms, as indeed the history of twentieth-century Egypt suggests they are doing. Thus Sayed Marei of the ancien régime, benefiting as he did from a network of rural clients, is an anachronism in contemporary Egypt. But of course the Sayed Marei of today has long since found functional substitutes for peasant clients, as have innumerable of his colleagues from the rural notability.

Given the coexistence of cyclical and linear change, the task of political anthropology is to discriminate between those forms that have passed into history and those that have been but temporarily eclipsed by other, more suitable types. The case of the Mareis suggests that the family, at least in Egypt, is sufficiently cohesive and adaptable to outlive even the most adverse of political circumstances.

Simultaneously, however, that very adaptability suggests that the family is responding to linear change as well. It may be predicted, therefore, that the family will continue to be of importance to Egyptian politics, but not necessarily in the same manner as it has been in the past.

As regards possible generalizations from this study of Egypt to other countries of the Middle East, John Waterbury's observations more than a decade ago remain appropriate. Concluding his study of Moroccan politics, he stated,

> The existence of general patterns of political behavior [in the Middle East] can be seen to flow logically from this shared social, cultural and historical background. Yet seldom has the relation between contemporary politics and the social organization and political culture of the Middle East been explicitly and extensively analyzed.[1]

Unfortunately both propositions remain accurate, for while linkages among contemporary politics and social organization and political culture have been investigated during the past decade, and while this study adds to that literature, much remains to be done. In particular, the political significance of family, regional, patron-client, and small-group loyalties must be studied in other than the Egyptian context if meaningful and correct generalizations on the political anthropology of the Middle East are to be made. This study suggests some relevant hypotheses and a method by which they may be investigated.

Appendix A

MAREI IBRAHIM NASR AND HIS DESCENDANTS THROUGH HIS FIRST WIFE

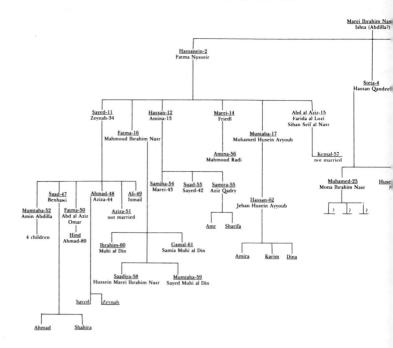

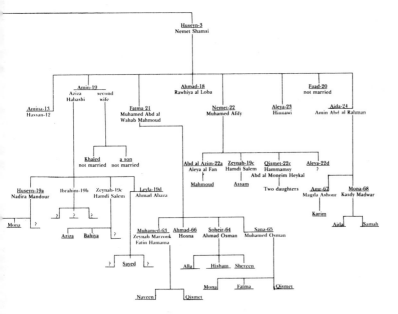

Appendix B

MAREI IBRAHIM NASR AND HIS DESCENDANTS THROUGH HIS SECOND WIFE

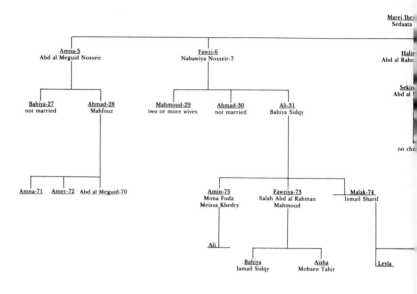

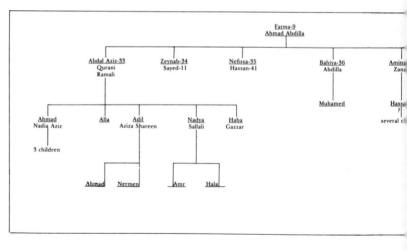

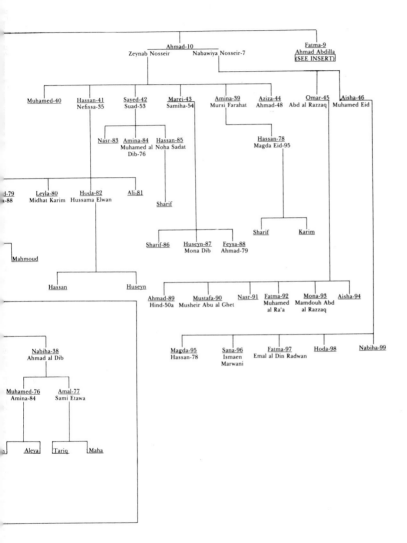

Appendix C

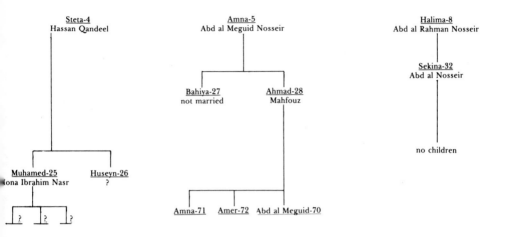

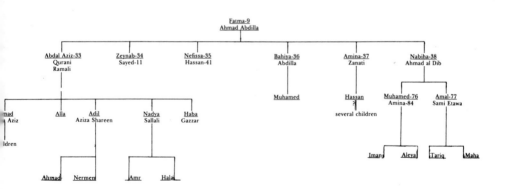

The Daughters of Marei Ibrahim Nasr and Their Sublineages

By his first wife, Marei Ibrahim Nasr had one daughter, Steta-4, who was married to Hassan Qandeel, a prominent landowner in the immediate neighborhood of Azizeha. Their eldest son, Muhamed-25, remained on the land managing the family estates. He married Mona Ibrahim Nasr, sister of his mother's brother's (Hassanein-2) daughter's (Fatma-16) husband, Mahmoud Ibrahim Nasr, the most prominent of the non-Marei Nasr. The second son, Huseyn-26, who took a degree in engineering, married yet another sister of Mahmoud Ibrahim Nasr before taking two additional wives. Although Hassan Qandeel, after marrying Steta Marei, had assisted his brother-in-law Hassanein in managing his estates, in the second and third generation the Qandeels and the Mareis, following patrilineal descent and lacking endogamous marriages between themselves, grew apart.

Marei Ibrahim Nasr's first child by his second wife, Amna-5, married Abd al Meguid Nosseir, who served as *umdah* of Kafr al Arbain as well as representative in the Gamiat al Ummumiya of 1891–94. After having a daughter, who died without marrying, and a son, the couple were divorced, and Amna and her son Ahmad-28 went to live in the household of her brother Ahmad-10 and his first wife Zeynab—not in the household of Ahmad and his second wife, Nabawiya. Amna's son Ahmad completed a degree in commerce at Cairo University in 1930 and went to work in 1932 in the Agricultural Credit Bank, newly created by Ali Marei's father-in-law, Prime Minister Ismail Sidqy. In later years Ahmad was to work for Sayed Marei in the same bank, renamed the Agricultural Cooperative Bank, and subsequently from 1975 for Sayed's half-brother, Omar-45, in the Feysal Islamic Bank, of which Omar was the managing director. In short, Ahmad became part of the family.

Halima-8, the second daughter of Marei Ibrahim Nasr by Sedaata Nosseir, also had bad luck with her marriage to a maternal cousin, Abd al Rahman Nosseir. Head of the Gamgara branch of the Nosseir, Abd al Rahman served in the Gamiat al Tishriya of 1914. After having one stillborn child, this couple was also divorced, and like her older sister Amna, Halima too went to live with her brother Ahmad, becoming the much loved aunt of Ahmad's children through Zeynab Nosseir.

Only Fatma-9, the youngest daughter of Marei Ibrahim Nasr, and the child closest in age to his son Ahmad, was to mother children who were to be reincorporated by marriage into the Marei lineage. Fatma married Ahmad Abdilla of Sanafen, whose mother was a sister of Fatma's father, Marei Ibrahim Nasr. Ahmad Abdilla was the Marei affine who later assisted his brother-in-law and cousin, Ahmad

Marei, in defeating Prime Minister Yehia Ibrahim Pasha in the 1923
election. Fatma and Ahmad Abdilla had one son and five daughters,
and three of these children had exogamous marriages to Sharqiya
notables, the most successful of which was that of their daughter
Nabiha to Ahmad al Dib, son of Sayed Ahmad Bey al Dib, a wealthy
Zagazig merchant who, prior to World War I, acquired a large estate
in Sharqiya (see Gabriel Baer, *Studies in the Social History of Modern Egypt*
[Chicago: University of Chicago Press, 1969], p. 225). Ahmad al
Dib's brother, a Wafdist from Zagazig, served in the 1945–49 parliament alongside Sayed Marei. Zeynab-34, the eldest daughter of
Fatma and Ahmad Abdilla, married her mother's brother Hassanein's
eldest son Sayed-11, while Nefissa-35, the next daughter, married
Hassan-41, eldest son of her mother's brother Ahmad. Fatma's
daughters thus served as additional bridges between the Hassanein
and Ahmad lineages. Another daughter, Bahiya-36, married her father's brother's son, thereby providing a link in this generation between the Abdillas and the Mareis.

In sum, of the children of the four daughters of Marei Ibrahim
Nasr, only those of the eldest, Steta, became isolated from the Marei
family. The two daughters who married Nosseirs ended up living
with their brother Ahmad after they were divorced by their husbands, and the sole offspring of this branch of the family who lived
to adulthood was raised by the Mareis in their household. Two of
Fatma's children were married within the Marei descent group, while
a third was married to an Abdilla, which is as close as one can come
without actually being a Marei. Thus, by a combination of chance
and choice, even the descendants of Marei Ibrahim Nasr through his
daughters have remained largely within the fold, not being hived off
into the patrilineages of their non-Marei fathers.

Appendix D

Estimate of the Size, Capital Value, and Annual Return of the Mareis'
Landholdings

For the purposes of this estimate we shall concentrate on the
holdings of the core group of the affinal set centered on Hassan-41,
Sayed-42, and Marei-43, since more information is available on this
group. The holdings of these individuals are on the average larger
than those of other members in the descent group, but they are
suggestive of the general range for the holdings of others as well.

On his death in 1942, Ahmad Marei left some 170 feddans in
Minya, 180 feddans next to Benha in Qalyubiya, 150 feddans in
Azizeha, 60 feddans in Saadin, and another parcel in Kafr al Arbain,
possibly as much as 200 feddans but probably not more than half
that amount. Since he had four sons and three daughters, the share
of each of the sons would have been not less than 120 feddans. Some
of the heirs added relatively small parcels to their holdings during the
1940s and 1950s, Sayed and Omar each purchasing 25 feddan farms
adjacent to the pyramids at Mansouriya in 1959. In addition to their
own holdings, title to which they could of course distribute to their
heirs at any time, thereby partially avoiding the violation of ceilings

imposed through past or expected agrarian reforms, all three of the brothers married women in the descent group who were themselves landowners. The eldest, Hassan, married Nefissa, the daughter of his father's sister Fatma, whose husband Ahmad Abdilla, owning some 400 feddans, was the largest landowner in the Abdilla village of Sanafen and who had but one male heir. Nefissa thus inherited some 135 feddans and possibly even more. Sayed and Marei married daughters of Hassan, who as the protector of the family estates in Azizeha and lacking a male heir would have left his daughters as much as 200 feddans each. Thus at the time of the first agrarian reform in 1952 each of these nuclear families would have owned well in excess of 200 feddans and possibly as much as 400. While some of that land was sold off in 1966–67, in all probability each of these nuclear families (remembering that their eldest children are now in their forties) owns something like 200 to 250 feddans. The legal limit of 100 feddans does not apply, because title to a very considerable amount of this land has already been turned over to heirs.

The vast bulk of land owned by the Mareis is planted with citrus orchards, for orange, grapefruit, and lemon trees require relatively little attention compared with field crops. They are also far more remunerative, because the government, which controls the price of all field crops, permits market forces to determine the price of citrus fruit, which is correspondingly relatively higher. While earnings per feddan vary from year to year and according to type of soil, age of tree, quality and quantity of necessary agricultural inputs, and so on, a rough idea of income derived per feddan is suggested by the yield for Marei orchards in Benha in 1976, which grossed £E575 per feddan and netted somewhere between £E300 and £E350. Taking the lower figure of 200 for total feddans owned and the lower figure of £E300 netted per feddan, the nuclear family of Sayed Marei, for example, would have derived a minimum of some £E60,000 in 1976 from its agricultural operations, or roughly $100,000. In a country where annual per capita income hovers around the $200 mark, this is a very sizable figure. It is high not only in relation to a peasant's earnings but also in relation to the earnings of other landowners as well, for fragmentation through inheritance and ceilings imposed through successive agrarian reforms means that relatively few nuclear families own more land than the Mareis, and many owners are not nearly such efficient farmers.

The total value of Marei rural real-estate holdings is difficult to estimate, for values vary according to proximity to urban centers, soil fertility, and other factors. Sayed Marei's horse farm in Mansouriya, for example, is worth in 1979 prices not less than £E20,000 per feddan and probably much more than this, because the area is being encroached upon by the Giza suburbs. Marei land in Sharqiya may be worth on the average £E3,000 to 4,000 per feddan. If the lower figure of £E3,000 is taken, the nuclear family of Sayed Marei owns not less than £E600,000 of rural real estate, or about $1 million. If all the rural landholdings of the descent group of Marei Ibrahim Nasr were added together, the total would clearly be worth many millions of dollars.

EPILOGUE

On October 6, 1981, the eighth anniversary of the Egyptian attack across the Suez Canal, President Sadat was assassinated while reviewing his troops. The hail of bullets and grenade fragments that felled the president also wounded Sayed Marei, who was in the front row of the reviewing stand and separated from Sadat only by Minister of Defense Abu Ghazzala. During his three-week convalescence in the Maadi military hospital, Marei offered his resignation as adviser to the president. President Hosni Mubarak accepted the resignation and nominated shortly thereafter Abd al Aziz Hegazy, Mustafa Khalil, and Mamdouh Salem to serve as counselors to the president. In distancing himself from Marei, Mubarak is indicating his intention to alter certain aspects of the regime he has inherited from Sadat. Whether this will result in the end of Sayed Marei's political career, or will prove to be just another temporary setback, remains to be seen.

NOTES

| PREFACE

1. For example, William R. Brown, *The Last Crusade: A Negotiator's Middle East Handbook* (Chicago: Nelson-Hall, 1980), p. 7, states:

> Social structure has important ramifications for public life in Arab countries. . . . One good example of how these relationships are expressed in public life can be found in the Arabic word mahsubiyya. The dictionary offers a definition "patronage" or "favored position," but it means much more than that. Mahsubiyya is the social institution by which members of an extended family (itself a protective instrument) serve their common purpose. With this device there is no compunction against using official position to favor a family member. Actions that otherwise seem irrational sometimes make sense when family ties can be discerned among participants in a set of political events.

Brown does not, however, go on to analyze the complexities of Middle Eastern politics in terms of *mahsubiyya.* Among social scientists interested in the Middle East, Samir Khalaf stands out as having argued consistently for the sociopolitical significance of kinship. See, for example, his most recent analysis of the Lebanese political elite in Jacob M. Landau, Ergun Özbudun, and Frank Tachau, *Electoral Politics in the Middle East* (London: Croom, Helm; and Palo Alto: Hoover Institution Press, 1980), pp. 243–71.

2. Among historians, a similar approach is known as prosopography, a form of collective biography in which "the family connections and the careers of a substantial number of persons in a given society and period are examined with a view to drawing conclusions about the political system or social structure" (G. W. Bowerstock, "The Emperor of Roman History," *New York Review of Books* March 6, 1980, pp. 8–13). For a discussion of the method, see Lawrence Stone, "Prosopography," *Daedalus* 100 (1971):49–79; and Arnold Toynbee, *A Study of History,* vol. 12: *Reconsiderations* (London: Oxford University Press, 1961), pp. 118, 121–24.

3. *Al Ahram* published twelve separate excerpts from those memoirs, the first appearing August 4, 1978. The memoirs, entitled *Political Papers,* were then published by al Ahram Publishing Company in Arabic. They will be referred to in notes as *MM.*

| INTRODUCTION

1. Leonard Binder, *In a Moment of Enthusiasm: Political Power and the Second Stratum in Egypt* (Chicago: University of Chicago Press, 1978).

2. See, for example, Robert Springborg, "Patrimonialism and Policy Making in Egypt: Nasser and Sadat and the Tenure Policy for Reclaimed Lands," *Middle Eastern Studies* 15 (January 1979):49–69; and Robert Springborg, "Patterns of Association in the Egyptian Political Elite," in George Lenczowski, *Political Elites in the Middle East* (Washington: American Enterprise Institute, 1975).

3. On Orientalism generally, see Edward W. Said, *Orientalism* (New York: Pantheon Books, 1978), and Bryan S. Turner, *Marx and the End of Orientalism* (Boston: Allen & Unwin, 1978). For critiques of the works cited in note 2, from the anti-Orientalist perspective, see Roger Owen, "Explaining Arab Politics," *Political Studies* 26 (December 1978):507–12, and Samir Naim, "Towards a Demystification of Arab Social Reality: A Critique of Anthropological and Political Writings on Arab Society," *Review of Middle East Studies* 3 (1978). For a critique from a somewhat different perspective, see Nazih N. M. Ayubi, *Bureaucracy and Politics in Contemporary Egypt* (London: Ithaca Press, 1980), pp. 464–79.

4. Karl Marx and Friedrich Engels, "Manifesto of the Communist Party," in Robert C. Tucker, *The Marx-Engels Reader,* 2d ed. (New York: W. W. Norton & Co., 1978), p. 475.

5. On this point, see James A. Bill and Carl Leiden, *Politics in the Middle East* (Boston: Little, Brown & Co., 1979), pp. 75–133.

| CHAPTER 1: THE MAREI FAMILY

1. See Abbas M. Ammar, *The People of Sharqiya: Their Racial History, Serology, Physical Characters, Demography and Conditions of Life* (Cairo: Publications de la Société Royale de Géographie d'Egypte, 1944), vols. 1 and 2.

2. The Tahawi are well known throughout Egypt as highly successful breeders of Saluqi dogs and racehorses. The extent of their landholdings is indicated by the fact that seven Tahawis appeared on the register of names drawn up in 1952–53 of those individuals whose landholdings were thought to exceed the new legal maximum of 200 feddans per individual or 300 per family, as imposed by the agrarian reform law decreed on September 9, 1952. On the list drawn up for the purposes of the second agrarian reform in 1961, in which the limit was lowered to 100 feddans per individual, eight Tawahi names appeared. Copies of the agrarian reform registers were made available to me by John Anderson, to whom I would like to express my appreciation.

3. Following Egyptian practice, I shall use the term "family" rather than "clan" or "tribe" when describing these large kinship units, some of which are several thousand strong.

4. Hassan Agha Abaza, who is referred to by contemporary Abazas as the true founder of their lineage in Egypt, was appointed sheikh of Sharqiya in 1812 by Ibrahim Pasha, Muhamed Ali's son and acting commander in chief. On his death in 1848–49, Hassan Agha Abaza owned some 4,000 feddan. One of his sons, Sayed Pasha Abaza, *mudir* (governor) of Beheira Province, left 6,000 feddan on his death in 1875–76. Since 1925 there have been Abazas in all Sharqiya parliamentary delegations and on occasion as many as one-third of all Sharqiya deputies have been Abazas. On this family, see Gabriel Baer, *Studies in the Social History of Modern Egypt* (Chicago: University of Chicago Press, 1969), pp. 7–9.

5. Due to a misinterpretation of the data, I stated in a previous publication that Marei Ibrahim Nasr had acquired only some 60–70 feddans. See "Sayed Bey Marei and Political Clientelism in Egypt," *Comparative Political Studies* 12 (October 1979): 259–88.

6. On the emergence of a class of native Egyptian landowners, described frequently as the *umdah* class, see Baer, *Studies;* Ali M. Barakat, "The Development of Agricultural Ownership in Egypt and Its Effects on the Political Movements" (in Arabic) (Ph.D. diss., Cairo University, 1972); Leonard Binder, *In a Moment of Enthusiasm: Political Power and the Second Stratum in Egypt* (Chicago: University of Chicago Press, 1978); Ibrahim Abu-Lughod, "The Transformation of the Egyptian Elite: Prelude to the Urabi Revolt," *Middle East Journal* 21 (Summer 1967):324–44; and Ali Disuqi, *Large Landowners and Their Role in Egyptian Society, 1914–1952* (in Arabic) (Cairo: Dar al Thiqafa al Gadida, 1975).

7. On the Nosseir, see Baer, *Studies,* p. 11.

8. L. B. Graffety-Smith, a British diplomat who visited the Delta in February 1929 to gauge nationalist feelings, sent to his superior in London the following report on his conversation with Mahmoud Bey Nosseir:

> Mahmoud Bey Nosseir, a portly, bottle-nosed Municipal Councillor *(umdah)* who after a lifetime in the Watanist Party turned Wafdist two months before the coup d'etat as the price of a senatorship that had not

time to materialize, told me that he has never been so popular in his life as now. Unknown admirers cheer him in the street; two workmen now do work that required four before his 'conversion'; his clerk is no longer absent through ill health half a dozen times a month; he feels in a word that he has not ratted in vain. . . . He thought . . . that there was an ugly undercurrent of disorder in popular feeling at present, and that if the Government were 'to make a bad mistake, or show itself suddenly weak,' there might be dangerous results. He was friendly disposed toward ourselves. 'If I could turn the English out of Egypt I would. But I know I can't, so let's be friends. (Great Britain, Public Records Office, FO 371/13841)

9. The family home in Kafr al Arbain had been built by Ahmad Nosseir about 1850. His daughter was Sedaata Nosseir, the mother of Ahmad Marei, who as a boy spent considerable time on his maternal grandfather's estate. Shortly after World War I, Abd al Meguid Nosseir, then the owner of Kafr al Arbain and the husband of Amna Marei, sister of Ahmad Marei, sold the estate to one Muhamed Bey Yussef, who in turn sold it to Fathalla Barakat, shortly to be appointed by his uncle Saad Zaghloul as minister of agriculture. Barakat, anxious to buy a large property in Bilbeis that had just been reclaimed, then sold the house and some 55 surrounding feddan to Ahmad Marei at a price of £E200 per feddan. In the following years, Ahmad Marei bought more land surrounding Kafr al Arbain.

10. The Qandeels did not succeed in electing a member of their family to parliament until Abd al Fattah Qandeel won the seat of Mashtul al Suq in 1969. It is interesting to note, however, that by 1961 the Qandeels' landholdings in Sharqiya probably surpassed those of the Nosseir, for while only one of the latter appeared on the list of some 3,800 names drawn up by the agrarian reform authorities, three Qandeels were listed, suggesting they were suspected of owning land in excess of the 100-feddan maximum. Neither the Qandeels nor the Nosseirs appeared on the 1952 list, which probably indicates their holdings were at that time not in excess of 200 feddans.

11. The Shamsis were of Circassian descent and had succeeded in electing their leader, Sheikh Ali Shamsi, to the second Maglis Shura al Nuwwab in 1870 and his brother Amin Shamsi Bey to the Maglis al Nuwwab of 1881 and to the Gamiat al Ummumiya of 1891 and 1896. Ali Shamsi Pasha, son of Sheikh Ali Shamsi, was elected to parliament in 1914, 1924, 1926, 1930, 1936, and 1938, while his brother Abd al Halim Shamsi was elected to parliament in all those years and in 1942 and 1950 as well.

12. On these two figures, and especially the latter, see Afaf Lutfi al-Sayyid-Marsot, *Egypt's Liberal Experiment, 1922–1926* (Berkeley: University of California, 1977).

13. On April 14, 1954, a decree was issued prohibiting from holding public office anyone who had held a cabinet post between February 1946 and

July 1952, which would, therefore, have precluded Sayed Marei from taking the post of chairman of the Higher Committee for Agrarian Reform had he succeeded, as he nearly did, in becoming minister of agriculture in 1950.

14. The eldest brother, Ahmad Nosseir Bey of Kafr al Arbain, had already in 1881 succeeded in winning election to the Maglis al Nuwwab, the first nationalist-inclined assembly to be composed predominantly of rural notables of *umdah* backgrounds. On this assembly, see P. J. Vatikiotis, *The Modern History of Egypt* (London: Weidenfeld & Nicolson, 1969), pp. 126–64. Ahmad Nosseir Bey's younger brother, Abd al Rahman, was later to serve in the Gamiat al Tishriya (Legislative Assembly) of 1914.

15. On the al Lozi family, see Baer, *Studies,* pp. 138–39.

16. Hamdi Seif al Nasr was also one of Makram Obeid's targets in his muckraking *Black Book,* published in 1942. Obeid leveled numerous charges of corruption at Seif al Nasr, the most novel being that Seif al Nasr had converted a wing of the Ministry of Agriculture, then located in what is now the Agricultural Museum, into a domicile for himself and his family. Employees of the ministry were, according to Obeid, used as domestics by the Seif al Nasrs. See Makram Obeid, *The Black Book of a Black Regime* (in Arabic) (Cairo, 1942), pp. 106–7.

17. Cable, Clark Kerr, January 15, 1924, Great Britain, Public Records Office, FO/E11499.

18. Ahmad's childrens' dedication to preserving family solidarity is further reflected by the marriages they arranged for their children. Hassan's eldest son, Ahmad-79, who holds a Ph.D. in nuclear engineering, was married to Marei's only daughter, Feysa-88, who has an English Ph.D. in biology. Sayed's daughter Amina-84 was married to her great aunt Fatma's grandson Muhamed al Dib-76.

19. The sensitive nature of relations between the two groups was made evident at the time of probate, for neither side wanted the execution of Ahmad's will to be the cause of open conflict. They proceeded therefore with great caution, taking three years and the compilation of a detailed list of Ahmad's assets (which took on the size of a Manhattan telephone directory) before dividing up the estate. In the end the two offspring of Ahmad and Nabawiya, defended by their half brother Ali-31, were given first choice of assets by the more numerous offspring of Ahmad and Zeynab, who were wary lest they be charged with ganging up on their half brother and sister.

20. Mustafa Abd al Razzaq, having made a career in religious politics in Egypt, was Sheikh al Islam and then minister of awqaf (religious endowments) in Muhamed Mahmoud's government in 1938–39, while his father and brother had been successful secular politicians, both being vice-presidents of the Liberal Constitutionalist Party.

21. Ali, educated at Cambridge, first met Bahiya on a skiing holiday in Switzerland with her brother Amin. They were married two years later, and Ali was immediately made secretary to the prime minister, his father-in-law. He was then given a top position in the Foreign Ministry, causing Cairo wags

of the day to comment that the degree which had entitled Ali Marei to the high-paying, prestigious job was a B.I.S. (bint [daughter] Ismail Sidqy).

22. Fawziya's eldest daughter was married to a grandson of Ismail Sidqy, while her younger daughter was married to a grandson of Murad Pasha Mohsen, who had made a career in palace politics under Kings Fuad and Farouk. It is interesting to note that aspiration for social status, rather than preservation of the patrilineage, determined with which lineage this branch of the family would identify. When in Cairo, Ali's children and grandchildren live in the Sidqy building along the Nile in Zamalek. The abundant memorablia in the several Marei/Sidqy flats into which the building is divided honors the Sidqys almost to the exclusion of the Mareis. Clearly male chauvinism in the form of adherence to the patrilineage is rejected when it conflicts with claims to higher social status through the matrilineage.

23. Significantly, none of the Mareis have been career army officers, a vocation of relatively low prestige. Only one female descendant of Marei Ibrahim Nasr married an officer. Amina-56, daughter of Marei-14 and his German wife, married Mamdouh Radi, an army colonel from Beni Suef.

| CHAPTER 2: MAREI MARRIAGE PATTERNS

1. See, for example, Raphael Patai, "Cousin Right in Middle Eastern Marriage," *Southwestern Journal of Anthropology* 11 (Winter 1955):371–90.

2. For an excellent discussion of this point, and of family and kinship in general, see Dale F. Eickelman, *The Middle East: An Anthropological Approach* (Englewood Cliffs: Prentice-Hall, 1981), pp. 105–34.

3. For greater elaboration of this argument, see Pierre Bourdieu, "Marriage Strategies as Strategies of Social Reproduction," *Annales,* July–October 1972, pp. 1105–25, reprinted in R. Forster and O. Ranum, eds., *Family and Society* (Baltimore: Johns Hopkins University Press, 1976), pp. 117–44. See also Roger M. Keesing, *Groups and Social Structure* (New York: Holt, Rinehart & Winston, 1975), p. 125.

4. Ibid., p. 141.

5. Ibid.

6. See Emrys Lloyd Peters, "Aspects of Affinity in a Lebanese Maronite Village," in J. G. Peristiany, ed., *Mediterranean Family Structure* (Cambridge: Cambridge University Press, 1976), p. 61. See also Gabriel Baer, *Population and Society in the Arab East* (New York: Praeger, 1964), pp. 57–69; Raphael Patai, "Structure of Endogamous Unilineal Descent Groups," *Southwestern Journal of Anthropology* 21 (1965):325–50; Robert F. Murphy and Leonard Kasdan, "The Structure of Parallel Cousin Marriage," *American Anthropologist* 61 (1959): 17–29; and Robert F. Murphy and Leonard Kasdan, "Agnation and Endogamy: Some Further Considerations," *Southwestern Journal of Anthropology* 23 (Spring 1967):1–14.

7. Bourdieu, pp. 120–21.

8. Hildred Geertz, "The Meanings of Family Ties," in Clifford Geertz,

Hildred Geertz, and Lawrence Rosen, *Meaning and Order in Moroccan Society: Three Essays in Cultural Analysis* (Cambridge: Cambridge University Press, 1979), p. 355.

9. Peters, "Aspects of Affinity," pp. 40–41.

10. Ibid., pp. 66–67.

11. Frederick Barth, "Father's Brother's Daughter Marriage in Kurdistan," *Southwestern Journal of Anthropology* 10 (1954):164–71. While Hassan was in fact the cousin and not the uncle of Sayed and Marei, in practice the effect of generational skewing was such that Hassan was in structural and behavioral terms cast within the role of uncle rather than cousin. On such intergenerational role changes, see Robert Cresswell, "Lineage Endogamy Among Maronite Mountaineers," in Peristiany, ed., *Mediterranean Family Structure*, pp. 105–6.

12. For a review of these arguments, see Fuad I. Khuri, "Parallel Cousin Marriage Reconsidered: A Middle Eastern Practice That Nullifies the Effects of Marriage on the Intensity of Family Relations," *Man*, December 1970, pp. 597–618.

13. Ibid.

14. Henry Rosenfeld, "Social and Economic Factors in Explanation of the Increased Rate of Patrilineal Endogamy in the Arab Village in Israel," in Peristiany, ed., *Mediterranean Family Structure*, pp. 115–36.

15. See, for example, Emrys Lloyd Peters, "Aspects of the Family Among the Bedouin of Cyrenaica," in M. F. Nimkoff, *Comparative Family Systems* (Boston: Houghton Mifflin Co., 1965). For a brief summary of rates of endogamy among various Middle Eastern populations, see Baer, *Population*, p. 65.

16. See Patai, "Cousin Right," esp. p. 379.

17. Ibid., p. 380.

18. Jacque Berque, *Les Arabes;* cited in Baer, *Population*, p. 65.

19. Ilse Lichtenstadter, "An Arab-Egyptian Family," *Middle East Journal* 4 (Autumn 1952):379–99.

20. There is, however, a recent study of marriage and social interaction among the urban poor of Bulaq, a slum quarter in Cairo. See Andrea Rugh, *Coping with Poverty in a Cairo Community* (Cairo: Cairo Papers in Social Science, 1979).

21. Khuri, "Parallel Cousin Marriage."

22. Cresswell, "Lineage Endogamy."

23. See Peters, "Aspects of Affinity."

24. On intergenerational functional equivalency in FBD marriage, see Cresswell, "Lineage Endogamy," pp. 105–6.

25. The Muhi al Din's estates are actually located on the Qalyubia side of the Sharqiya-Qalyubiya border, but the primary focus of the Muhi al Din's activities has been in Sharqiya Province.

26. Abd al Fattah al Lozi did serve briefly on the Wafdist central committee in Damietta. See Marius Deeb, *Party Politics in Egypt: The Wafd and Its Rivals, 1919–1939* (London: Ithaca Press, 1979), p. 156.

CHAPTER 3: MAREI FAMILY SOCIAL AND ECONOMIC BEHAVIOR

1. A. R. Radcliffe-Brown, "Introduction," in A. R. Radcliffe-Brown and C. D. Forde, eds., *African Systems of Kinship and Marriage* (London: Oxford University Press, 1950), reprinted in Jack Goody, *Kinship: Selected Readings* (Baltimore: Penguin Books, 1971), p. 121.

2. Peter C. Dodd, "Family Honor and the Forces of Change in Arab Society," *International Journal of Middle East Studies* 4 (January 1973):40.

3. Ibid., pp. 40–54.

4. The distaste with which such behavior is viewed is suggested by a rumor campaign in the mid-1970s directed against Sayed Marei in an attempt to discredit him and the Sadat regime. The rumors were to the effect that Marei was having affairs with teenage girls.

5. Dodd, "Family Honor," p. 49.

6. *MM* (see Preface, note 3), pp. 506–7.

7. Sequestration, or the seizure of an individual or family's assets for crimes specified or even unspecified, became increasingly common in Nasser's Egypt after 1961 and especially during 1966–67, when the Committee for Liquidation of Feudalists was active. The practice was outlawed after Sadat came to power.

8. For speculation on the causes and eventual termination of the Committee for the Liquidation of Feudalists, see John Waterbury, *Egypt: Burden of the Past / Options for the Future* (Bloomington: Indiana University Press, 1978), pp. 239–40.

9. That Marx's schema with economics as substructure and politics as superstructure should be inverted to properly understand the dynamics of power in the Middle East is argued in James A. Bill and Carl Leiden, *Politics in the Middle East* (Boston: Little, Brown & Co., 1979), pp. 75–133.

10. Sayed Marei and his family also derived considerable income from their Arabian horse stud farm in Mansouriya, which has in recent years been managed by Nasr Marei, Sayed's son. The *Studbook,* vol. 4, published by the Egyptian Agricultural Organization in 1975, lists all registered purebred Arabian horses held by the major stables in Egypt between 1971 and 1975. According to the *Studbook,* in this period the Mareis owned forty-two purebred Arabians, of which at least three were sold to overseas interests. Since that time the rate of sales has increased dramatically, as have prices. By 1980, al Badia, the Mareis' stud farm, had become the most prestigious of the numerous stud farms in Egypt. For a description of it and its bloodstock, see the special issue devoted to Egyptian Arabian horses of *Arabian Horse World* 20 (June 1980):257–79, 328–36, 394, 434.

11. Anwar Sadat dubbed Marei "the Father of Egyptian Agrarian Reform" in a speech defending him against attack by students, delivered to the Cairo University General Federation of Students. Cited in *Foreign Broadcast Information Service: Near East and North Africa,* February 2, 1977.

12. The several small enterprises which Sayed Marei owns and which are scattered around Cairo and the Delta were in the late 1970s targets for attack by terrorists opposed to the regime. On July 11, 1979, the Lebanese daily *al Safir* quoted a statement by an anti-Sadat organization, al Samedoun, claiming responsibility for a fire in Shubra al Kheima in which three small factories, all owned by Sayed Marei, were destroyed by fire and eleven people were killed. Al Samedoun also threatened to strike at other plants which Sadat had "turned into American-Israeli interests" (quoted in *Arab Report,* August 1, 1979, p. 20). In May 1976, a fire occurred at Sayed Marei's farm at Barania. Police investigated but determined that "the cause may have been some boys playing with matches" (*al Ahram,* May 5, 1976).

| CHAPTER 4: MAREI FAMILY POLITICAL BEHAVIOR

1. See Assam al-Disuqi, *Large Landowners and Their Role in Egyptian Society, 1914–1952* (in Arabic) (Cairo: Dar al Thiqafa al Gadida, 1975); and Robert Mabro, *The Egyptian Economy, 1951–1972* (Oxford: Oxford University Press, 1974), pp. 60–62.

2. The tie to Misr al Fatat was primarily through the party's former publicist, Muhamed Sobieh, who in 1947 shifted his allegiance to the Saadist Party, where he edited the party's paper, *al Shaab.* Sobieh and Sayed Marei became friends, and after the revolution Marei hired Sobieh as director of public relations for the Higher Committee for Agrarian Reform. The Marei connection to the Moslem Brothers was through Omar Marei-45, who throughout his life has been active in religious circles in Egypt.

3. There are currently some ten thousand voters in Azizeha, of whom as many as three-quarters are Nasrs. It is imperative, therefore, that the Mareis remain on close terms with their Nasr relatives, lest a feud open the door to a rival politician.

4. See Gamal Abd el Nasser, *The Philosophy of the Revolution* (Buffalo: Economica Books, 1959), pp. 28–29.

5. On Zulfikar Sabry's activities during the Nasser era, see R. Hrair Dekmejian, *Egypt Under Nasser: A Study in Political Dynamics* (Albany: State University of New York Press, 1971), pp. 172, 219; see also P. J. Vatikiotis, *Nasser and His Generation* (London: Croom, Helm, 1978), pp. 165–66, 306, 309.

6. On the Kafr al Sheikh and Beni Suef experiments and their implications, see Patrick O'Brien, *The Revolution in Egypt's Economic System: From Private Enterprise to Socialism, 1952–1965* (London: Oxford University Press, 1966), pp. 141–47.

7. For a retrospective account of Nasser's pilgrimages to the agrarian reform areas at this time, see "The First Caravan," an article by Taher Hassan Dura, deputy minister of agriculture, which appeared on the twenty-fifth anniversary of the agrarian reform in *al Ahram,* September 8, 1977. See also *al Ahram,* September 10, 1954.

8. Marei's evasiveness in an interview published in *Oktober,* August

14, 1977, pp. 26–31, suggests the sensitivity of the issue. Asked if it was true that some members of his family "get high positions in the state," Marei responded: "Lies and pure slander." Further defending himself, he reviewed the careers of his sons and brothers, omitting in each case the posts which they had obtained as a result of the open-door economic policy.

9. Muhamed Sid Ahmed's book *After the Guns Fall Silent,* which was addressed to the question of what might happen after a peace treaty was signed with Israel, caused an uproar in Egypt when it was first published in 1975. It was then translated into English and published in London by Croom, Helm, Ltd., 1976.

CHAPTER 5: NONFAMILIAL UNITS OF POLITICAL SOLIDARITY AND INTERACTION

1. Ilse Lichtenstadter, "An Arab-Egyptian Family," *Middle East Journal* 4 (Autumn 1952):379–99.

2. On *ezab* and their owners, see Leonard Binder, *In a Moment of Enthusiasm: Political Power and the Second Stratum in Egypt* (Chicago: University of Chicago Press, 1978), pp. 106–8, 216–55.

3. Parliamentary election returns are to be found in *al Akhbar,* July 6, 1957.

4. Lutfi Wakid served as editor of the Unionist Progressive Party's paper, *al Ahali,* in 1978. The leader of that party was Khaled Muhi al Din.

5. Jean Lacouture, *Nasser* (New York: Knopf, 1973), p. 70.

6. Three Tarhutis lost a total of more than 750 feddans in the 1952 agrarian reform, and two of them, plus another of their family members, lost more land in the 1961 reform.

7. Mark Neal Cooper, "The Transformation of Egypt: State and State Capitalism in Crisis, 1967–1977" (Ph.D. diss., Yale University, 1979), p. 976.

8. On *shillal,* see Clement Henry Moore, "Clientelist Ideology and Political Change: Fictitious Networks in Egypt and Tunisia," in Ernest Gellner and John Waterbury, *Patrons and Clients in Mediterranean Societies* (London: Duckworth, 1977), pp. 255–74; Robert Springborg, "Sayed Bey Marei and Political Clientelism in Egypt," *Comparative Political Studies* 12 (October 1979):-259–88; and Robert Springborg, "Patterns of Association in the Egyptian Political Elite," in George Lenczowski, *Political Elites in the Middle East* (Washington: American Enterprise Institute, 1975), pp. 83–108.

9. *MM* (see Preface, note 3), p. 52.

10. "Five Hours with Sayed Marei," *Oktober,* August 14, 1977, pp. 26–31 (in Arabic).

11. Fikry Makram Obeid, interview, October 15, 1977.

12. On this experience, see *MM,* pp. 53–54.

13. "We military people know one another quite well. We know that one man is a soldier while another man has nothing to do with soldiering. This is particularly true of military men who graduate from the same class.

To us, graduates of the same class are like one family, and even more so because we all live and mingle together. Therefore, we know everything about one another." Taken from the 35th installment of Anwar al Sadat's memoirs, *Foreign Broadcast Information Service: Egypt,* July 28, 1977.

14. *MM,* pp. 547–48.

15. Ibid., pp. 625–26.

16. Mustafa Far, interviews, July 21, October 7, and October 14, 1977.

17. Hafiz Awad, interview, July 23, 1977.

18. Muhamed Salmawi, interviews, July 17 and September 5, 1977.

19. Ibid., and Hussein Murad, interview, September 30, 1977.

20. *MM,* and Sayed Marei, interviews, April 15, August 4, and November 3, 1977.

21. On political clientelism, see Steffen W. Schmidt, et al., *Friends, Followers, and Factions: A Reader in Political Clientelism* (Berkeley: University of California Press, 1977); and Gellner and Waterbury, *Patrons and Clients.*

22. See Alex Weingrod, "Patrons, Patronage, and Political Parties," in Schmidt, et al., *Friends, Followers, and Factions,* pp. 323–36; and Springborg, "Sayed Bey Marei."

23. Richard P. Mitchell, *The Society of Muslim Brothers* (New York: Oxford University Press, 1966), p. 66.

24. In 1968, for example, they worked together in what proved to be a futile attempt to win election to the Higher Executive Committee of the Arab Socialist Union. See *MM,* pp. 570–91.

CHAPTER 6: SAYED MAREI'S POLITICAL PERSONAE IN THE ANCIEN RÉGIME

1. Afaf Lutfi al-Sayyid-Marsot, *Egypt's Liberal Experiment: 1922–1936* (Berkeley: University of California Press, 1977), p. 205.

2. Abd al Tawab Abd al Hay, interview with Sayed Marei, *The Broadcast Magazine,* October 18, 1958 (in Arabic).

3. Ibid.

4. *MM* (see Preface, note 3), p. 48.

5. *Parliamentary Debates* (in Arabic, hereafter *Debates*), April 9, April 23, April 30, June 18, 1945, and February 25, 1946.

6. During a parlimentary debate in 1946, he was accused by another deputy of being a communist. See *MM,* pp. 104–6.

7. *Debates,* April 15, 1947.

8. Ibid.

9. Ibid., December 15, 1947.

10. *MM,* pp. 105–7.

11. The spread of black rust fungus in the wheat crop provided Marei the opportunity to question Minister of Agriculture Ghaffar Pasha's competence (*Debates,* June 11, 1945), while an outbreak of hoof-and-mouth disease among cattle supplied him with ammunition to attack palace politician and

then minister of agriculture Hussein Inan (*Debates,* February 4 and May 21, 1946). Inan also came under attack from Marei for mishandling agricultural price supports (*Debates,* April 8, 1946). Following Ghaffar Pasha's return to the cabinet in December 1946 as minister of agriculture, Marei stepped up his harassment, asking Ghaffar why the quantity of potatoes exported was less than that agreed upon (*Debates,* May 26, 1947), why a fertilizer plant had not been built in Nag Hamadi (*Debates,* June 15, 1947), why the government had ceased its distribution of superphosphate (*Debates,* December 8, 1947), and so on.

12. Sayed's brother, Marei Ahmad Marei, was later, as a result of the July 1961 Socialist Decrees, to have some of his shares confiscated by the government. Rawhiya Al Loba Marei, Sayed's first cousin Ahmad-18's wife, also lost a substantial portfolio, which originally had belonged to her husband, as a result of the July decrees. See Mahmoud Murad, *Who Ruled Egypt?* (in Arabic) (Cairo: Madbuly, 1975), pp. 87, 90, 92, 115, 130.

13. *Debates,* June 10, 1946.

14. Ibid., January 6, 1947.

15. Ibid., May 12, 1948.

16. On these early and unsuccessful efforts for agrarian reform, see Gabriel Baer, *A History of Landownership in Modern Egypt* (London: Oxford University Press, 1962), pp. 201–19.

17. *MM,* pp. 102–4.

18. Baer, *History,* p. 87.

19. *Debates,* February 19, 1947.

20. Perhaps the most interesting thing in the report of the Committee of Financial Affairs is the interesting statistic for agricultural ownership and its maldistribution among the people. That distribution I consider to be the cause of the spread of poverty and want among the classes. It is also the cause of the decrease of national income to such a degrading level. Every reform for the improvement of the standard of the people should be based upon these statistics, because the great majority of the people own nothing and the rest own a feddan or less. Therefore we should improve the distribution of ownership. I find that since the great majority of this country are agricultural workers who own nothing, then the first step in reform should aim for the improvement of the standard of the agriculture worker. (*Debates,* [March 3, 1948])

21. Ibid., February 25, 1946.

22. Ibid., February 19, 1947.

23. *MM,* pp. 102–4.

24. *Debates,* March 3, 1948.

25. Ibid.

26. Ibid., February 19, 1947.

27. Ibid., February 14, 1949.

28. Ibid.

29. Ibid., March 3, 1948.

| CHAPTER 7: THE EARLY NASSER ERA

1. *MM* (see Preface, note 3), p. 205.

2. Ibid., p. 208. Aissa Serag al Din served in the late 1970s as Egypt's ambassador to Denmark.

3. Abd al Wahhab Ezzat, interviews with Clement Henry, May 4 and June 3, 1973. I would like to thank Clement Henry for making his interview notes available to me.

4. For an indication of Magdi Hassanein's feelings toward Marei, see his *The Desert and Its Wealth* (in Arabic) (Cairo: Dar al Thiqafa al Gadida, 1975).

5. Those "close observers" are numerous agronomists who were young civil servants at that time and who prefer to remain anonymous.

6. There exist numerous accounts of the initial confrontation between the agrarian reform authorities and landowners. The most authoritative is Sayed Marei, *Agrarian Reform in Egypt* (Cairo: Imprimerie de l'Institute Français, 1957), pp. 44–48.

7. See, for example, Harry Hopkins, *Egypt the Crucible: The Unfinished Revolution of the Arab World* (London: Secker & Warburg, 1969), pp. 102–4.

8. See, for example, ibid.; Jean and Simone Lacouture, *Egypt in Transition* (London: Methuen & Co., 1958), pp. 340–56; and Peter Mansfield, *Nasser's Egypt* (Baltimore: Penguin Books, 1965), pp. 174–83.

9. Keith Wheelock, *Nasser's New Egypt* (New York: Praeger, 1960), pp. 74–94.

10. For a retrospective account of this event, see Taher Hassan Dura, "The First Caravan," *al Ahram,* September 8, 1977. On that occasion, Gamal Salem, when asked by a Reuter's correspondent who the father of the agrarian reform law was, responded that it was he who had drafted it, thanks to the five years he had spent in a hospital in England and the United States following an air crash. "Shut up in a room with no one to talk to he had worked on that project. Then, after five years, he had produced the law. He paid tribute to Dr. Abdul Razzak el Sanhury, president of the State Council, Dr. Abdul Galal el Emary, minister of finance and economy, Dr. Abdul Razzak Sidky, minister of agriculture, and Dr. Sayed Marei [*sic*], member of the National Production Council, for their part in that reform." *Egyptian Gazette,* July 26, 1953.

11. On this occasion the Cairo dailies carried a picture of Marei talking with Nasser and Salah Salem at the party held to celebrate Peasants' Day.

12. For Hassanein's account of the project, see *The Desert and Its Wealth.* For other descriptions, see Hopkins, *Egypt,* pp. 128–39, 309–25; Martin Flavin, "Egypt's Liberation Province: The Beginning of a Beginning," *The Reporter,* November 3, 1955, pp. 23–29; and Robert Springborg, "Patrimonialism and Policy Making in Egypt: Nasser and Sadat and the Tenure Policy for Reclaimed Lands," *Middle Eastern Studies* 15 (January 1979): 49–69.

13. Aziz Sidqy, for example, began his career as a consultant to the

Liberation Province Organization, as did Osman Badran, who was to serve as minister of agriculture and/or land reclamation in the early 1970s.

14. See Hopkins, *Egypt,* pp. 128–39; Flavin, "Egypt's Liberation Province"; and Doreen Warriner, *Land Reform and Development in the Middle East: A Study of Egypt, Syria, and Iraq* (London: Oxford University Press, 1962), pp. 49–54, 200–201.

15. *Al Ahram,* March 6, 1955. See also Springborg, "Patrimonialism," pp. 53–56.

16. On this meeting of Nasser and Marei and its aftereffects, see *MM,* pp. 324–39.

17. *Parliamentary Debates* (in Arabic), August 27, 1957.

18. The most detailed account of this affair is found in Abd al Latif Baghdady, *Memoirs* (in Arabic) (Cairo: Al Maktab al Masri al Hadith, 1977), vol. 2, pp. 7–27.

19. *Al Ahram,* July 11, 1958, and *MM,* p. 337.

20. *Al Ahram,* April 20, 1961, and May 11, 1961.

21. See, for example, Patrick O'Brien, *The Revolution in Egypt's Economic System: From Private Enterprise to Socialism, 1952–1965* (London: Oxford University Press, 1966), pp. 118–20.

22. *MM,* pp. 380–86.

23. Ibid., pp. 364–72.

24. See Robert Springborg, "New Patterns of Agrarian Reform in the Middle East and North Africa," *Middle East Journal* 31 (Spring 1977):127–42.

25. Marei, *Agrarian Reform in Egypt.*

26. Kemal al Din Hussein, interview, October 24, 1977; *MM,* pp. 411–21.

27. Anthony Nutting, *Nasser* (London: Constable, 1972), p. 307.

28. *MM,* pp. 433–38.

29. Ibid., pp. 427–33.

30. *Nasser's Speeches* (Cairo: Ministry of Information, 1963), p. 385.

31. *MM,* pp. 438–40.

32. Ibid., p. 434. Isolation refers to a situation of near house arrest, whereby the individual is sacked from all his posts, put under surveillance, and possibly vilified publicly. It becomes widely known that continued association with the person in disgrace would be politically unwise and possibly even personally risky, hence all but the closest associates of the person in isolation discontinue contact with him. Because political power in the Egyptian elite rests almost exclusively on extensive personal connections rather than on institutional affiliations, isolation is an effective means of undermining personal power bases.

CHAPTER 8: THE LATE NASSER ERA

1. *MM* (see Preface, note 3), pp. 456–58.

2. Ibid., p. 458.

3. Ibid., p. 462.

4. In addition to the latent tension in the Sabry-Marei relationship,

experiments begun in 1963 under Sabry's auspices in Kafr al Sheikh and Beni Suef governorates for the purpose of collectivizing agriculture under the guise of "supervised cooperatives" had greatly exacerbated tension between the two men. On those experiments see Patrick O'Brien, *The Revolution in Egypt's Economic System: From Private Enterprise to Socialism, 1952–1965* (London: Oxford University Press, 1966), pp. 141–47.

5. See R. Hrair Dekmejian, *Egypt Under Nasser: A Study in Political Dynamics* (Albany: State University of New York Press, 1971), pp. 157–60.

6. The transcript of these discussions was published in *al Tali'a,* March 1965, pp. 9–26 (in Arabic).

7. Ibid., p. 23.

8. Ibid., pp. 23–24.

9. Ibid., p. 24.

10. *MM,* pp. 471–74.

11. Marei's attack in *al Ahram* focused on several specific issues and was couched in terms sufficiently guarded that Abu al Nour could not complain convincingly to Nasser that he was being insulted before the newspaper's one million readers. Marei argued that commodity prices were too low and that state interference in the marketing of crops was proving to be counterproductive. It should be noted that marketing was a highly contentious issue, for Abu al Nour had spread the system of "cooperative" marketing, which Marei himself had initiated in the agrarian reform areas on certain crops, to cover all field crops and the entire country. "Cooperative marketing" was in reality a euphemism for the compulsory delivery of crops to government warehouses for which peasants received fixed and generally low prices. Marei also pointed to the negative terms of trade between urban and rural areas and cited statistics on national income which revealed the relative poverty of rural Egypt. He argued that changes would have to be made if production were to be increased. He further indicted Abu al Nour's and Kishin's ministries for not providing essential technical assistance to improve yields of corn, a staple in rural areas. Contrasting this to technical assistance provided for cash crops, and especially cotton, Marei implied that Abu al Nour, Kishin, et al. were callous in their disregard for the welfare of peasants. Marei went on to impugn Abu al Nour's technical capabilities, arguing that cropping policies were inappropriate from the standpoint of a cost-benefit analysis and that not enough had been done to stimulate production of animal protein and hence to alleviate shortages of eggs, meat, and milk. See *al Ahram,* July 11, 12, and 13, 1964.

12. In an aside, Marei directed implicit criticism at Abu al Nour for having curried peasants' favor by having had passed Law 138 of 1964, which canceled all obligations for the repayment of remaining principal and interest due on agrarian reform lands. In that the political context of the debate had shifted grounds, Marei was now defending the state's interest, whereas some months earlier, in the articles cited above, he had been indicting Abu al Nour for disregarding producers' problems. Ibid., March 7, 8, and 11; April 5, 6, 7, and 8; and May 11, 1965; see also O'Brien, *Revolution,* p. 138.

13. On Egyptian professional syndicates, see Donald M. Reid, "The Rise of Professions and Professional Organization in Modern Egypt," *Comparative Studies in Society and History* 16 (January 1974):24–57; Clement Henry Moore, *Images of Development: Egyptian Engineers in Search of Industry* (Cambridge: MIT Press, 1980), pp. 47–54; and Clement Henry Moore, "Professional Syndicates in Contemporary Egypt: The 'Containment' of the New Middle Class" (Paper presented to the Middle East Studies Association annual conference, November 1973). For a more specific treatment of the syndicate of agricultural engineers, see Robert Springborg, "Professional Syndicates in Egyptian Politics, 1952–1970," *International Journal of Middle East Studies* 9 (October 1978):275–95.

14. Ibrahim Shukry, interview, July 17, 1977.

15. *MM,* p. 503.

16. Ibid., pp. 503–4.

17. Ibid., pp. 504–6.

18. Ibid., pp. 513–14.

19. Ibid., pp. 508–12.

20. Ibid., pp. 528–30.

21. Ibid., pp. 530–33.

22. Ibid., pp. 525–33.

23. *Al Ahram,* June 25, 1967.

24. Ibid., November 28, 1967.

25. Ibid. See also his reply to questions from deputies in *al Ahram,* December 21, 1967.

26. See *al Tali'a,* March, 1965, pp. 9–26.

27. For a general discussion of agricultural issues, see *al Tali'a,* October 1972. On cooperatives specifically, see in the same issue "Agricultural Cooperation in Egypt: Its Development and Present Condition," pp. 56–62; and Muhamed Mahmoud Abd al Raouf, "The Development of Agriculture Through Cooperation," pp. 62–66. For an analysis of the cooperative system by a Western expert that appeared at this time, see René Dumont, "Les Problèmes Agraires de la R.A.U.," *Politique Étrangère* 33 (1968):143–79.

28. *MM,* pp. 530–31.

29. Ibid., p. 531.

30. Ibid., pp. 532–33.

31. Ibid., pp. 579–91.

32. Ibid., pp. 601–3.

33. *Al Ahram,* August 23, 1971.

34. Abd al Raouf, "Development of Agriculture," p. 62.

35. Dekmejian, *Egypt,* p. 262.

36. *An Nahar Arab Report,* August 24, 1970.

37. Munir K. Nasser, *Press, Politics, and Power: Egypt's Heikal and Al Ahram* (Ames: Iowa State University Press, 1979), pp. 59–60.

38. Ibid., pp. 67–69.

39. *An Nahar Arab Report,* August 31, 1970.

CHAPTER 9: FROM TECHNOCRAT TO PARTY BOSS AND DIPLOMAT UNDER SADAT

1. During the Nasser era, 131 people held ministerial portfolios, for an average of 7 per year. From 1970 to 1979, 186 different individuals served in the cabinet, for an average of 20.6 per year. Under Nasser, ministers served on average 44 months, compared to 21 months under Sadat.

2. *MM* (see Preface, note 3), pp. 645–56.

3. On this phase of the Marei-Sidqy battle, see *ibid.*, pp. 627–35.

4. *Al Tali'a,* June 1972, pp. 11–32.

5. *Arab Report and Record,* January 15–31, 1972.

6. *Al Ahram,* February 17, 1972.

7. Ibid., January 19, 1972.

8. Ibid.

9. Ibid., January 20, 1972.

10. Ibid., January 23, 1972.

11. Ibid., February 17, 1972.

12. Ibid., February 23, 1972.

13. *Al Tali'a,* May 1972, pp. 124–30.

14. Ibid., pp. 117–20.

15. See, for example, Abu Sayf Yussef, "The Starting Point in the Movement of the Masses," ibid., pp. 121–34.

16. Ibid., pp. 49–50.

17. *Al Ahram,* March 11, 1972.

18. *Al Tali'a,* May 1972, pp. 13–20.

19. Ibid., pp. 86–116.

20. Ibid., pp. 21–49.

21. Ibid., June 1972, pp. 95–96.

22. Ibid., pp. 63–64.

23. Ibid., pp. 80–81.

24. The transcript of this particularly vitriolic meeting was never published. It was, however, circulated privately in Cairo, and Clement Henry managed to obtain a copy. I would like to thank him for making it available to me.

25. *Al Ahram,* June 3, 1972.

26. See his speech in ibid., July 19, 1972.

27. See *The Second Session of the ASU General National Congress* (Cairo: Ministry of Culture and Information, n.d.).

28. On this law and on the process of liberalization between 1971 and 1976, see Ali E. Hillal Dessouki, *Democracy in Egypt* (Cairo: American University in Cairo, 1978). See especially Sayed Marei, "Political Evolution from the One-Party to the Multi-Party System," pp. 38–41, in ibid.

29. For example, see his address to the Giza Women's Organization, *al Ahram,* December 18, 1972. See also his address in Minya, *al Ahram,* December 20, 1972.

30. Account based on interviews with Aziz Sidqy, September 7, 1977, and Mustafa Gabaly, September 26, 1977, and in *MM,* pp. 675–76.

31. See David Hirst, "New Class Saps Old Ideals," *The Guardian,* March 6, 1973.

32. For a particularly scathing criticism of the land reclamation program, see Muhamed Sobieh, "After Seven Years," *The Agricultural Magazine* (in Arabic), April–May 1972, pp. 1–5.

33. *Al Tali'a,* May 1972, pp. 49–85.

34. *Al Ahram,* May 16, 1972.

35. *Al Gumhuriya,* January 10, 1973. The interview actually took place some two weeks prior to the publication of the transcript.

36. See the interview of Sayed Marei in *al Watan,* December 22, 1976.

37. Ibid.

38. *MM,* pp. 676–78.

39. Ibid., pp. 678–79.

40. See *The Times* (London), December 12 and 13, 1972.

41. Ibid., February 5, 1973.

42. Alvin Z. Rubinstein, *Red Star on the Nile: The Soviet-Egyptian Influence Relationship Since the June War* (Princeton: Princeton University Press, 1977), p. 222.

43. *Arab Report and Record,* April 1–15, 1973, p. 152.

44. Ibid., pp. 720–36.

45. Ibid., pp. 738–56.

46. On the World Food Conference and Marei's role in it, see Thomas G. Weiss and Robert S. Jordan, "Bureaucratic Politics and the World Food Conference," *World Politics* 28 (April 1976):422–39. See also Edwin McC. Martin, *Conference Diplomacy: A Case Study—The World Food Conference, Rome, 1974* (Washington: Georgetown University, 1979).

47. The principle underlying IFAD was that of marrying petro dollars and Western technology more efficiently to exploit under- and poorly-utilized agricultural resources of the Third World, with the example of Sudan offered repeatedly by Marei as the most promising case in point. OECD countries, OPEC countries, and LDCs agreed to the idea represented by IFAD, and in the months following the Conference the necessary funds for it to be established were raised. The three blocs, however, found it more difficult to agree on IFAD's internal structure than they had on the need for it. Eventually it was agreed to divide voting power between the three blocs, thereby putting OPEC countries in a key pivotal position. Arguing the case that IFAD's activities would be a boon to the industrialized West in that they would stimulate demand for agricultural technology, Marei fostered the creation of IFAD in a structurally somewhat ambiguous context so that the organization itself had to work out its relations with the World Bank, International Monetary Fund, the U.S. Agency for International Development, and so on. While this ambiguity has led to contentiousness within IFAD in recent years, as OECD countries and LDCs have struggled for control over it, it has enabled IFAD to emerge as one of the principal lending organiza-

tions identified more with the needs and demands of the Third World as opposed to those of the First World.

48. "World Food Conference," *United Nations Monthly Chronicle* 11 (March 1974):29–33.

49. In an interview given in August 1977, some two months after he stepped down as president of the World Food Council, Marei commented on the opposition by First World countries to his methods.

> This was a matter of life and death, not just giving speeches and individuals and countries showing off. So I thought of something new to the United Nations, and that was planning a food strategy, which was actually done. But a lot of countries, especially the big ones, considered this to be interference in their affairs. Some of the representatives of these countries announced to my face that the secretariat should stick to its job as a secretariat and should not try to force its opinions on the members of the conference since they are representatives of the countries. But during this meeting I said that it should be understood that when I accepted my work as a secretary general to this conference I was answering the call of a hungry child in Africa. . . . I also said that I thought that I would be thanked for the effort of the secretariat instead of being criticized. What should have been discussed was the acceptance, rejection, or amendment of the strategy we planned, and not our right to plan it. At the end I said that this meeting should have been held in Africa, not in an air-conditioned room in Rome. (*Oktober,* August 14, 1977, pp. 26–31 [in Arabic])

The difficulties Marei faced from the FAO are suggested by the following appraisal of the conference by two American academic observers of it:

> The most energetic criticisms of the proposal for a World Food Authority to implement the resolutions of the Conference were advanced by the FAO Secretariat. This is not surprising, since it is a rare institution that would welcome a rival in its own realm of confidence. What was unusual, however, was the extent to which the FAO pursued its lobbying efforts. Even after it became clear that the proposed World Food Authority would be rejected by the Conference as a follow-up mechanism, the FAO continued to fight the idea of any such organ and to propose that it undertake the primary responsibility for follow-up procedures itself. (Weiss and Jordan, "Bureaucratic Politics," p. 429)

50. His suppleness and considerable leadership ability is suggested by the following observation:

> It apparently mattered little to him that the two most important institutional frameworks to emerge from the World Food Conference—the International Fund for Agricultural Development and the World Food Council—actually represented the rationale and even the language of

his own proposed World Food Authority, but that the credit for these innovations, publicly at least, went elsewhere. . . . He 'steered' not 'pushed,' the national delegations to consider and approve financial and supervisory institutional responses similar to those that he had originally suggested. (Ibid., pp. 433–34)

51. He launched the appeal in 1976, and by December 1977 the required $1 billion had been raised, thanks to a last-minute supplementary donation from the OPEC Special Fund. This was not the end of IFAD's troubles, however, for the First World pressed for "co-financing," a euphemism for relying on conventional aid organizations like the World Bank and the International Monetary Fund, which have stringent lending criteria. LDCs preferred that IFAD develop autonomously. A further dispute arose between the OECD and OPEC countries over who was to foot the bill for replenishing IFAD's capital, the first installment of which falls due in 1981. As president of the World Food Council, and even since stepping down from that role in June 1977, Marei has been assisting IFAD President Abd al Mohsen al Sudairy, a Saudi, in attempting to work out compromises to these conflicts. On IFAD, see *The Middle East,* June 1978, pp. 158–59, and March 1980, p. 58.

52. Sayed Marei and Saad Hagrass, *If the Arabs Want* (in Arabic) (Cairo: Dar al Ta'awun, 1975).

53. Sayed Ahmed Marei, *The World Food Crisis* (London: Longman, 1975).

54. See, for example, his speech to the Food Security Conference in Cairo, *al Ahram,* September 25, 1977.

55. *Oktober,* August 14, 1977, pp. 26–31.

56. Ibid., and *The Middle East,* November 1978, p. 132.

57. See, for example, *al Ahram,* June 24, 1975.

58. From interviews with American, British, and Australian officials. The brief biographical sketch of Marei in the files of the British Embassy in Cairo alludes to that government's opposition to his reelection as president of the World Food Council: "In the same month (January 1974), he was appointed secretary-general of the U.N. World Food Conference due to be held later in 1974, but he did not give up his Egyptian posts and activities, accepting the speakership of the People's Assembly even before his U.N. job was over."

59. *Al Ahram,* March 12, 1977.

60. Ibid., May 13, 1977.

| CHAPTER 10: SPEAKER OF THE PEOPLE'S ASSEMBLY

1. Mark Neal Cooper, "The Transformation of Egypt: State and State Capitalism in Crisis, 1967–1977" (Ph.D. diss., Yale University, 1979), pp. 917–1030.

2. *Al Ahram,* October 19, 1975.

3. It should also be noted that upon Sadat's return from Jerusalem on November 21 he was accompanied in his open-top limousine in his triumphal drive from the airport to the presidential palace by Sayed Marei and Hosni Mubarak, vice-president.

4. *Al Ahram,* November 21, 1977.

5. These sessions, attended by the author, were held in early December.

6. *Al Ahram,* November 2, 1974.

7. Marei's reasoning was as follows:

> The question is: Does this fixed opposition represent anything at this stage? I believe that it cannot represent anything or become completely fixed except after the parties recur, if they ever do. Then there will be party opposition. Let us ask ourselves another question. What is the result of party opposition? It will oppose everything. That is opposition for opposition's sake only. We have examples in our history, the best of which is the stand of the party opposition before the Revolution— I was a member in the parliament then—toward the electrification of the Aswan Dam and what disasters it will bring to the dam and the whole country. Although the majority were with the government, there were hesitations. The hesitation remained until the 23rd July Revolution came and executed the project, and none of the disasters the opposition cited took place. (Ibid., May 16, 1975).

8. Ibid., February 3, 1976.

9. Ibid., February 6, 1976. He also took the opportunity presented by this interview to deride parties and those who were calling for their creation: "I was associated with the parties before the revolution. Those who speak of the parties today as though they are the ideal picture of democracy and who want to compare what took place in the 20 years of the revolution with what was present in the past, to this I say 'no.' The past was not purely positive."

10. *Al Qabas,* March 19, 1976. Following the issuing of the committee's report, Marei leapt into the fray to defend its recommendations, the composition of the committee itself, and its rejection of parties. In an interview with Samy Metwally of *al Ahram* (May 15, 1976), Marei, ignoring Metwally's questions, spoke what was on his mind:

> First, I would like to answer those who said that the organizations [referring to the three *minabar*] were created from above, that is, from the authority. This is not true. Let us recall together the steps that led to the formation of these organizations. . . . When the issue of *minabar* was brought up, a committee for political work was formed. The nature of the work of this committee did not at all require a new popular election because it gathered 50 members of the People's Assembly who

were directly elected and 50 members from the Central Committee, who were also elected. . . . The question is, where is the role of the authority in this?

Those who say that the establishment of political organizations is a play say so for personal reasons, for at one time they themselves called for the formation of parties. . . . After that we heard them lecturing or saying that the political organizations will not provide democracy. This is a premature judgment since it is only natural to allow the organizations a chance to practice and maybe the coming elections of the People's Assembly will be a test of the effectiveness of these organizations.

11. Ibid., May 8, 1976.
12. Ibid., May 15, 1976.
13. Ibid., October 14, 1976.
14. Ibid., September 15, 1976.
15. Ibid., October 14, 1976.
16. *Al Akhbar,* June 6, 1976.
17. Ibid., February 28, 1978.
18. Gamal Oteify, interview, October 11, 1977.
19. Sayed Marei, interview, November 3, 1977.
20. For example, he opened the special meeting of the ASU National General Conference with the following remarks:

It is fortunate to have this meeting while the Islamic nation is celebrating the memory of the Prophet's *hijra* [flight from Mecca], the memory of his starting the struggle for the victory of Allah's religion and raising the word of truth. He left for succeeding generations an ample amount of the spirit of struggle. As we celebrate this feast we promise to carry the flame of struggle for liberating our land, for supporting our principles, and for the victory of our Arab and Islamic peoples (*al Ahram,* February 17, 1972).

21. Ibid., March 17, 1977.
22. *Al Watan,* December 22, 1976.
23. *Arab Report and Record,* January 15–31, 1972.
24. Bill Schmidt, Middle East Correspondent for *Time* magazine, interview, October 16, 1977.
25. See especially his interview with Fahmy Huweidy, *al Ahram,* January 17, 1975.
26. Lutfi al Kholi, interview, August 5, 1977.
27. Muhamed Salmawi, interview, September 5, 1977.
28. Abu Seif Yussef, interview, August 5, 1977.
29. See, for example, the interview of Sayed Marei in *Al Ahram,* January 17, 1975. See also Cooper, "Transformation of Egypt," p. 398.
30. Lutfi al Kholi, interview, and Marei Ahmad Marei, interview, August 11, 1977.

31. *Al Ahram,* November 10, 1976; Hilmy Murad, interview, August 30, 1977.

32. *Al Ahram,* November 12, 1976.

33. Hilmy Murad, interview, August 30, 1977.

34. *Al Ahram,* February 15, 1977.

35. Parliamentary Debates (in Arabic), June 12, 1977.

36. Interviews with Hilmy Murad, Abu Seif, and others.

37. Abd al Aziz Hussein is the younger brother of Ahmad Hussein, a prominent minister of social affairs at the end of the ancien régime and the Revolutionary Command Council's first ambassador to the United States. From a wealthy landowning family, Ahmad Hussein married the only daughter of Abboud Pasha, Egypt's leading entrepreneur in the 1940s and early 1950s. Abd al Aziz Hussein resigned his portfolios of Agriculture and Sudanese Affairs in October 1977 in protest against an agreement between an American agribusiness firm and the Egyptian government calling for the establishment of a joint-venture agri-industrial project. Hussein let it be known through private channels that his reason for resigning was that he was excluded from the final negotiating session at which the contract was signed and at which bribe money changed hands. Present at that session, and representing the Egyptian government, were Osman Ahmad Osman and President Sadat.

38. Shortly after the election, Salah al Abd purchased a farm of several feddans adjacent to the Giza Pyramids, for which he paid some £E35,000 per feddan.

39. *Al Ahram,* January 14, 1975.

40. Ibid., February 11 and January 15, 1975.

41. *Al Ahram,* May 16, 1975.

42. See, for example, Abbas al Aswani, "A Point of View: The Press and the ASU," *Ruz al Yussef,* December 22, 1975; and "The Secretary General of the ASU Tries to Suppress Ruza to His Will," *Ruz al Yussef,* December 8, 1975.

43. Phillip Ghallab, "The Picture of the ASU as Its Leaders Present It," *al Tali'a,* June 1975, p. 20.

44. Sayed Marei, interview, August 4, 1977.

45. *Al Ahram,* February 3, 1976.

46. Ibid., March 20, 1976.

47. Ibid., March 24, 1976.

48. See his interview with Fahmy Huweidy in *al Ahram,* January 17, 1975.

49. *Al Hawadith,* May 15, 1975, cited in Raphael Israeli, *The Public Diary of President Sadat* (Leiden: E. J. Brill, 1979), vol. 2, p. 875.

50. *Al Ahram,* July 30, 1975.

51. Ibid., October 19, 1975.

52. Ibid., October 24, 1974.

53. Ibid., November 3, 1975.

54. Ibid., March 20, 1976.

55. Ibid., May 8, 1976.

56. That Marei's dissatisfaction with the government's policy went unnoticed at the mass level is suggested by the various slogans chanted against him in the January 18–19 demonstrations and riots. The attack on Marei became so virulent at this time that Sadat, in a meeting with the General Federation of students on February 2, spoke out in his defense during a question-and-answer session, which went as follows:

STUDENT: We need an example set for us, and we want reform regardless of the method.

SADAT: An example, where?

STUDENT: In all the state positions, sir.

SADAT: Give an example. What are you afraid of?

STUDENT: We could mention, for example, some places where they usually appear, such as the People's Assembly—Sayyid Mar'i in the People's Assembly. I believe that the majority of students oppose the presence of Sayyid Mar'i in the Assembly because of his behavior and what has been said about it more than once, whether in the press or other information media. The contradictions began with his behavior.

. . .

SADAT: . . . I will provide the country all the facts in order that we may put an end to all the talk, defamation, and the campaign of doubt such as the example you gave me about Sayyid Mar'i. Sayyid Mar'i has worked with the regime since the beginning. You heard me telling you on 25 December that the person who introduced Mar'i was Jamal Salem. Mar'i was the one who proposed the first, second, and third agrarian reform laws and implemented them. He was a minister throughout the Nasir regime and was later made a deputy prime minister. What is wrong with him now? Is he no longer good? . . .

The communists want and a group among you wants to cast doubts on the regime. They take the speaker of the Assembly and say: This man is a feudalist and such and such are his qualities. . . .

Is it that Sayyid Mar'i became a subject of doubt only after he became my in-law, as one member of the People's Assembly wrote? The Assembly member concerned did not want to mention Anwar al Sadat by name because there is nothing against me. Everything about me is very simply well known and clear to you. I am prepared to answer anyone. But to involve me, it was necessary to beat around the bush and make allegations against Sayyid Mar'i and say that he was unacceptable. For your information only, the only person who was a parliamentarian before the Revolution took place is Sayyid Mar'i. . . . Sayyid Mar'i had always been a member of the parliament prior to the revolution. He is the one who prepared the agrarian reform laws. The whole issue is casting doubts on the entire command, that is all. (*Foreign Broadcast Information Service,* February 2, 1977.)

57. On the New Wafd, see Donald M. Reid, "The Return of the Egyptian Wafd, *1978*," *International Journal of African Historical Studies* 12 (1979): 389–415.

58. *Al Akhbar*, March 22, 1978.

59. *Al Ahram,* March 29, 1978.

60. Ibid., May 28, 1978, and *al Akhbar,* June 14, 1978.

61. *Al Ahram,* June 27, 1978.

62. *Events,* October 17, 1978, p. 19.

63. *Al Hawadeth,* October 13, 1978, p. 14.

| CHAPTER 11: CONCLUSION

1. John Waterbury, *The Commander of the Faithful: The Moroccan Political Elite —A Study in Segmented Politics* (London: Weidenfeld and Nicolson, 1970), p. 320.

INDEX

1957–1976, 93–96; 1969, 181; 1976, 79–80, 214, 219, 225, 230, 237

elite(s): xxv, 9, 12, 15, 26, 83, 91, 122, 149, 155, 156, 161, 163, 171, 175, 188, 229; Arab descended, 4; of Sharqiya, 97; provincial, 3, 125; urban professional, 20. *See also* political elite

Elwan, Hussama, 81

Elwan, Sheikh Muhamed, 80–82, 91, 93, 146

Elwan(s), 47, 80–82, 91, 93

Emary, Gamal al, 142

encysting, 8, 46

endogamy: 5, 16, 27, 32–34, 38–40, 40–44; lineage, 40; rate of, 42, 43, 46; patrilineal, 36

England, 16, 20, 121–22, 133, 219

English, 16, 133, 155

Europe, 20, 56, 110, 124

European, 13, 44, 133

exogamy, 33

ezba (pl. *ezab*), 90

Ezza, 5

Ezzat, Abd al Wahhab, 141–42

Fahim, Muhamed, 159

Fahmy, 48

Fahmy, Abd al Aziz, 10, 26, 37

Fahmy, Ismail, 107

Fahmy/Omar family, 37

Falluga, 75

family(ies): xiii–xv, xxv–xxviii, 3, 5, 10, 23, 99, 105, 164, 243–45; affinal sets in, 55–57; as communication network, 84–88; as political organization, 71–73; connections, 109, 125–26, 164, 243; Egyptian, 27, 98; honor, 32, 51–52, 54; in Middle East, 39; influence, 178; in Third World, 27; nests, 73, 76, 82–83, 88; notable/landowning, 18, 90–91, 101, 103; nuclear, 57–58, 256; patrimony, 21; rift/feud in, 22, 124; Sharqiya, 90–98; social and economic behavior, 49–55, 58–70; solidarity, 23, 27, 124; substitutes for, 100, 105; tree, xv,

49, 50–51. *See also* lineage, Marei; marriage

Faqi, al family, 172–73, 180

Faqoos, 94–96

Far, Muhamed Disuqi, 101

Far, Mustafa, 98, 101–2, 104

Far, Zeynab, 102

Farahat, Hassan-78, 25

Farahat, Mursi, 24, 47, 56, 59

Farahat(s), 47

Far(s), 101–2

Fawzy, Mahmoud (agronomist), 110, 151

Fawzy, Mahmoud (Prime Minister), 100, 107, 164, 188–89, 206

Fawzy, Muhamed, 187

Feysal Islamic Bank, 53, 66, 68, 92, 252

Fiat, 205

First World, 208–9, 211

Fisha, 40

Foda, 48

Food and Agriculture Organization (FAO), 78, 102, 110, 208–9, 229

France, 10, 15

Free Officer(s), 74–75, 77, 80, 85–86, 94, 139, 142–43, 147, 155–56, 170, 203, 215, 231

French, 13, 21, 155

Fuad, Ahmad, 141, 165

Fuad I secondary school, 74, 99, 103, 123

Gabaly, Mustafa, 198–200, 229

Gamgara, 5–6, 75, 89, 125, 252

Gamiat al Tishriya, 252

Gamiat al Ummumiya, 6, 252

Garden City, 27

Gazzar, Fikry, 172

Geertz, Hildred, 34

genealogical links, 49–50, 55

genealogy, 32, 35, 50

generational skewing, 16

German(s), 13, 16

Germany, 16

Gezira Sporting Club, 103

Gezirat al Saud, 3

Ghaffar, Abd al, 130, 199

Ghali, Mirrit, 134–35

among Christians and Moslems,
40; arranged, 29–30, 35, 52; connections based on, 22, 48, 99, 131,
220; cousin, 32–33, 35, 44, 46; endogamous, 7, 17, 25–27, 35–38,
41–42, 44–45, 47, 49, 252; exogamous, 5, 7, 17, 25–26, 30–31, 35–
38, 41–43, 47–48, 72, 253; father
brother daughter (FBD), 37–40,
46; in the Middle East, 32–34, 38,
40; Marei-Sadat, 186; negotiations, 32; partners, 8
Marsot, Afaf Lutfi al-Sayyed-,
122
Marx, xxvii
Marxist(s), 86, 217, 223
Masa', al, 171
Mashour, Abdulla Ahmad, 80,
94–96
Mashour, Mashour Ahmad, 79–80,
95–97, 109
Mashour, Salem, 79
Mashour(s), 79–80, 94, 97
Mashtul al Suq, 80, 95
matrilineage, 24, 35–36
matrilineal, 34, 37
matrilineality, 7
Mazhar, Suleiman, 171
Mecca, 197
Menoufiya, 40, 60–61, 110, 173,
199, 230
Middle East, xiii, xxvi–xxviii, 161,
164, 207–8, 243, 245
Middle Easterners, 33
minbar (pl. *minabar*), 190, 195, 214–
15, 218–19, 234, 237–38
Minshiya, 81
Minshiya al Bakri, 160
Minya, 25, 60, 110, 255
Minya al Qamh, 4, 11–12, 78, 80,
89, 95–96, 113
Misr al Fatat, 72, 127, 133, 145, 171,
224–25
Misr Cotton Export Company, 70
Misr Dairy Company, 70
mode of production: asiatic, xxvii;
capitalist, xxvii
Morocco: family ties in, 34; politics
in, 245
Moscow, 230

Moslem Brotherhood, 25, 72, 81,
126–27, 133, 224–25
Moslem Brothers, 165, 172
Moslem inheritance laws, 58, 60
Moukhabarat, 81
Mubarak, Hosni, 235, 258
muhandis, 129–30
Muhi al Din, Abd al Aziz, 74, 76, 99,
237
Muhi al Din, Fuad, 237
Muhi al Din, Khaled, 37, 47, 75, 86,
94, 141–42, 171, 192, 195, 215,
240
Muhi al Din, Kholi, 74
Muhi al Din, Samia, 75
Muhi al Din, Sayed, 75
Muhi al Din, Zakariya, 37, 47, 74–
76, 81, 83, 99, 139–41, 175
Muhi al Din(s), 37, 47, 73–76, 78,
81, 85, 99
Mukhtar, Ahmad, 93
Murad, Ahmad, 103, 142
Murad, Hilmy, 67, 225–28, 239
Murad, Hussein, 64, 98, 103–4, 135,
142
Murad, Mustafa Kamel, 186, 203
Musawwar, al, 79, 86
Muslimani, Muhamed Fathi al, 93

Nagd, 4, 8, 53
Nahhas, 139
Napoleonic invasion, 4
Nasr, Ali, 53
Nasr, Gamal, 75
Nasr, Ibrahim, 4
Nasr, Ibrahim-60, 75
Nasr, Mahmoud Ibrahim, 17, 37,
252
Nasr, Marei Ibrahim: 4, 6–14, 16,
18–19, 22–24, 27, 35–37, 41, 51,
101, 252–53; descendants of, 42–
49, 52, 55, 60, 66, 76; descent
group of, 41, 50–51, 257; lineage
of, 36, 124
Nasr, Mona Ibrahim, 252
Nasr, Mumtaha-59 (Marei), 75
Nasr, Nasr Ibrahim, 4, 8
Nasr, Salah, 173
Nasr, Sharif, 8
Nasr, Sheikh Ashour Muhamed, 239